EXCISE SYSTEMS

SIJBREN CNOSSEN

EXCISE SYSTEMS

A Global Study
of the Selective Taxation of
Goods and Services

THE JOHNS HOPKINS UNIVERSITY PRESS
Baltimore and London

Manufactured in the United States of America

The Johns Hopkins University Press, Baltimore, Maryland 21218
The Johns Hopkins Press Ltd., London

Library of Congress Catalog Card Number 77–1407
ISBN 0–8018–1962–8

Library of Congress Cataloging in Publication data
will be found on the last printed page of this book.

For Miep and Mem,
and to the Memory of Heit

CONTENTS

    TABLES

ACKNOWLEDGMENTS

This treatise would not have been written but for the encouragement and advice of Richard Bird of the University of Toronto, who saw the need for it and, more important, believed that it could be done. I am indebted to the Fiscal Affairs Department of the International Monetary Fund for providing a stimulating environment in which to work; the support of Richard Goode, the Department's Director, did much to make this study possible. Special mention should also be made of the interest shown by Hendrik Hofstra of Leyden University.

Thanks are due to Luc De Wulf, John Due, Charles McLure, Oliver Oldman, Carl Shoup, Alan Tait, Gunnar Tómasson, Johannes van der Poel, William White, and Dik Wolfson, who commented on parts of the manuscript and drew my attention to relevant literature. They have all been generous with their time.

Chapter 2 draws on my "Sales Tax and Excise Systems of the World," published in *Finanzarchiv*; and on "The Role and Structure of Sales Tax and Excise Systems," which appeared in *Finance and Development*, and was reprinted in *Weekblad voor Fiscaal Recht*. Chapter 6 is based on my "Capacity Taxation: The Pakistan Experiment," published in *IMF Staff Papers*. These articles, as well as the main body of Chapters 3, 7 and 8, were originally prepared for the International Monetary Fund; permission for publication is gratefully acknowledged. The remainder of the treatise was completed under a grant from the Netherlands organization for the advancement of pure research (Z.W.O.).

Joslin Landell-Mills gave valuable assistance in editing the manuscript and Ralla Christie devoted many hours of cheerful effort to getting the typescript in order.

The responsibility for whatever faults remain rests, of course, with me.

EXCISE SYSTEMS

CHAPTER 1

INTRODUCTION

Selective taxes on goods and services, often referred to as excises, are among the oldest forms of taxation in the world. In China, at the time of the Han dynasty, excises were levied on tea, liquor, fish, and on reeds used for fuel and thatching. Salt and iron were also considered convenient sources of government revenue and their production was organized as a government enterprise so that all net proceeds would accrue solely to the state. During the Mauryan period in India, excises were imposed on liquor and salt, and later coverage was expanded to perfumery, indigo, cotton carding, soap making, edible oil and printed cloth. The salt excise was considered a gold mine for the European sovereign during the Middle Ages, because sources of supply were few and could be controlled easily. In Europe, the prominence of excise taxation in the sixteenth and seventeenth centuries owed much to the Dutch, whose duties on beer, sugar, salt, spirits, and other goods were called *excijsen*.[1] In fact, excise taxation was so widely applied that an English observer noted that "a fish dish eaten in Holland pays 30 excises."[2] From *la terre classique de la fiscalité*, as Holland was called at that time, excise taxation spread to other European countries. Many German states, for instance, followed the Dutch example and the apparent success of the "new imposts" also led to their introduction in England.

In Europe, during the nineteenth century, many of the "small" excises (so called because they yielded comparatively little revenue) were abolished or absorbed into more general taxes on goods and services, often referred to as sales taxes, that were widely introduced in the first quarter of this century. The "big" excises—for instance, on tobacco products, alcoholic beverages, sugar, and later petroleum products and soft drinks—remained, but little attention has been given to them in the professional literature. The ostensible simplicity of the excise base and the forms of imposition have caused some to devote greater analytical and empirical efforts to taxes held to be intellectually more challenging, even if sometimes less relevant to policy issues. In recent years the focus has been primarily on structural aspects related to the introduction or modification of the value added form of sales taxation in the European Economic Community (EEC). But the EEC is now in the process of harmonizing the excise systems of its member countries and this should focus the attention again on the selective taxation of goods and services.

Elsewhere, the excise form of taxation is still in full bloom, notably on the Indian subcontinent and in the Far East, but also in some Middle Eastern and Latin American countries, whose systems sometimes cover more than a hundred items. These areas are where most of the world's population lives, and obviously the workings of their excise systems have important implications for revenue, income distribution, and the allocation of resources.

WHY STUDY EXCISE TAXATION?

One of the main arguments in this book is that in many instances excises may be more effective as a tax and a tool of social and economic development policies than many other taxes that are comprehensive in design but turn out to be incomprehensible and capriciously

1

applied in practice. The case for excise taxation may be briefly sketched on the basis of well-established goals and criteria of a good tax.[3]

The Issue of Progressivity

A widely accepted principle of taxation is that burdens should be distributed progressively, that taxes as a percentage of individual income should rise as a person's income rises. Excises have generally been regarded as unsuitable for effecting a fairer after-tax distribution of income. Indeed, they have often been reviled, sometimes savagely, for falling more heavily on the poor than on the rich. This may well have been the case, but the almost automatic association of excises with a regressive tax burden distribution may have prematurely encouraged taxes that are more equitable in intent but not necessarily in effect, and may have also obscured the potential for progressivity in excise design.

Ferdinand Lassalle's tax polemic published in Germany in 1863 is an interesting example of the views on the income redistribution effects of excise taxation that still prevail in many countries.[4] Lassalle, a strong believer in the inevitability of the class war between capital and labor, saw excises (levied at that time in Germany on salt, cereals, beer, meat, and heating fuel) and related taxes as enabling the bourgeoisie to exempt capital from taxation and leave the burden of the cost of the public household for the poor to pay. He pointed out that these taxes could be absorbed into the prices of excisable commodities so that buyers would be unaware they were paying them. Lassalle cited the salt excise as particularly onerous and regressive, since the poor used more salt than the rich in order to add flavor to their miserable diets.[5] Moreover, he argued, so-called luxury taxes either fell on widely consumed items and hence could not be called luxury taxes, or indeed qualified as such but then would not yield any revenue; excises on silk and furs were important examples in Lassalle's time.

Lassalle's observation on the salt excise would appear correct, but his views on the taxation of luxury goods and services do not stand up to closer scrutiny. Excise systems covering goods and services that are major items in the household budgets of middle-income and high-income groups, but not in those of the poor, should exhibit a progressive incidence over some part of the income range and also yield substantial revenues. A pertinent example today are the various taxes and charges in the motoring field.

Interestingly enough, at the time that Lassalle published his polemic, luxury taxes on coaches, horses, menservants, dogs, armorial designs and other indices of luxurious consumption in England were a mainstay of its tax structure, and it has been pointed out that they formed the basis of Pitt's "triple assessment" which stood at the cradle of modern income tax. Elsewhere at that time it was argued that the existence of class-differentiated consumption patterns should be exploited to put most of the excise burden on the rich. According to the argument, the basic foods of the poor should be exempted, the middle class should pay tax through an excise on meat, and the rich should be taxed most heavily through excises on tobacco, brandy, aquavit, wine, and precious articles.[6] Obviously, the objectives of taxation and the form and structure of related instruments change over time and differ from place to place. But after allowing for this, it is clear that selective taxes on luxury goods and services should be given more serious consideration, especially in countries where for practical reasons progressive income and wealth taxes cannot yet be administered successfully.

The Efficiency Criterion

The second well-established principle of a good tax is that it should further, or at least interfere as little as possible with, the "optimum" conditions for production and exchange. As first formulated by Vilfredo Pareto, the central thesis of the efficiency criterion is that resources should be allocated in such a way that there would not be an alternative arrangement under which somebody would be better off without anybody being worse off. During the past thirty-five years, the excise tax has been singled out in the professional literature as especially inefficient because the price distortion it causes induces a consumer to purchase some good that has an inferior ranking on his preference scale. An excise, the conclusion was, leads to an excess burden that could be avoided if instead a general tax on consumption or income were levied that would not interfere with consumer preferences.

In recent years, though, there has been a growing recognition that the excess burden argument has less validity than seemed to be the case. James Buchanan and Francesco Forte have demonstrated that in a multiperiod setting in which anticipated spending patterns fluctuate more than anticipated income receipts, an individual who has to meet a fixed tax obligation would prefer to pay a single excise on a residual and postponable item of consumption rather than any other tax—whether levied as a lump sum, on income or on general consumption expenditures.[7] Assume an individual has the same annual income over a ten-year period, but that his expenditures are highest in years one through five when his children are in college. The theorem suggests that the individual will prefer to pay his tax in the later years when basic needs are low and the marginal utility of income is therefore also low. A tax structure that could provide this choice would consist of an excise on a pleasure boat, for instance, or on some other luxury good whose consumption is not essential and can be postponed. This institutional approach to taxation, which has not been fully developed, reflects an older philosophy that selective taxes on goods and services expand the range of options available to a potential taxpayer.[8] Perhaps the element of choice in taxation will become important again in countries that have broad-based income and sales taxes that affect nearly everyone.

The excess burden argument is one aspect of the theory of optimal commodity taxation that seeks to choose taxes in such a way as to maximize the resulting consumer welfare. Another example is the use of selective taxes to promote the efficient use of resources in a social welfare sense, defined to include intangibles affecting the quality of life. For instance, excises could be designed to internalize the cost of the harmful effects on the environment caused by the production or consumption of certain products. Furthermore, there is a need to design selective taxes that approximate the cost of using roads; this is one of the guiding principles for harmonizing the motor fuel and vehicle tax systems of the member countries of the EEC.

Revenue Sufficiency and Flexibility

Essential characteristics of a good tax are that its yield is adequate in relation to budgetary needs (revenue sufficiency), that it is responsive to changes in these needs (flexibility), and stable in relation to the level of economic activity (elasticity). The costs of administering and paying the tax should also be low. On the whole, the big excises meet the revenue sufficiency criterion well. In most countries sales volumes are large and demand is inelastic (an excise-induced rise in price does not greatly reduce volume); factors which have made these excises reliable sources of revenue. Collection costs are usually low—sometimes lower than for any other tax—because production is concentrated in large manufacturing units that are easy to control. On the other hand, many small excises have been criticized for yielding relatively little and being expensive to collect, and it has been alleged that here the excise method of collection that relies on physical controls is at a disadvantage compared to the sales tax method that is based upon self-assessment. However, much would seem to depend on the degree of taxpayer cooperation in a country. Where this is not generally voluntarily forthcoming, self-assessment is obviously an illusory concept and enforcement must fall back on the excise method.

Excises have often been faulted for their lack of elasticity for two reasons. First, as economic development proceeds, the share in income of expenditures on items like tobacco products declines; therefore, the argument goes, so will excise receipts, given that the same ad valorem rate is maintained. However, the assertion does not allow for changes in commercial and consumption patterns that take place concurrently. With rising income more people are likely to buy, for instance, market-processed cigarettes that are easy to tax rather than the home-produced tobacco products that an excise has difficulty in reaching. Moreover, the alleged drawback does not hold for excises on petroleum products, luxury goods and services, the consumption of which as a proportion of income generally rises faster than income. Second, excises are often associated with specific rates (fixed amounts per unit of production) which, unlike ad valorem rates, must be adjusted when prices rise if the real value of receipts is to be maintained. If the adjustment process is slow, receipts will show a lag; this issue also needs further examination.

Simplicity and Certainty

Another important feature of a good tax is simplicity in design and certainty in operation. Fortunately, the choice is not always one of either/or, but if it were, then it could be that "the certainty of what each individual ought to pay is, in taxation, a matter of so great importance, that a very considerable degree of inequality, it appears, I believe, from the experience of all nations, is not near so great an evil as a very small degree of uncertainty."[9] Simplicity and certainty go hand in hand and the excise method of taxation appears to meet both requirements well. The tax base is obvious, readily understood by the tax official and the taxpayer, and generally not susceptible to varying interpretations by either party. The physical characteristics of the excisable products that form the basis for the computation of the tax liability usually leave little room for argument. This should reduce the scope for arbitrary decisions by the tax collector who may not be able to refer to court decisions or professional literature and must rely on the letter of the law for assessment purposes. It compares favorably with the provisions of income and sales tax laws that, relative to the conditions in developing countries, are often unclear, overly sophisticated and insufficiently attuned to business practices. In dualistic economies the modern versions of these laws simply cannot encompass the wide diversity of social and economic conditions which they confront. Broad-based sales taxes, too, will involve substantial interference with business and trade as opposed to excise systems that concentrate on a few important commodities.[10] It may be that the excise method of taxation as an intermediate form of tax technology is more capable of being implemented successfully than seemingly more advanced forms of taxation.[11] Equity and efficiency are highly desirable in taxation, but certainty is compelling.

ORGANIZATION OF THE BOOK

The following chapters present a general survey and appraisal of excise taxation throughout the world. Although the emphasis is on selective taxes on goods and services, reference must of course be made to sales taxes as the principle alternative form of taxation; they are twin branches of the same tree. Excise and sales tax systems in socialist economies have been excluded from the review, however, first because data were not sufficient, and second because the role of taxation in centrally planned economies differs fundamentally from that in market-oriented or mixed economic systems.[12]

With a phenomenon as multifarious as the excise one, some definition and classification is an essential prerequisite to analysis. This is covered in the second chapter. From a wide survey of the kinds of goods and services subject to selective taxes, it is possible to describe the composition of excise systems, and from there to make a general classification of every country's excise system according to its coverage. There is also a survey of the form, manner and extent of sales taxation, which makes it possible to define each country's overall approach to the taxation of goods and services. Following this general survey, the third chapter explores the revenue aspects of excise systems—sufficiency and elasticity, overall and for individual items, with some attempt to explain intercountry variation in yield.

The fourth chapter surveys and analyzes the evidence on the income redistribution effects of excise taxation and indicates the scope for achieving a less regressive or more progressive burden distribution. Some observations are also made on the theory of excise incidence and on the requirements for progressivity in excise taxation. Much of what is said in this chapter should also apply to sales taxes that have graduated rate schedules. In fact, excises might have been defined to include that part of a sales tax that exceeds the standard sales tax rate. (In addition, a lower than standard or zero sales tax rate (exemption) might be viewed as a negative excise, or subsidy.) Although such an analysis might usefully be undertaken for a single country, information for a wider application of this approach is simply lacking.

The effects of various excises on the allocation of resources are reviewed in the fifth chapter. Because the excise is so diverse and its goals so different, the subject matter had to be divided into separate topics. The headings that cover areas with wider application include a review of the state of the art on the excess burden of excise taxation and the need for coordination with import duties; here again much of the argument would also be relevant to the sales tax field. There is also a more general discussion on the employment implications of excise taxation—a topical matter since the role of taxation in maintaining or furthering the use of labor-intensive production techniques has recently come to the fore. More specific excise subjects are the treatment of road user charges and taxes, effluent charges and energy taxes, and excises on sumptuary goods.

Following the general analytical presentation in these two chapters, the sixth chapter considers the specific economic and administrative effects of presumptive excise taxation, largely on the basis of a novel experiment being undertaken in Pakistan. There the government introduced a highly interesting form of excise taxation based on the capacity output of production units, in the belief that this would be an incentive to increase production. The validity of the economic argument is examined, as are the difficulties of measuring capacity output properly. Here too, a closer look is taken at the effects of an excise on producer equipment.

A widespread but little discussed variant of excise taxation is the use of government enterprises, particularly for the production or sale of tobacco and alcohol products, to transfer resources to the state. These "fiscal monopolies" are treated in the seventh chapter. This purely institutional form of excise taxation that shows kinship with commodity taxes in socialist economies, warrants full separate treatment; first, therefore, there is a discussion of the rationale and forms of fiscal monopolies, followed by a review of the extent to which they are used throughout the world. Then fiscal monopolies are evaluated in terms of their revenue sufficiency, management aspects, and the pricing policies they pursue.

One of the advantages of the excise method of taxation is its more certain administration, and a detailed discussion of this aspect is included in Chapter 8. Although the equity and economic effects of sales and excise taxation are often the same, the analysis reveals a sharp difference between excise taxation with compliance ensured through physical controls and sales taxes that rely upon checks on accounts for enforcement. The salient features of excise control are discussed first, followed by a review of possible problems in levying the excises. Separate sections are devoted to administrative issues arising in connection with selective taxes on services and in the motoring field.

This broad survey and analysis is completed by an appraisal of the role of excise taxation in the ninth and concluding chapter. More explicit recognition is given here to political and social factors that shape the structural development of excise taxation. Here too excises are compared with other taxes, notably those on sales and income, and the comparative advantages and disadvantages regarding the equity, efficiency and administration of each tax are reviewed; possible influences of these taxes on economic growth and stability are also considered. A summary of the major arguments in the book concludes the chapter.

Systematic and comprehensive information on the structure of excise and sales tax systems in 126 countries is provided in two appendixes to the book: Appendix A—Excise Systems, and Appendix B—Sales Tax Systems. Excise systems are classified on the basis of their coverage, sales taxes according to the levels of trade at which they are imposed. Both systems are further categorized in the light of certain accepted redistributive and allocative criteria relating to the treatment of basic necessities, luxury items, and producer goods; their coverage of services is also dealt with. Appendix C, Tax Revenue Statistics, contains pertinent information on the contribution to government tax revenues of excise systems and of other taxes in eighty-two countries for which sufficient data were available.

CHAPTER 2

CLASSIFICATION AND OVERVIEW OF EXCISE AND SALES TAX SYSTEMS

The nature of excises must be explored before analysis can proceed, and principles and objectives formulated. To which goods and services do governments apply selective taxes? How are they applied and to what extent? On the basis of this information it should be possible to identify essential similarities and to organize the numerous forms and manners in which tax liability arises into relatively homogeneous groupings. These, in turn, can form the basis for an analysis of the nature and effects of selective taxes. Excises must also be differentiated from general taxes on goods and services, which are often called sales taxes.[1] No special virtue attaches to the terminology developed here. Any attempt at formal classification is by nature arbitrary and alternative schemes may have equal merit.[2]

THE DEFINITION OF EXCISES

Broadly speaking, the distinguishing features of excise taxation are selectivity in coverage, discrimination in intent, and some form of quantitative measurement in determining the tax liability.

Selectivity of Coverage

Taxes are commonly classified according to the kind of action that creates the liability or the nature of the base on which the tax is levied. Taxes on goods and services may include "all taxes and duties levied on the production, sale, transfer, leasing, and delivery of goods and rendering of services, or in respect of taxes on the use or ownership of goods or permission to use goods or perform activities."[3] Within this major tax category a distinction is made between selective and general taxes, depending upon the range of goods and services included in the statutory base. Selective taxes include excises, fiscal monopoly profits, as well as taxes on betting and gambling stakes and on specified services. Sales, turnover, or value-added taxes are examples of general taxes. A further subcategory covers taxes on the ownership or use of goods as distinct from taxes on the goods themselves, and taxes on permission to perform certain activities. Examples are the important recurrent or user taxes on motor vehicles, and taxes on licenses to sell alcoholic beverages; these taxes are also selective in nature.

Selective taxes on goods are normally labeled excises, but those on services are usually referred to by the kind of activity being taxed. In the motoring field, selective taxes on petroleum products are generally called excises, but various license and registration duties are usually grouped under motor vehicle taxes. In the United States, a broad application of the excise label has long been accepted, while economists reserved it for the taxes on commodities, and legal writers and courts extended it to include levies imposed in connection with various acts, transactions, or permission to carry on certain activities.[4] History appears to support a broad interpretation. In seventeenth century England, the term excise or new impost was not only applied to eatables, drinks, tobacco, and other goods, but also to houses, trades (hackney coaches, hawkers), bachelors, and services performed in connection with burials, births, and marriages.[5] Although this usage seems rather wide as it includes elements of property taxation and government charges, for ease of expression and exposition it should be acceptable to consider all selective taxes on goods, services, and motor vehicles part of excise systems.[6] Furthermore, general taxes on goods and services will be referred to as sales taxes. On the whole, this terminology appears justified, although sales taxes are sometimes referred to as general excises and excises as selective sales taxes. Finally, customs and import duties, and export and exchange taxes, may also be called selective taxes, but they are not included here.[7]

The scope of coverage, then, emerges as the most useful distinction between excises and sales taxes. Under an excise system, taxable commodities are individually enumerated in the law; under a sales tax, on the other hand, the tax base is typically defined to include all commodities for sale other than those specifically exempted.[8] In practice, coverage may be similar, particularly between an excise system with extended coverage and a sales tax with a large number of exemptions. The excise systems of the Indian subcontinent, for instance, are much broader in scope than the sales taxes in Australasia.[9] The selective nature of excises implies that rates are determined separately for each commodity, in contrast to a sales tax which applies the same rate or a few rates to all commodities or all items of a particular group of commodities.

Discrimination in Intent

In Anglo-Saxon tax literature, selectivity in coverage has usually been considered the main distinguishing feature of excises, and little attempt has been made to consider further refinements. This characteristically undogmatic approach to tax definitions contrasts with European work which has attempted greater precision by making effects and consequences an essential element of the classification.[10] Even though excises are difficult to define according to results, they are nevertheless often imposed precisely because they are discriminatory in intent. They are not normally designed solely for revenue purposes, but are often also justified on other grounds, or viewed as serving a special purpose. This contrasts with sales taxes which have mostly been introduced to meet general revenue needs, and are, therefore, "general" in intent if not in effect.[11]

Various reasons may be advanced to support the imposition of excise-type levies.

1. Excises may be justified to control the consumption of items that are considered immoral or unhealthy, prime examples being sumptuary goods such as tobacco products and alcoholic beverages. At one time or another similar reasons have been given for the excise taxation of playing cards, fireworks, cabaret admissions, and betting and gaming activities. But in the case of sumptuary goods the objective is difficult to attain, since the demand for tobacco products and alcoholic beverages is relatively inelastic. Another reason is that sumptuary excises are alleged to charge consumers for external diseconomies associated with the consumption of cigarettes and liquor.

2. Excises may be imposed on nonessential or luxury items considered proxies for taxpaying capacity. The most obvious examples are the luxury excises on cosmetics, perfumes, jewelry, and furs, but in developing countries selective taxes on electrical appliances and various entertainment-related goods fulfill a similar role. In addition, excises on services such as those related to foreign travel, restaurants, hotels, admissions, and club dues would fall within this category.

3. Excises in the motoring field may be designed and rationalized as service charges for the use of roads. If governments provide services, the consumption of which is

excludable, then prima facie it seems fair that beneficiaries should pay for them in proportion to their use.[12] Such payments are also referred to as benefit levies or user charges. The benefit principle is used to rationalize the various road user charges and taxes, although benefits are only partly discernible and charges only an imperfect approximation of price. Transportation taxes, for example on air fares and freight, may be similarly justified.

4. Related to the sumptuary excises are regulatory type levies, designed to improve efficiency in the use of resources. Examples are the pollution taxes that have recently received so much attention. Like sumptuary excises, these levies are also designed to internalize external diseconomies generated by the producer or consumer, but unlike excises generally no moral or ethical reasons underlie the objective of a reduction in consumption. A difference, too, is that here the main aim is regulation, whereas revenue is an important objective of sumptuary excises.

5. Excises on raw materials have been justified as preventing waste or inducing growing high-yielding plants. The reasoning is that the assumption in excise design of a fixed relationship between inputs and output should lead to an improvement in the quality of inputs, or the design of methods of production which economize on raw materials because the generation of additional output would be free of tax. The sugar excise in Germany has been cited as an example, as has the more recent system of presumptive excise taxation in Pakistan.[13]

6. Recently, the use of selective taxes to promote employment has come to the fore. It is hypothesized that aggregate employment can be increased directly through alterations in the factor mix, or indirectly by changing the product mix. For instance, excises might be imposed on capital equipment that has strong labor-displacing effects, or more generally, higher taxes might be levied on goods that are produced with capital-intensive technology to induce a shift of consumer demand toward more labor-intensive products. In view of the high rates of unemployment in developing countries, these approaches deserve attention.

7. Even more specifically linked to certain objectives are various levies or cesses on agricultural products which are applied to finance research and trade promotion activities, or as price compensation measures, or to facilitate the enforcement of special regulations—relating for instance to adulterated butter or the distribution of narcotics. Examples are the agricultural cesses and duties in Australia and India, the butter levy in the United States, and the tax-cum-subsidy schemes involving dairy products in Finland and Sweden. Generally a direct revenue objective is absent; unlike fees and charges, however, proceeds are not used directly to defray the expenses of the regulating agency.

To be sure, some excises have been introduced solely for revenue purposes, the main consideration being that they could be administered more readily than other taxes. The age-old excise on salt used to be called a gold-mine for revenue purposes, but excises on matches, sugar, edible oil, kerosene, soft drinks, textiles, and cement have been considered just as lucrative. On the whole, large sales volume, few producers, inelastic demand, ready definability, and no close substitutes (unless these can be included in the base) are the requirements for separate excise taxation.[14]

Quantitative Measurement

The sumptuary or regulatory features of excise taxation usually imply the use of some form of physical control or measurement by the excise authorities to determine the tax liability and ensure compliance with the law. For instance, the premises of cigarette producers and alcoholic beverage manufacturers are almost always closely policed by excise staff, but this form of compliance control is also suitable for other excises. In some instances, excise staff may be replaced by metering devices that record the quantities produced, and numbered tickets issued, for instance in the case of admissions. Obviously, measurement is essential in the case of excises on pollutants. For most excises the control and enforcement procedures that are prescribed by statute are typically attuned to the peculiarities of each production process or the manner in which a particular service is rendered. Quantitative measurement and physical control may be considered additional distinguishing features of excise taxation.

The form of control for excises contrasts with that for sales taxes under which, at least in name, liabilities are almost always verified through checks upon written records. Recently, the trend in industrial countries has been to shift excise control to books of account, but even then statutory provisions for quantitative checks are retained in full force, as exemplified by the updating of excise legislation in the Netherlands in the sixties.

Domestic Goods, Imports, and Exports

Historically, excise taxation has been associated with domestically produced commodities, any countervailing duty on goods coming from abroad being incorporated in the import duty. But present practice differs. Thus, a number of countries—Ethiopia, Turkey, and most francophone African countries, for example—designate the countervailing import duties as excises. Mali refers to its taxes on petroleum products and liquor as excises, although the products are wholly imported. Egypt and the Sudan levy excises on certain commodities, whether of domestic origin or imported, but call the levy at the import stage a "consumption duty" to distinguish it from the domestic excise. Still other countries impose duties primarily on unmanufactured products that are all imported.[15] The usual treatment in OECD literature is to regard the duties on tobacco, alcohol and petroleum products levied at the import stage as excises. That custom is also followed in this study.

Under sales taxes, imports are included in the base, except in Barbados and Ghana. However, the rates that are applied may differ from the domestic duty. With few exceptions, exports are exempted both under excises and sales taxes.[16] Under a sales tax this may involve a refund of the tax paid prior to the export stage, whereas with an excise levy goods are generally exported from bonded factory premises. Little effort, however, is made to free exports from excises on auxiliary materials (such as petroleum products) and services. Generally, excisable goods are not included in the sales tax base, except in continental European and French-speaking African countries.

Stamp Duties, Fees, and Charges

Stamp duties, fees, and charges are closely related to excises. Stamp duties are levied on the documentary evidence of specified financial and capital transactions, including official papers, deeds, mortgages, receipts, and bank checks, usually at a fixed rate but sometimes at differentiated rates depending upon the value of the transaction.[17] Fees and charges are payments for, but usually do not exceed the cost of services performed or privileges granted by government from which a special measurable benefit is derived.[18] Like some excises, fees and charges are specific purpose levies, but though the specific purpose is a secondary objective for excises, since revenue is usually the first, it is the exclusive justification for levying fees and charges; driving license and passport fees are good examples. On the other hand, license duties payable by producers of and dealers in excisable goods are designated excises in this study; in some countries they are an important source of revenue.[19]

Sales taxes must also be distinguished from related levies. Thus business, occupation, or license taxes measured by gross receipts are not considered sales taxes here. Although these taxes are probably identical to low-rate turnover taxes in terms of economic effects, they are often justified as a government charge for the privilege of carrying on a business, trade, or profession, are not meant to be passed on to consumers, and are usually levied at fractional rates. Examples are the gross receipts taxes in Argentina, Brazil, Nicaragua, and Venezuela.

It should be reemphasized that the distinctions made here are inherently arbitrary. In practice, differences may be minimal, as with the tax bases of excises and sales taxes. Historical biases may also obscure the issue—the French taxing tradition for instance clearly favors sales taxes over excises, whereas countries following the British tradition have shown a preference for excise taxation. Furthermore, excises, particularly those of the regulatory kind, often shade off into related license fees and charges. The revenue aspects of the latter may in turn become so important that they might appropriately be considered excises. Stamp duties may also be extended far beyond the rather limited number of legal and commercial documents with which they are customarily associated and come to resemble gross receipts or sales taxes. Examples are the stamp taxes of Greece, Guatemala, Paraguay, and Portugal; some of these taxes also have elements of income and payroll taxes. Although in form, therefore, the excise systems of countries following one or another pathway may appear to diverge quite widely, in reality differences may be minimal.

CLASSIFICATION OF EXCISE SYSTEMS

Excises may be classified into broad categories of selective taxes on goods, on services, and on motor vehicles; these three groupings comprise an excise system. Furthermore, tobacco products, alcoholic beverages, and petroleum products have been referred to as traditional excise goods (the corresponding duties are traditional excises), and other goods subject to excises have been called nontraditional excise goods.[20] This terminology can be employed for a systematic identification of the composition of excise systems and subsequently of the forms that they may take.

Composition and Forms of Excise Systems

A comprehensive list of goods and services that may be subject to excises in various countries of the world is set out below. Obviously, some commodities mentioned in the list can be placed under more than one heading: industrial countries may view electrical appliances, radios, and television sets as seminecessities while they are luxury goods elsewhere. Motor vehicles could be classified justifiably under luxury goods, but their importance warrants separate consideration. Similarly, entertainment duties could be designated excises on luxury services, together with, for instance, foreign travel and tourist-related levies including those on hotels and restaurants. A somewhat different grouping could also be made if certain articles were considered proxies for other excisables—matches and lighters for tobacco, tubes for radios, playing cards for gambling—or if items were classified on the basis of relative substitutability, for instance, soft drinks for beer.

Selective taxes on goods

Traditional excise goods
1. Tobacco products: unmanufactured tobacco, cigars, cheroots, cigarettes, pipe and cigarette tobacco, chewing tobacco, snuff

2. Alcoholic beverages: beer, wine, vermouths, cider, perry, mead, spirits, liqueurs, cordials

3. Hydrocarbon oils: crude petroleum, spirit, kerosene, fuel, lubricating oils, natural gas

Foods and nonalcoholic beverages

4. Sugar: beet sugar, cane sugar, syrups, molasses, caramel, confectionary, liquorice, sweetened food preparations, saccharine

5. Soft drinks: spa waters, aerated waters, lemonades, orangeades, fruit juices

6. Other foods and nonalcoholic beverages: coffee, tea, cocoa, salt, spices, edible oils, margarine, dairy products, ice cream, cereals, rice, flour, bread, biscuits, fruits, meat, fish

Other nontraditional excise goods

7. Textiles and miscellaneous nonfood items: textiles, footwear, matches, soap, detergents, cutlery, glassware, furniture, pharmaceuticals, playing cards

8. Luxury goods: cosmetics, perfumery, jewelry, furs, electric household appliances, refrigerators, air-conditioning units, radios, television sets, clocks, watches, musical instruments, phonographic records, photographic equipment, toys, sporting goods, fireworks

9. Producer goods: cement, building materials, paints, enamels, metals, plastics, coal, wood, paper, rubber, jute, cables, batteries

Selective taxes on services

Services

10. Transportation, travel: freight and passenger services, foreign travel, airports

11. Banking, insurance: banking services, checks, credit balances, insurance policies, insurance premia, fire protection

12. Miscellaneous services: electricity, gas, water, telephone, telegraph, restaurants, hotels, tourism, advertisements

Betting, gaming, entertainment

13. Gambling, sweepstakes, lotteries

14. Entertainment: admissions to casinos, night clubs, cabarets, theaters, sporting events, club dues, fishing, hunting, and dog licenses

Selective taxes on motoring

Motor vehicles

15. Road use: motor vehicle licenses, registration duties, transfer taxes, special duties on cars, tires, tubes, tolls, vehicle tonnage

On the basis of the classification of this list, Appendix A—Excise Systems, gives for each country the various goods and services on which excises are imposed. Because they are taxed in virtually all countries, traditional excise goods, entertainment services, and motor vehicles are not identified separately. But many countries also levy excises on other goods and services. Thus from a review, it appears that sugar, salt, soft drinks, and their substitutes are the most widely excised food products. Of 115 countries known to impose nontraditional excises, 65 collect an excise on sugar, 29 on salt, and 71 on soft drinks. Matches, another highly favored product, are subject to an excise in as many as 65 countries. Like salt, its inelastic demand features and implicit revenue properties made it commonly subject to tax in early times; presently mechanical lighters are often taxed concurrently. At least 17 governments collect an excise on playing cards that can only yield a little revenue. Among luxury items, cosmetics, perfumery, and toilet articles are subject to excises in at least 27 countries and jewelry in 20 countries. Producer goods that are taxed frequently—by at least 27 countries—include cement and building materials. Among services, a separate levy on insurance is imposed in 40 countries; travel in one form or another is taxed in 50 countries; hotel and restaurant services in 31 countries. Some excises are peculiarly regional, including the taxation of biscuits in East Africa, wheat flour in Central American countries, and dairy products and pharmaceuticals in Scandinavia.

As shown below, in the list of forms of excise systems, depending upon the range of goods and services covered, excise systems may be of the limited, intermediate, or extended type. While all types of excise systems include selective taxes on traditional goods, motor vehicles, entertainment services, and items like sugar, soft drinks and cement, the coverage of intermediate excise systems usually extends to a number of other nontraditional excise goods such as textiles, paints, cosmetics, perfumery and some services such as insurance and travel. Extended excise systems include, in addition, a large number of selective taxes on luxury and producer goods. As is clear, the systems may overlap and sometimes the distinctions become blurred, particularly when a country employs a large number of selective levies that have strong regulatory features but yield little revenue. Appendix A indicates the form of excise system for each country, and the extent to which governments have monopolized the production or distribution of products or services that are subject to excises elsewhere.

Forms of excise systems

Limited excise systems comprise at least the traditional excise goods: tobacco products, alcoholic beverages, and petroleum products as well as motor vehicles and various forms of entertainment. In addition, some food products such as sugar, salt, soft drinks and, for instance, matches, cement, or insurance may be included. However, all in all, the coverage of limited systems would not exceed ten to fifteen commodity groups with closely related products (various petroleum products, or sugar and saccharine, for instance) being treated as one excisable item.

Intermediate excise systems consist of between fifteen and thirty commodity groups. In addition to the items covered under limited systems, they include more food products such as various dairy and grain products. Other items of widespread consumption, such as textiles, footwear, and pharmaceuticals, may also be covered, as well as a few luxury items, for instance, cosmetics and perfumes. The producer goods that may be part of intermediate systems are cement, building materials, paints, and varnishes. As a rule, a number of services such as insurance, banking, transportation, and public utilities are taxed.

Extended excise systems comprise more than thirty commodity groups spanning almost the whole range of production activities in a particular country. In addition to the items taxed under intermediate systems, many luxury and producer goods are excisable. Invariably, high excises are imposed on electrical and gas-operated appliances, radios, television sets, and musical and photographic equipment. Extended systems are the only excise systems that cover a wide range of producer goods: steel and aluminum products, plastics and resins, rubber products, wood products, and sometimes machinery.

Excise Rate Schedules

"A tax scheme addressed to any taxpayer is a list of statements relating quantities of payments required from him to selected objective conditions."[21] For an excise, the payment may be a specified amount per unit produced, sold or consumed, and the conditions may be the number, volume, weight, strength, length, or other physical characteristics of the excisable commodity. When the rate is expressed as a fixed amount per unit, it is called a unit tax or specific excise. Alternatively, the payment may be a specified proportion of the possible values of the commodity, in which case it is called an ad valorem excise. The value may be based on the invoice price of the commodity, but more often it is a constructive or appraised value determined by the excise authorities.

Several relationships between payments and conditions are possible. A specific excise may be the same regardless of the volume of production or the range of possible values, but an additional condition may specify that the rate does not apply unless the production or unit price exceeds a specified amount. More generally, bracketed specific rates are levied when the fixed amount of the excise varies for different price brackets or volumes of production. Similarly, ad valorem rates may be expressed as a uniform percentage for the whole production or price range possible, but they may also vary with specified production or price brackets and accordingly may be called bracketed ad valorem rates.

The level of an excise rate may be expressed in its relation to the price of the commodity, preferably the actual (rather than constructive) retail price; the ratio may be called the effective excise rate. The effective rates of most specific excises fall with rising prices; an exception is the bracketed specific rate schedule under which the average effective excise rate for one price bracket is higher than the effective rate of the preceding bracket. Most ad valorem rates are proportional to price, except the bracketed ad valorem rate that rises with higher price brackets.

Several of these variations in rate schedules occur in practice, and it is not unusual to find combinations of specific and ad valorem rates. Excises on petroleum products, sugar, and soft drinks may be of the simple specific type solely based on volume, but additional conditions are often made that make the rate dependent on the nature of the petroleum products (gasoline versus diesel oil), the sugar content (white versus brown sugar), or the kind of soft drink (aerated water versus fruit juice). An interesting example of bracketed specific rates are the cotton yarn and fabric duties on the Indian subcontinent that condition the amount of excise per square yard on the fineness of the fabric (superfine, fine, medium, coarse) and the nature of the processing (bleached, printed, mercerized, or embroidered). Similarly, for yarn, the duty rises with the number of counts per pound. An unusual bracketed specific rate is in effect for matches in Pakistan, related to the number of sticks per box and the number of boxes produced per day. In the EEC most excises on beer vary with the volume of production.

Luxury goods and services usually attract simple ad valorem rates, because of great variations in form, quality, and price of the excisable commodity. Bracketed ad valorem rates are not unusual either, though. In Japan for instance, luxury goods with a retail price below a specified amount are exempted, and in New York City low-priced theater admissions are similarly free of excise. In Pakistan, multiple bracketed ad valorem rates apply to soap, batteries, and electric tubes. Tobacco products, tea, and coffee are often taxed under rate schedules that combine a uniform specific excise per weight unit with a bracketed ad valorem schedule based on various possible retail prices.

The effective rates on traditional excise goods are high in most countries. In industrial countries, duties on cigarettes and liquors may be 70 per cent of the retail prices of these products. In July 1974, the effective rate on gasoline averaged 48 per cent in industrial countries, compared to 40 per cent in developing countries.[22] Generally, rates are lower for nontraditional goods and services with the exception of perfumes and cosmetics that also attract heavy excises.

CLASSIFICATION OF SALES TAX SYSTEMS

Taxable commodities pass through various stages of production and distribution on their way from primary producer to consumer, and sales taxes may be imposed at one or more of these stages; accordingly, they may be called single-stage or multistage taxes. Sales taxes collected at the manufacturers, wholesale, or retail level are single-stage taxes, and turnover and value-added taxes are multistage levies. In addition, various hybrid forms are imposed that ostensibly aim at the retail level, but exclude small retailers for practical reasons. Below are shown the various forms of sales taxation found throughout the world in their approximate order of historical appearance.

Forms of sales taxation

Turnover taxes: collected on sales at all or nearly all production and distribution stages; on account of their cumulative effects these taxes are also referred to as cascade taxes.

Production taxes: collected on sales by producers to wholesalers, retailers, or other producers; transactions prior to the sale by the last producer are often partially exempted or taxed at reduced rates:

a. French-type production taxes: exempt domestically produced raw materials and intermediate goods as well as imported goods that have not been further processed.

b. Other production taxes: exempt producer goods or apply reduced rates, while trading activities per se are excluded from the tax.

Manufacturers taxes: collected on sales by manufacturers to wholesalers or retailers, including occasional direct sales to consumers. While capital goods are usually exempted outright, various techniques have been designed to counter the cumulative effects of the taxation of raw materials and intermediate goods:

a. The suspension method: permits the tax-free purchase of inputs by traders and manufacturers registered for that purpose, tax being levied when products leave the "ring" and are sold to unregistered persons.

b. The subtraction technique: allows for a deduction of taxable purchases from taxable sales; this can be done for:

(1) physically incorporated inputs only; or

(2) on some other basis such as a deduction for inputs taxed at the same rate as the finished product.

c. The tax credit principle: provides for a credit for tax paid on purchases against tax payable on sales.

Wholesale taxes: collected on sales by the last wholesaler or manufacturer to retailers, including occasional direct sales to consumers. Capital goods are usually exempted outright, while the suspension method applies to raw materials and intermediate goods.

Retail/wholesale taxes: (hybrid systems) collected on the sales of retailers to final consumers and of wholesalers or manufacturers to retailers whose operations are considered too small for separate taxation. Producer goods are treated similarly as under wholesale taxes.

Retail taxes: collected on sales by retailers to final consumers, including wholesalers or manufacturers selling occasionally to consumers; producer goods are generally excluded by definition.

Value-added taxes: collected on sales at all or nearly all production and distribution stages, with each stage receiving a credit for tax paid on purchases from the preceding stage:

   a. The EEC model: extends through the retail stage and provides for a credit for tax paid on all producer goods.

   b. Other types: may not cover the retail stage and sometimes do not give credit for tax paid on certain fixed assets.

In addition to the trade level at which they are imposed, sales taxes may be distinguished on the basis of features designed to eliminate competitive distortions. As is well known, a sales tax that applies to each transaction becomes cumulative in its effect on prices and the effective tax rate will differ depending upon the number of transactions involved. The classic example is the turnover tax that has widely differing effective rates and distorts producer choices because it favors integrated over nonintegrated forms of business and self-production over subcontracting.

Cumulative or cascade effects may be avoided by applying tax only once to each good on its way from producer to consumer. Single-stage taxes succeed in this, but competitive distortions remain, because taxable firms are induced to push as many functions forward as possible so that their value will not be included in the taxable price. Moreover, effective rates will still vary to the extent that distribution margins are not included in the taxable price—for instance, the rate will be lower on luxury goods with relatively high margins and higher on necessities with relatively low margins. Obviously, the tax will eliminate competitive distortions better and achieve more uniformity in effective rates the closer its impact is to the point of final sale to the consumer, because potential variations in trading functions and margins will be smaller; variations are zero at the retail stage. On the whole, in the order in which they are listed here, each sales tax discriminates less than its predecessor between different forms of economic organization.

In eliminating cumulative effects, the concern is mainly with avoiding taxation of commodities that are purchased from previous production or distribution stages. These commodities may be called producer goods; they include production inputs such as raw materials and intermediate goods that are physically incorporated in the product or lose their identity in the process of production or distribution, or items such as machinery that are used in more than one production process, as well as commodities that are simply traded further.

By definition no attempt is made to exclude producer goods under multistage turnover taxes, although capital goods may be exempted. In the case of production taxes, however, various rules limit the cumulative effects that arise from the taxation of successive production and distribution stages.[23] Thus, under one variant, modeled after the French production tax, an exemption is provided for domestically produced raw materials and intermediate goods as well as for imported goods that have not been further processed.[24] Other countries with multistage production taxes partially exempt producer goods or apply reduced rates, while trading activities per se are excluded from the tax. Consequently, these taxes have multistage features, but these are less pronounced than they are under the pure turnover taxes that apply to all transactions at the same rate.

Under single-stage taxes, capital goods, being relatively easy to identify and used primarily for business purposes, are commonly exempted outright. However, raw materials and intermediate goods can often be applied to production as well as consumption purposes;[25] consequently, various techniques have been designed to counter the undesirable effects of cumulative taxation. Thus, under the suspension method, manufacturers and wholesalers, registered for that purpose, can buy or import their inputs free of tax, tax being levied only when products are sold to unregistered entities, usually at the point of sale to the last wholesaler or the retailer. The subtraction technique, incorporated in some manufacturers taxes, allows for a deduction of taxable purchases from taxable sales; this can be done for physically incorporated inputs only, or on a wider basis. Under a closely related principle, credit is given for the tax paid on purchases against the tax payable on sales.

Under a retail tax, the taxation of producer goods can be avoided almost entirely by defining taxable sales as sales for use or consumption, and not for resale. Under sales taxes of the retail/wholesale type the suspension method is usually adopted for inputs, while capital goods are exempted outright. Under the value-added tax, the tax credit method is universally applied to the tax paid on both inputs and capital goods.[26] This is fully accomplished under the model adopted in the EEC that extends through the retail stage, but elsewhere no credit is given for the tax on certain capital goods, while the retail stage may not be taxable.[27]

Sales tax systems of individual countries are listed in Table 1 in Appendix B. Each system is characterized by the stage at which the tax is imposed, the most common or standard rate of tax[28] and certain structural aspects relating to the treatment of basic necessities, luxury goods, producer goods and services, which are categories also used in classifying excisable commodities. Under most sales taxes, basic necessities are either exempted or subject to reduced rates.[29] Luxury goods may or may not be discriminated against and accordingly may attract higher rates of tax or be subject to the standard rate. The methods used in eliminating or mitigating cumulative effects that arise from the taxation of producer goods are also indicated, or if no such efforts are made, the extent to which producer goods are taxed is shown. The last column deals with the treatment of services. Where appropriate, the degree of rate differentiation in the relevant legislation is indicated, together with the coverage of each category of goods and services.[30]

OVERVIEW OF EXCISE AND SALES TAX SYSTEMS

An overview of the excise and sales tax systems in 126 countries is given in Table 2:1. Here the classification is by region, and for clarity the sales tax system in each country and the standard rate are indicated first, followed by the nature of the excise system. To complete the overview, the revenue importance of each system is also given, but discussion is deferred until the next chapter.

As shown further in Table 2:2, one half of all countries have limited excise systems that comprise traditional excise goods, motor vehicles, entertainment services, and a few other products. Geographically, this form of excise system is heavily concentrated in North and West Africa and in South America. The large number of countries that levy a wider range of excises is surprising. In fact, more than two out of five users extend the coverage beyond the commodities included under a limited system. The widespread and intensive use that is made of excises indicates that they are considered an important form of taxation in many countries.

More specifically, one out of four countries operates an intermediate excise system, but geographically they are predominantly a European and Central, East and South African phenomenon. In Europe various food products are widely taxed as well as other items of widespread consumption. In Central Africa the excise systems comprise the *tax unique* that is imposed on goods produced and traded in the Central African Customs and Economic Union; it replaces the import duties and sales taxes collected previously.[31] Extended excise systems that comprise virtually all industrial activities in a country are mainly found in Asia, the Caribbean and Central America. In Asia they include the excise systems of the Indian subcontinent and the commodity taxes in China (Taiwan), Japan, and Korea.[32] In the Caribbean, this form comprises the consumption and purchase taxes of the countries belonging to the Caribbean Community (Caricom) that impose selective taxes on products for which trade restrictions and

Table 2.1. Sales Tax and Excise Systems of the World[1]

Country	Nature of Sales Tax	Standard Sales Tax Rate (Tax-Exclusive)	Excise Coverage	Sales Tax	Total	Traditional Excise Goods
North and West Africa						
Algeria	Manufacturers[2]	25	Limited	. . .	. . .	(. . .)
Dahomey (Bénin)	Manufacturers[3]	15.6	Limited	4	10	(9)*
Gambia, The	No sales tax	—	Limited	—	. . .	(. . .)
Ghana	Manufacturers[4]	11.5	Extended	8	21	(13)
Guinea	Manufacturers[3]	7.5	Limited	. . .	. . .	(. . .)
Ivory Coast	Manufacturers[2]	20.2	Limited	26	10	(9)*
Liberia	No sales tax	—	Limited	—	7	(5)*
Libya	No sales tax	—	Limited	—	. . .	(. . .)
Mali	Manufacturers[3]	25	Limited	24	11	(7)*
Mauritania	Manufacturers[3]	9.9	Limited	25	10	(9)*
Morocco	Manufacturers[2]	17.6	Limited	26	23	(17)
Niger	Manufacturers[3]	22	Limited	28	9	(8)*
Nigeria	No sales tax	—	Extended	—	14	(6)
Senegal	Manufacturers[2]	12.4	Limited	34	18	(16)*
Sierra Leone	No sales tax	—	Intermediate	—	26	(24)
Togo	Manufacturers[3]	11.1	Limited	. . .	. . .	(. . .)
Tunisia	Manufacturers[3]	16.8	Limited	25	17	(15)
Upper Volta	Manufacturers[3]	21.9	Limited	21	12	(11)*
Central Africa						
Burundi	Turnover	2	Limited	. . .	. . .	(. . .)
Cameroon	Production[5]	9.6	Intermediate[6]	. . .	. . .	(. . .)
Central African Republic	Production[5]	11.7	Intermediate[6]	. . .	. . .	(. . .)
Chad	Production[5]	15.6	Intermediate[6]	14	18	(9)*
Congo	Production[5]	15.2	Intermediate[6]	. . .	. . .	(. . .)
Equatorial Guinea	Turnover	3	No excises	. . .	—	(—)
Gabon	Production[5]	7.5	Intermediate[6]	. . .	. . .	(. . .)
Rwanda	No sales tax	—	Limited	—	. . .	(. . .)
Zaïre	Production	10	Limited	8	6	(5)*
East and South Africa						
Botswana	Manufacturers[2]	10	Limited	. . .	. . .	(. . .)
Ethiopia	Production	5	Intermediate	16	26	(17)
Kenya	Manufacturers[4]	15	Intermediate	—[7]	34	(26)
Lesotho	Manufacturers[2]	10	Limited	. . .	. . .	(. . .)
Malagasy Republic	Manufacturers[2]	13.6	Limited	20	18	(18)*
Malawi	Production	15	Limited	. . .	. . .	(. . .)
Mauritius	No sales tax	—	Limited	—	37	(31)
Somalia	No sales tax	—	Intermediate[6]	—	31	(13)*
Sudan	No sales tax	—	Extended[6]	—	. . .	(. . .)
Swaziland	Manufacturers[2]	10	Limited	. . .	. . .	(. . .)
Tanzania	Manufacturers[4]	12	Intermediate	11	31	(22)
Uganda	Manufacturers[4]	10	Intermediate	16	29	(18)
Zambia	No sales tax	—	Intermediate	—	10	(10)*
Middle East						
Afghanistan	No sales tax	—	Intermediate[6]	—	. . .	(. . .)
Bahrain	No sales tax	—	No excises	—	—	(—)
Egypt	No sales tax	—	Extended[6]	—	. . .	(. . .)

Table 2.1 (continued).   Sales Tax and Excise Systems of the World[1]

Country	Nature of Sales Tax	Standard Sales Tax Rate (Tax-Exclusive)	Excise Coverage	Sales Tax	Total	Traditional Excise Goods
					Revenue Importance (In Per Cent of Total Tax Revenues)	
	Structure				*Excise System*	
Iran	No sales tax	—	Intermediate	—	10	(8)
Iraq	No sales tax	—	Intermediate	—	. . .	(. . .)
Israel	Value-added	8	Extended[6]	12	12	(8)*
Jordan	No sales tax	—	Extended[6]	—	. . .	(. . .)
Kuwait	No sales tax	—	No excises	—	—	(—)
Lebanon	No sales tax	—	Limited	—	23	(19)
Oman	No sales tax	—	No excises	—	—	(—)
Qatar	No sales tax	—	No excises	—	—	(—)
Saudi Arabia	No sales tax	—	No excises	—	—	(—)
Syria	No sales tax	—	Intermediate	—	18	(10)
United Arab Emirates	No sales tax	—	No excises	—	—	(—)
Yemen Arab Republic	No sales tax	—	Limited	—	. . .	(. . .)
Yemen, P.D.R.	No sales tax	—	Limited	—	. . .	(. . .)
South Asia and Far East						
Bangladesh	Manufacturers[4]	20	Extended	. . .	. . .	(. . .)
Burma	Production	10	Limited	. . .	. . .	(. . .)
China (Taiwan)	Turnover	2	Extended[6]	6	42	(21)
India	Turnover	0.5-3	Extended	15	51	(24)
	Manufacturers[4]	5-7				
Japan	No sales tax	—	Extended[6]	—	26	(17)
Korea	Turnover	1-2	Extended[6]	7	37	(18)
Nepal	Retail/wholesale	8	Extended	15	16	(11)*
Pakistan	Manufacturers[4]	20	Extended	6	38	(24)
Sri Lanka	Production	5	Limited	11	27	(24)
South-East Asia						
Indonesia	Production	10	Limited	12	19	(17)
Laos	Production[5]	7.2	Limited	. . .	. . .	(. . .)
Malaysia	Manufacturers[4]	5	Intermediate	—[7]	35	(22)
Papua New Guinea	No sales tax	—	Limited	—	. . .	(. . .)
Philippines	Production	7	Limited	21	16	(14)
Singapore	No sales tax	—	Limited	—	40	(24)
Thailand	Production	7	Limited	21	28	(22)
Caribbean and Central America						
Bahamas	No sales tax	—	Limited	—	. . .	(. . .)
Barbados	Retail	5	Extended[6]	—[7]	19	(14)
Costa Rica	Value-added	8	Extended[6]	15	23	(17)
Dominican Republic	No sales tax	—	Intermediate	—	29	(20)*
El Salvador	No sales tax	—	Intermediate[6]	—	28	(21)
Grenada	No sales tax	—	Extended[6]	-	. . .	(. . .)
Guatemala	No sales tax	—	Limited	—	28	(23)
Haiti	No sales tax	—	Extended	—	. . .	(. . .)
Honduras	Value-added	3	Limited	7	28	(23)
Jamaica	No sales tax	—	Extended[6]	—	28	(19)
Nicaragua	Retail/wholesale	6	Extended[6]	8	41	(27)
Panama	Value-added	5	Limited	—[7]	28	(16)
Trinidad and Tobago	No sales tax	—	Extended[6]	—	22	(9)*

Table 2.1 (continued). Sales Tax and Excise Systems of the World[1]

Country	Nature of Sales Tax	Standard Sales Tax Rate (Tax-Exclusive)	Excise Coverage	Sales Tax	Total	Traditional Excise Goods
South America						
Argentina	Value-added	16	Intermediate	17	32	(25)
Bolivia	Value-added	5	Limited	6	13	(11)*
Brazil	Manufacturers[2]	8	Limited	50	17	(15)
	Value-added	12.3-17.6				
Chile	Value-added	20	Limited	32	9	(8)*
Colombia	Manufacturers[2]	15	Limited	8	15	(14)
Ecuador	Value-added	4	Limited	10	16	(11)
Guyana	Manufacturers[4]	10-20	Limited	. . .	. . .	(. . .)
Paraguay	Retail/wholesale[4]	3	Limited	5	20	(17)
Peru	Manufacturers[2]	20	Limited	. . .	15	(10)*
Surinam	No sales tax	—	Limited	—	. . .	(. . .)
Uruguay	Value-added	20	Intermediate[6]	19	27	(17)
Venezuela	No sales tax	—	Limited	—	8	(7)
North America and Australasia						
Australia	Wholesale[4]	15	Limited	7	19	(13)
Canada	Manufacturers[4]	12	Limited	16	12	(7)
	Retail	5-8				
Fiji	No sales tax	—	Limited	—	. . .	(. . .)
Mexico	Turnover	4	Intermediate	11	17	(7)*
New Zealand	Wholesale[4]	20	Limited	8	14	(13)
South Africa	Manufacturers[2]	10	Limited	7	19	(16)
United States	Retail	2.5-7	Limited	6	15	(8)
Western Samoa	No sales tax	—	No excises	—	—	(—)
European Economic Community (EEC)						
Belgium	Value-added	18	Limited	31	15	(12)
Denmark	Value-added	15	Intermediate	18	25	(16)
France	Value-added	17.6	Intermediate	38	21	(16)
Germany	Value-added	11	Intermediate	22	21	(16)
Ireland	Value-added	20	Limited	11	41	(36)
Italy	Value-added	12	Intermediate	22	36	(25)
Luxembourg	Value-added	10	Limited	. . .	. . .	(. . .)
Netherlands	Value-added	18	Limited	22	15	(11)
United Kingdom	Value-added	8	Limited	8	25	(21)

import duties were lifted by agreement.[33] Most of the eight countries that do not levy excises at all are located in the Middle East where alternative sources of revenue are available in the form of oil revenues or oil transit dues.

A breakdown of sales taxes is provided in Table 2 in Appendix B. The most favored form appears to be the variant imposed at the manufacturing stage. Thirty-two countries, or 37 per cent of all those with sales taxes, collect the tax at this level. For developing countries this tax is probably the easiest to administer as it is collected at a level where the number of taxpayers is smallest and record keeping the best; the close relationship with previously imposed production excises, and the corresponding duties collectible at the import stage are other administrative

Table 2.1 (concluded). Sales Tax and Excise Systems of the World[1]

| | Structure | | | Revenue Importance (In Per Cent of Total Tax Revenues) | | |
| | | | | | Excise System | |
Country	Nature of Sales Tax	Standard Sales Tax Rate (Tax-Exclusive)	Excise Coverage	Sales Tax	Total	Traditional Excise Goods
Europe (non-EEC)						
Austria	Value-added[8]	18	Intermediate	25	19	(13)
Cyprus	No sales tax	—	Limited	—	37	(24)
Finland	Wholesale[4]	12.4	Intermediate	20	25	(18)
Greece	Manufacturers[3]	8	Extended	12	31	(23)
Iceland	Retail	20	Intermediate	. . .	. . .	(. . .)
Malta	No sales tax	—	Limited	—	. . .	(. . .)
Norway	Value-added[8]	20	Intermediate	31	21	(12)
Portugal	Wholesale[4]	10	Intermediate	12	29	(13)
Spain	Turnover	2	Intermediate[6]	. . .	. . .	(. . .)
Sweden	Value-added[8]	17.6	Intermediate	13	21	(14)
Switzerland	Retail/wholesale[4]	5.6/8.4	Limited	9	20	(13)
Turkey	Manufacturers[3]	Var.	Intermediate	20	30	(19)

Sources: Appendices A, B, and C.

[1]Information on structural aspects relates to the beginning of 1977; however, some source material was of older date and sometimes incomplete. Revenue data are averages covering fiscal years 1969–71; — indicates that revenue is nil; . . . mean that data are not available; * means that data are incomplete.

[2]Cumulative effects mitigated through tax credit principle.

[3]Cumulative effects mitigated through subtraction technique.

[4]Cumulative effects mitigated through suspension method.

[5]French-type production tax.

[6]Excise system includes wide range of selective taxes known as *taxe unique* (francophone Africa), consumption tax (Afghanistan, Caribbean, Central America, Egypt, Somalia, Sudan), additional tax (Jordan), commodity tax (Far East), purchase tax (Israel), or luxury tax (Spain, Uruguay).

[7]Sales tax introduced subsequent to the fiscal years for which revenue data were collected.

[8]Value-added tax based on EEC model.

advantages.[34] The variant is particularly popular in Africa where two out of every three countries use it. The countries that impose manufacturers taxes are approximately evenly divided among the various techniques to eliminate cumulative effects. The subtraction technique, limiting deductions to inputs which are physically incorporated in produced goods, is exclusively a francophone African phenomenon. Closely related are the production taxes that are found in fourteen countries, six of which were formerly associated with France.

Only four countries impose the sales tax at the wholesale stage and four collect the tax at the retail stage. Four countries operate hybrid forms of sales taxes of the retail/wholesale type. Twenty-two countries, or 25 per cent of those with sales taxes, now have a value-added tax; they

Table 2.2. Regional Distribution of Excise Systems

Region	No Excises	Limited Excise Systems	Inter-mediate Excise Systems	Extended Excise Systems	Total
North and West Africa	—	15	1	2	18
Central Africa	1	3	5	—	9
East and South Africa	—	6	6	1	13
Middle East	6	3	4	3	16
South Asia and Far East	—	2	—	7	9
South-East Asia	—	6	1	—	7
Caribbean and Central America	—	4	2	7	13
South America	—	10	2	—	12
North America and Australasia	1	6	1	—	8
European Economic Community (EEC)	—	5	4	—	9
Europe (non-EEC)	—	3	8	1	12
Total Number of Countries	8	63	34	21	126
Per Cent of Total	6	50	27	17	100

Source: Table 2.1.

— denotes that excises or a particular form of excise system are not found.

are mostly found in the EEC and associated countries, although a few developing countries also impose this form of sales tax. Seven countries still levy multistage turnover taxes.

Of the 126 countries surveyed, 42 countries, or 1 out of 3, do not impose a sales tax at all. These countries are found mostly in the Caribbean, the Middle East, and Africa. As indicated, most Caribbean countries operate extended excise systems instead of a sales tax, and in the Middle East broad based consumption taxes are not needed since alternative sources of revenue are available; in many African countries the economic base is probably too small to justify the introduction of a sales tax, and import duties together with selective excises still fulfill the revenue function adequately.

The degree to which sales tax and excise systems interact in each country can be ascertained from Appendixes A and B. Allocative and redistributive criteria have probably been more consciously considered under sales taxes than under excise systems. Under sales taxes, basic necessities are either exempted or attract a lower rate, although the effect may be nullified by the regressive excises that are imposed separately. Most countries tax luxury items at enhanced rates of sales tax; very few apply luxury excises except under extended excise systems. With the exception of multistage turnover and production taxes, most sales tax systems attempt to eliminate the cumulative effects arising from the taxation of successive stages of production and distribution. Cascading is less of a problem under most excise systems as these are mainly single-stage taxes imposed on a limited number of items for direct consumption. Services are generally included under sales taxes that follow French taxing traditions; the opposite holds for countries that have adopted features of the British tax system. Financial services and services related to entertainment are often subject to separate excises. Border tax adjustments are made under both systems, that is, countervailing duties are levied on imports and exports freed from tax.

CHAPTER 3

REVENUE ASPECTS OF EXCISE SYSTEMS

Excises are important in most countries simply because they make such a large contribution to tax revenue. In a representative sample of developing and industrial countries, excises on average contribute 25 per cent of total tax revenue, which is more than sales or income taxes. India's extended excise system, for instance, brings in more than 50 per cent of combined central and state government tax revenues, and Ireland collects 36 per cent of tax revenue (or 10 per cent of gross national product) from only three items: tobacco products, alcoholic beverages, and petroleum products.

This chapter takes a closer look at the revenue aspects of excise systems. First comes a review of the scope and quality of the basic data. Next is a cross-section analysis of the role of excise systems in the tax structure, considering their relative contribution to total tax revenue, comparing it to the revenue importance of sales taxes, and reflecting on the response of excises to changes in income and revenue needs. The last part deals with the revenue composition of excise systems, the revenue importance of selected excisables and regional patterns of excise taxation.

A NOTE ON REVENUE DATA

Based on the classification developed in Chapter 2, excise data have been collected and tabulated for eighty-two countries. Data for sixty-three of these countries were complete enough to be used for further analysis. Three-year averages (generally covering fiscal years 1969–71) were used to eliminate possible fortuitous variations. An attempt was made to include receipts for all levels of government—central, provincial, and local—wherever possible.[1] The role of excise systems is related to the contribution of other indirect taxes and data have also been gathered for sales taxes, import duties, export duties, stamp and registration duties, and other indirect taxes—a catch-all category—as well as for total tax revenues, gross national products, and per capita incomes. The basic data are given in Appendix C—Tax Revenue Statistics, together with some further notes on source material and data classification.

Essentially, the data on excise receipts refer to the revenues collected from the selective taxes alone. However, in the important cases of tobacco products, alcoholic beverages, and petroleum products (also referred to as hydrocarbon oils), the statistics include as far as possible collections from the sales tax[2] and the import duty.[3] The data on the taxation of traditional excise goods in different countries are thus fully comparable, but data on receipts from nontraditional goods and services refer only to revenues from domestic excises on these items. The amount of the revenues shown for the latter is an indication whether a country's excise system is of the limited, intermediate, or extended type; of course, for a more complete judgment, the level of excise rates would also have to be taken into account.

A limitation on the data presented here is that while revenues on excise goods, traditional and nontraditional, and to a lesser extent on motor vehicles can usually be readily ascertained from government publications, it is often difficult to obtain disaggregated data for excises collected on financial and entertainment services. In a number of cases, therefore, receipts from these have perforce been included under a general heading "nonclassified selective taxes."

An attempt was made to explain variations in the contribution of excises to total tax revenue in various countries by looking for economic and institutional characteristics which might have a bearing on the level of excise taxation, but this was largely unsuccessful. For one thing, economic data were inadequate in most cases to establish reliable cross-section samples. For another, it is generally not possible to quantify the numerous institutional factors—tastes, traditions, ideological views, to name a few—that influence the ability and willingness to pay and collect excises. However, results are shown whenever the coefficients of the independent variables are significant, have the expected signs, and when the explained variances are noteworthy.

Finally, two terms that are used in this chapter require some explanation. The term "excise share" refers to the percentage contribution of excises to total tax revenue and thus indicates a country's dependence on this form of taxation relative to others. On the other hand, the term "excise ratio" refers to excises as a percentage of gross national product.

REVENUE IMPORTANCE OF EXCISE SYSTEMS

Table 3:1 contains the empirical evidence of the revenue importance of excise systems in a cross section of sixty-three countries. Some differences in the role of excise systems may be related to the level of economic development, and the countries have therefore been grouped as low-income or high-income, according to the essentially arbitrary dividing line of US$600 per capita annual income. As coverage affects the role excise systems play in revenue earning, there is a distinction within each income group between limited, intermediate, and extended systems. Subtotals are given for receipts from the following: traditional goods providing the bulk of excise receipts and for which coverage is most comprehensive; nontraditional goods that determine to a large extent the difference between the three types of excise systems; and services and motor vehicles, whose contribution depends largely on the stage of a particular country's economic development.

Contribution to Total Tax Revenue

Table 3:1 reveals three features which merit further attention: the overall yield of excise systems, the differences in yield between low-income and high-income countries, and the broad variations in the composition of excise systems between and within these two groups. Clearly, excise systems are a very important tax category, contributing on average one-fourth of total tax revenue. Within excise systems themselves, taxes on traditional goods are the most important, contributing 18 per cent of tax revenue. In contrast, excises on nontraditional goods are only 2 per cent of total revenues, though those on services and motor vehicles run to 5 per cent. The differences in coverage of the various types of excise systems are reflected in their contributions to revenue: limited excise systems contribute 21 per cent, intermediate systems 25 per cent, and extended systems 34 per cent. It is interesting that the excise share of traditional goods tends to be greater as the scope of excise systems in general expands.

Low-income countries are generally more dependent on excise taxation than the high-income group: the former collect 27 per cent of their tax revenue in the form of excises and the latter 23 per cent.[4] The difference of 4 percentage points is the algebraic sum of a fall in the share of excise goods of 6 percentage points (approximately equally divided between traditional and nontraditional goods), and a rise in the share of selective taxes on services and

Table 3.1. Revenue Importance of Excise Systems, 1969–71[1]

Nature of Excise Systems	Number of Countries	Traditional Goods (1)	Nontraditional Goods (2)	Total Goods (3=1+2)	Services, Motor Vehicles, Other (4)	Total Excise Systems (5=3+4)
		In Per Cent of Total Tax Revenue				
Low-Income Countries	33	**19.3**	**3.7**	**23.0**	**3.8**	**26.8**
Limited	15	19.0	0.8	19.8	2.6	22.4
Intermediate	11	19.0	3.9	22.9	3.9	26.8
Extended	7	20.6	9.4	30.0	6.3	36.3
High-Income Countries	30	**16.1**	**0.9**	**17.0**	**5.8**	**22.8**
Limited	16	15.0	0.3	15.3	5.3	20.6
Intermediate	10	16.0	1.3	17.3	6.0	23.3
Extended	4	20.8	2.4	23.2	7.0	30.2
All Countries	63	**17.8**	**2.3**	**20.1**	**4.8**	**24.9**
Limited	31	16.9	0.6	17.5	4.0	21.5
Intermediate	21	17.6	2.6	20.2	4.9	25.1
Extended	11	20.7	6.8	27.5	6.6	34.1
		In Per Cent of Gross National Product				
Low-Income Countries	33	**2.72**	**0.51**	**3.23**	**0.55**	**3.78**
Limited	15	2.77	0.12	2.89	0.38	3.27
Intermediate	11	2.64	0.53	3.17	0.60	3.77
Extended	7	2.74	1.32	4.06	0.85	4.91
High-Income Countries	30	**3.52**	**0.19**	**3.71**	**1.23**	**4.94**
Limited	16	3.32	0.05	3.37	1.05	4.42
Intermediate	10	3.68	0.32	4.00	1.48	5.48
Extended	4	3.90	0.46	4.36	1.34	5.70
All Countries	63	**3.10**	**0.36**	**3.46**	**0.87**	**4.33**
Limited	31	3.05	0.09	3.14	0.72	3.86
Intermediate	21	3.14	0.43	3.57	1.01	4.58
Extended	11	3.16	1.01	4.17	1.03	5.20

Source: Appendix C.

[1]Simple arithmetic averages. US$600 per capita per annum is taken as the dividing line between low-income and high-income countries. See Table 3.2 for the countries included in this table.

motor vehicles of 2 percentage points. The fall in the excise share of nontraditional goods from 4 per cent to less than 1 per cent in high-income countries is noteworthy, even though the number of intermediate and extended systems does not change materially compared to low-income countries. This is presumably because many high-income countries levy a large number of regulatory or protective excises that yield little revenue.

That low-income countries show a greater dependence on excise taxation than high-income countries appears to indicate that the nature of excise systems changes with the stage of economic development. Of course, there are exceptions. Particularly in low-income countries, the preference for excise taxation is partly a function of the unavailability of other readily accessible tax bases. Countries with exportable mineral resources, for example, may find it more convenient to meet revenue requirements from export taxes and related levies.[5] Also, as pointed out in Chapter 2, historic biases obscure the issue of excises versus sales taxes. For instance, countries following the French tradition show a preference for sales taxes over excises, whereas those following the British generally favor excise taxation.

It should be emphasized that these observations concern the relative preference for excises over other forms of taxation. A different picture emerges from Table 3:1 if instead the importance of excises is measured against gross national product. Excise ratios in these terms are higher in high-income countries: 5 per cent as against less than 4 per cent in low-income countries. The ratio for services and motor vehicle taxes more than doubles—which is to be expected since tax bases are largely a function of economic development—but the excise ratio for traditional goods is also higher, which is not so predictable. Presumably excisable bases are broader and effective excise rates are higher in the high-income group. This fits with the general postulate that most things are taxed more heavily in high-income countries.

Comparison with Sales Taxes

It is well known that the share of indirect taxes in total tax revenue is on average lower for high-income countries than for low-income countries: 55 per cent and 76 per cent, respectively, for the countries included in Table 3:1. Moreover, there are important shifts in the revenue shares of individual indirect taxes. Thus, the average shares of import duties (8 per cent) and export taxes (virtually nil) are proportionately much lower in high-income countries than those in low-income countries (21 per cent and 11 per cent, respectively). In addition, as already noted, the excise share falls 3 percentage points. On the other hand, the contribution of the sales tax to total revenue is on average greater in high-income countries: 14 per cent versus 11 per cent in low-income countries.[6]

Even in high-income countries the share of sales taxes in total tax revenue rarely exceeds that of excise systems. Thus, in the sample of sixty-three countries, of which forty-seven have sales taxes, the sales tax share is higher than that of the excise system in only eleven countries, and of these nine are high-income countries.[7] In those low-income countries that have sales taxes, the share of excise systems in tax revenue is on average 1.7 times higher than the share of sales taxes. For high-income countries the comparable ratio is 1.2.

Excise revenues are all the more significant since in many low-income countries the sales tax in fact amounts to little more than a supplementary import duty. This is because there is no local production of the taxed items, such production is exempted, or because sales tax rates levied on imports are higher than rates on domestic goods. For instance, in Bangladesh, Burma and Nepal, 90 per cent of the sales tax is collected on imports. A similar situation exists in francophone African countries, where between two-thirds and three-fourths of the sales tax is collected in the customs house. Comparable percentages for other countries are: Tanzania, 84 per cent; Pakistan and Uganda, 70 per cent; Nicaragua and the Philippines, 67 per cent; Ghana and Indonesia, 55 per cent.[8]

The same point can also be made by comparing the yields of excises with sales taxes relating to the domestic base. Particularly in low-income countries the revenue from that part of the sales tax levied directly on domestic production is often not nearly as great as receipts from a single traditional excise good. For instance, in Uganda the excise collected on either tobacco products or alcoholic beverages is as great as domestic sales tax collections, while hydrocarbon oils yield twice as much revenue. In Pakistan the domestic sales tax yields little more than one-tenth of the excise on hydrocarbon oils. In Nicaragua the ratio between the yields of domestic sales taxes and each of the traditional excise goods is about 1 to 3. Furthermore, in most low-income countries sales tax collections derive mainly from typical excise goods: sugar, soft drinks, cement, or textiles—which demonstrates further how small the domestic tax base is in these countries. In Indonesia, for example, where domestic sales tax collections are in any case only slightly more than half the excise yield of tobacco products, 40 per cent of the sales tax is collected from sugar (on which an excise is also imposed) and rubber, and 25 per cent from building construction (which is often taxed through an excise on cement).[9] In Pakistan 60 per cent of domestic sales tax receipts derives from goods that are also subject to excises.

These findings not only affirm the revenue significance of excise systems, they also have implications for tax policymakers relating to the choice between selective and general taxes on goods and services. Although the demonstration effect of the "success" of broad-based sales taxes in industrial countries does appear to recommend them to developing countries (even though their economies are not broad-based), in fact a broad-based sales tax is unwarranted if the manufacturing sector consists of only a few industries.[10] Given the context of rudimentary accounting methods and unsophisticated administrative skills in these countries, the fact that selective taxes are easier to administer is a crucial consideration.

Buoyancy and Elasticity of Excise Systems

The buoyancy of a tax may be defined as the percentage change in tax receipts that accompanies a 1 per cent change in income (gross national product). This measures the ability of a tax to respond to changes in the level of economic activity and the need for revenues; this flexibility is important for many countries since it can help to avoid deficit financing. Buoyancy includes the "automatic" change in tax revenue in response to income fluctuations (called its built-in income elasticity), as well as discretionary changes in tax structure and rates, or improvements in compliance and enforcement.[11] The built-in responsiveness of a tax to income can be low either because the tax is inelastic with respect to its base or because the base is inelastic with respect to income. To isolate these effects, the elasticity of a tax is partitioned into its two components: the tax-to-base elasticity and the base-to-income elasticity.[12]

In a major work on the tax performance of a sample of thirty developing countries, Raja Chelliah concluded that in the period 1953–55 to 1966–68, excises and sales taxes displayed the highest buoyancy of all taxes.[13] The average share of excises (defined as only excises on goods) in the total tax revenue increased from 17.9 per cent to 19.6 per cent over this period. Although this was less than the increase in the share of sales taxes (6.9 per cent to 12.9 per cent), it is impressive if allowance is made for the high initial revenue position of excises in most countries.

Table 3:2 shows the buoyancy coefficients and elasticities of various excise receipts in seven countries. For most excises, the buoyancy coefficients exceed unity, confirming Chelliah's finding that excise revenues have grown faster than income. A comparison with the corresponding built-in elasticities shows that this is largely the result of discretionary changes in tax rates. Noteworthy is the high buoyancy coefficient of the extended excise system in India, where several products were added to the base in the period under review. In general, the elasticities for excises on tobacco products and alcoholic beverages are lower than those for petroleum products and motor vehicles. The high income elasticity of demand for products related to the motoring field is shown by the base-to-income elasticities that exceed unity in most cases. On the whole, the figures shown in the table should be interpreted with caution, because of the difficulties in eliminating the effects of discretionary changes, selecting an appropriate proxy base where data on the legal base could not be obtained, and generally because of the statistically unsatisfactory results of the regression equations.

Table 3.2. Selected Countries: Buoyancy and Elasticity of Excise Systems

Country, Author (Date of Publication), Period of Estimate, and Excises Covered	Buoyancy Coefficients	Built-in Elasticities		
		Tax-to-Income Elasticity	Tax-to-Base Elasticity	Base-to-Income Elasticity
India				
Sahota (1961); 1951/52–1957/58				
Central Excise Duties	3.99	1.61	. . .	. . .
Motor Vehicle Tax	2.25	1.92	. . .	. . .
Uganda[1]				
Ghai (1966); 1948–63				
Tobacco, Beer, Spirits, Sugar,				
Matches	1.41	. . .	. . .	. . .
Paraguay[2]				
Mansfield (1972); 1962–70				
Excises	0.39	0.39	. . .	. . .
Cigarettes	. . .	–0.01	0.44	0.54
Beer, Wine, Soft Drinks	. . .	0.68	0.58	1.54
Ivory Coast				
De Wulf (1975); 1965–73				
Tobacco (Domestic)	0.94	. . .	. . .	. . .
Alcoholic Beverages (Domestic)	1.88	. . .	. . .	. . .
Fuel	1.73	0.77	0.71	1.06
Malaysia				
Chand (1975); 1960–71				
Tobacco	0.52	0.12	0.13	0.88
Alcoholic Beverages	0.39	0.25	0.27	0.88
Petroleum	1.58	1.03	0.46	2.23
Sugar	1.68	1.52	1.72	0.88
Motor Vehicle Fees	1.90	1.40	0.63	2.23
Peru				
Chand and Wolfe (1973); 1960–71				
Excises	1.41	0.70	0.67	1.05
Tobacco	2.36	1.09	1.89	0.27
Alcoholic Beverages	1.13	0.44	0.61	0.70
Gasoline	1.28	0.95	2.25	0.39
Bank Overdrafts	0.48	0.48	0.56	0.82
United Kingdom				
Baas and Dixon (1974); 1950/51–1970/71				
Tobacco	0.57	0.18	1.08	0.05
Beer	0.46	0.22	0.83	0.26
Spirits	1.06	0.67	1.18	0.55
Wines	1.10	0.78	0.71	1.09
Oils and Petrol	1.57	0.86	0.39	2.01
Betting and Gaming	1.05	0.37	. . .	. . .
Motor Vehicles	1.61	1.02	0.97	1.04

Sources: See bibliography.

. . . denotes that data are not available.

[1]Similar results were obtained for the buoyancy of the excise systems of Kenya and Tanzania in Lübbe Schnittger, "Taxation and Tax Policy in East Africa," in Peter Marlin, ed., *Financial Aspects of Development in East Africa* (München: Weltforum Verlag, 1970), p. 76. The studies on East Africa all argue that the built-in elasticities of the various excise systems also exceeded unity.

[2]The level of the statistic $\bar{R}^2$, which measures the goodness of the fit of the functional relationship that is being measured, was extremely low for all figures shown.

Recently, a more immediate policy concern has been with the adjustment of the tax system to price changes, in order to protect the real value of government receipts. Because the large excises are often levied at specific rates without discretionary adjustments, nominal tax payments remain unchanged, and so with rising prices the real value of receipts falls. This has happened in many member countries of the Organisation for Economic Co-operation and Development (OECD) where excise shares and ratios fell in the period 1968–73.[14] Therefore it has been proposed that ad valorem rates should replace specific rates, or alternatively that specific taxes should be indexed. Developing countries, in particular, might achieve this best if the ad valorem rates were applied to the constructive value of excise goods, for instance an appraised average retail value.

But the system of physical controls should be maintained, because in times of inflation this enforcement mechanism may be more helpful in maintaining the real value of tax liabilities than the voluntary compliance procedures of sales and income taxes. There are virtually no collection problems with excises because goods are not released until tax payment has been made. With sales or income taxes on the other hand, in times of money depreciation there is a substantial incentive to delay the payment of tax liabilities, or, more generally, to evade tax, and attempts to do so are likely to be more successful than in the case of excises. At least this would seem to be borne out by the Indonesian experience during the inflation of the sixties, when the real value of excise receipts fell less than that of other taxes. Recently, too, sales and income tax collections have shown a lag, because in times of inflation the targets set for these taxes on a national basis and subsequently allocated to individual tax offices actually act as ceilings rather than as stimuli on collections. This defect is not inherent in the excise collection machinery whose assessments are based on actual production and price movements. Of course, much depends on institutional conditions, but in a situation of scarce administrative skills, sales and income tax collections sometimes suffer more from inflation than excises.[15]

REVENUE COMPOSITION OF EXCISE SYSTEMS

Below, the role of excise systems in the tax structure of individual countries and the revenue aspects of individual excise items is considered. Regional excise patterns are also reviewed and special attention is focused on what are called here the traditional excise goods, as well as on a few other items that have deep roots in history.

Receipts by Country

Table 3:3 shows the contribution of each excise category to total tax revenue in the sixty-three countries referred to at the beginning of the chapter, grouped in twelve regions with common socio-economic characteristics. Within each region, countries are ranked in order of excise yield. For each country the nature of the excise system has been indicated.

Among individual countries, India has the most productive excise system in terms of revenue. More than half her total central and provincial government revenue is derived from selective taxes on goods and services. Similarly productive and extended systems are operated in Pakistan, China (Taiwan), and Nicaragua. The revenue potential of even a limited excise system is obvious in Cyprus, Ireland, Mauritius, and Singapore, where more than one-third of total tax revenue is collected in the form of excises. One-third of all the countries in the sample actually collect over one-fifth of total tax revenues in the form of traditional excises on tobacco products, alcoholic beverages, and hydrocarbon oils. Ireland collects as much as 36

Table 3.3. Sixty-Three Countries: Contribution of Excise Systems to Total Tax Revenue, 1969-71 (in per cent)

Region, Country, and Nature of Excise System[1]	Total Excise System	Tobacco Products	Alcoholic Beverages	Hydrocarbon Oils	Subtotal Traditional Excise Goods	Sugar	Soft Drinks	Other Foods and Non-alcoholic Items	Textiles and Miscellaneous Items	Luxury Goods	Producer Goods	Services	Gambling, Entertainment	Motor Vehicles	Non-classified Items
Indian Subcontinent															
India (E)	50.8	5.4	4.2	14.6	24.3	2.8	0.1	1.3	5.9	0.7	6.8	2.9	1.4	4.0	0.6
Pakistan (E)	38.3	6.9	0.8	16.2	23.9	1.3	0.3	2.6	4.7	0.4	3.0	0.2	—	1.7	—
Far East															
China (Taiwan) (E)	41.6	9.8	6.5	4.6	20.9	1.8	0.5	4.0	1.9	3.2	3.9	0.5	1.6	3.1	0.1
Korea (E)	37.5	7.6	5.5	5.0	18.2	2.0	0.2	0.1	2.8	1.6	2.3	5.2	2.5	2.4	0.6
Japan (E)	25.8	4.6	5.3	6.8	16.7	0.4	0.1	—	—	1.2	—	2.1	0.4	4.5	—
South-East Asia															
Singapore (L)	40.3	8.1	7.1	8.9	24.0	1.7	—	—	—	—	—	2.4	2.9	7.9	1.5
Malaysia (I)	34.7	7.6	3.6	10.4	21.6	2.7	—	—	—	—	—	—	—	9.5	0.9
Thailand (L)	28.1	8.6	4.1	9.6	22.3	—	0.9	—	—	—	0.3	—	3.0	1.4	0.2
Sri Lanka (L)	27.4	11.1	8.1	4.8	24.0	—	—	1.8	—	—	—	—	0.7	0.8	—
Indonesia (L)	19.1	9.7	0.1	7.7	17.5	1.6	—	—	—	—	—	—	—	—	—
Philippines (L)	15.7	6.0	3.2	5.1	14.2	—	—	—	—	—	—	—	0.6	0.9	—
Middle East and North Africa															
Turkey (I)	30.3	—	9.5	9.7	19.2	2.5	—	—	—	—	—	6.7	—	0.8	1.1
Lebanon (L)	23.5	4.8	0.4	13.5	18.7	—	—	—	—	—	1.0	—	0.1	3.6	—
Morocco (L)	23.1	6.3	—	10.9	17.2	3.0	—	—	—	—	—	—	—	0.6	2.2
Syria (I)	18.0	5.1	0.6	3.8	9.6	2.7	—	0.6	—	—	1.8	0.6	—	2.7	—
Tunisia (L)	17.4	10.5	—	4.8	15.3	—	—	2.1	—	—	—	—	—	—	—
Iran (I)	10.0	1.5	0.9	5.3	7.7	0.7	0.1	0.1	—	0.1	—	0.5	—	0.9	—
Eastern Africa															
Mauritius (L)	37.0	9.0	12.5	9.6	31.1	—	0.6	—	—	—	—	—	1.7	4.1	0.1
Kenya (I)	33.7	5.5	8.1	12.5	26.1	3.7	0.6	0.1	1.2	—	0.2	—	0.1	1.8	—
Tanzania (I)	31.4	6.6	5.1	10.1	21.8	3.3	0.4	—	1.8	—	0.1	0.3	0.4	3.1	—
Uganda (I)	28.6	4.9	4.0	9.1	18.0	5.8	0.4	0.1	1.7	—	0.1	0.3	0.2	1.8	—
Ethiopia (I)	26.2	1.3	5.6	10.4	17.3	3.1	—	2.0	2.7	—	—	—	0.3	0.5	0.2
Malagasy Rep. (L)	18.3	3.6	14.6	—	18.2	—	—	—	—	—	—	—	—	0.1	—

Western Africa															
Sierra Leone (I)	26.3	8.4	3.8	12.1	24.2	0.1	—	—	0.1	—	0.1	—	0.2	1.4	—
Ghana (E)	21.3	3.8	2.6	7.0	13.4	—	—	3.6	—	—	—	0.4	0.3	1.3	2.3
Senegal (L)	18.5	2.3	1.6	12.4	16.4	—	—	—	—	—	—	—	0.2	0.6	1.4
Caribbean and Central America															
Nicaragua (E)	41.2	8.3	9.7	8.6	26.6	1.4	2.1	1.5	—	—	1.2	0.3	0.3	1.5	6.3
Dominican Rep. (L)	28.7	8.0	10.7	1.6	20.3	—	0.3	—	—	—	—	1.2	4.1	2.9	—
Jamaica (E)	28.4	6.4	7.8	4.7	19.0	0.3	0.4	0.5	1.0	0.3	0.2	0.7	2.2	2.8	1.1
Guatemala (L)	28.1	4.5	10.9	7.8	23.3	—	1.2	—	—	—	—	—	—	2.0	1.6
Honduras (I)	28.1	3.3	14.4	5.0	22.7	0.9	0.9	—	—	—	—	—	—	2.0	1.7
El Salvador (I)	28.0	4.5	10.1	6.7	21.3	1.9	—	—	—	—	—	—	1.5	1.9	1.4
Panama (L)	27.8	2.3	8.0	5.7	16.0	—	—	—	—	—	—	—	11.9	—	—
Costa Rica (E)	23.5	3.4	7.4	5.9	16.7	0.2	0.9	0.3	—	—	0.8	—	—	—	4.6
South America															
Argentina (I)	32.0	8.7	2.1	14.4	25.1	—	0.7	—	—	0.5	—	0.9	0.7	4.0	—
Uruguay (I)	26.7	6.9	4.1	6.2	17.2	—	1.4	—	—	0.9	—	4.0	2.6	0.6	—
Paraguay (L)	19.6	4.0	5.1	8.4	17.5	—	—	—	—	—	—	0.1	—	—	2.1
Colombia (L)	15.5	4.0	4.5	5.7	14.3	—	—	0.2	—	—	—	1.5	0.2	0.3	0.3
Brazil (L)	16.7	6.0	1.5	7.2	14.6	—	—	—	—	—	—	0.1	—	0.4	0.2
Chile (L)	9.4	3.8	0.7	3.5	8.0	—	—	—	—	—	—	0.1	0.5	0.6	0.1
Venezuela (L)	7.8	2.5	3.5	1.2	7.3	—	—	—	—	—	—	0.2	—	0.3	—
Mediterranean															
Cyprus (L)	37.0	11.3	2.9	9.9	24.2	—	—	0.2	—	—	—	0.2	3.6	8.3	0.5
Italy (E)	35.7	7.1	1.3	16.4	24.8	0.4	—	2.0	—	—	0.9	1.6	1.6	2.0	2.4
Greece (E)	31.2	8.7	3.3	10.7	22.7	2.2	—	—	—	—	—	0.5	—	4.8	1.1
Portugal (I)	29.3	5.2	1.1	6.5	12.8	—	0.4	0.1	—	—	—	3.9	0.7	0.3	10.9
France (I)	21.0	2.8	2.9	10.3	16.1	0.2	0.1	0.3	0.1	—	—	2.1	1.0	1.2	—
Israel (L)	11.8	2.5	1.0	4.9	8.4	—	—	—	—	—	1.1	0.9	0.1	1.3	—
Northern Europe															
Ireland (L)	40.8	12.0	14.4	10.0	36.3	—	0.2	—	—	—	—	0.1	0.7	3.4	—
Finland (I)	25.2	4.3	8.2	5.5	18.0	0.3	0.3	0.7	1.5	—	—	0.4	0.9	2.9	0.3
United Kingdom (L)	24.9	7.1	5.7	8.4	21.2	—	—	—	—	0.5	—	—	0.8	2.8	0.1
Denmark (I)	24.6	6.3	5.7	4.3	16.3	0.6	0.3	0.1	0.2	—	—	0.3	0.3	5.8	0.1
Sweden (I)	21.5	3.5	6.0	4.1	13.6	—	0.4	—	—	—	—	3.3	0.7	3.5	—
Norway (I)	21.1	3.0	5.2	4.3	12.5	—	0.3	0.6	—	—	—	0.6	0.1	4.6	2.3
Germany (I)	20.6	4.9	3.8	7.3	16.0	0.1	0.1	0.7	—	—	—	0.7	0.5	2.4	0.1
Switzerland (L)	19.7	3.9	1.8	7.7	13.4	0.1	0.3	—	—	—	—	0.9	0.3	3.2	1.6
Austria (I)	19.0	3.9	2.4	6.3	12.6	—	0.9	1.0	—	—	—	2.3	0.3	1.6	0.3
Belgium (L)	15.1	3.0	1.8	7.1	11.9	0.1	0.3	—	—	—	—	0.8	0.5	1.6	—
Netherlands (L)	14.7	2.9	2.2	5.7	10.8	0.1	—	—	—	—	—	—	0.2	3.6	—

Table 3.3 (concluded). Sixty-Three Countries: Contribution of Excise Systems to Total Tax Revenue, 1969–71 (in Per Cent)

Region, Country, and Nature of Excise System[1]	Total Excise System	Tobacco Products	Alcoholic Beverages	Hydrocarbon Oils	Subtotal Traditional Excise Goods	Sugar	Soft Drinks	Other Foods and Non-alcoholic Items	Textiles and Miscellaneous Items	Luxury Goods	Producer Goods	Services	Gambling, Entertainment	Motor Vehicles	Non-classified Items
Australasia and South Africa															
Australia (L)	19.1	3.7	5.6	4.2	13.5	—	—	0.3	—	—	—	0.4	1.6	3.2	0.1
South Africa (L)	18.6	5.6	7.7	3.2	16.5	—	—	—	—	—	—	—	—	2.1	—
New Zealand (L)	14.4	4.1	3.2	6.0	13.3	0.2	—	—	—	—	—	—	1.0	—	—
North America															
United States (L)	15.3	2.2	3.2	2.7	8.2	—	—	—	—	—	—	4.2	0.3	1.7	0.9
Canada (L)	12.3	0.7	2.1	4.1	6.9	—	—	—	—	—	—	0.3	0.2	4.8	—

Source: Appendix C.

— denotes that revenue is nil, or less than half the final digit shown.

[1] L = Limited; I = Intermediate; E = Extended. The classification of the nature of excise systems is based on observations for the years 1969–71, for which data were collected. As shown in Appendix A, as of 1977 the status has been changed for four countries: the Dominican Republic and Italy now have intermediate excise systems; the system in Honduras is of the limited type and at present Israel has an extended excise system.

per cent of all tax revenue from these three items—probably the highest share in the world. Mauritius collects 31 per cent of tax revenue from traditional excise goods.

Table 3:3 shows that apart from those countries with extended excise systems, the excise share is greatest in small countries. Small countries may be forced to rely more heavily on excises than on sales or income taxes for various reasons. Generally, the manufacturing base is small, and so income or sales taxes cannot be a very productive source of revenue, an aspect that may be compounded by the openness of the economy. Services may be important (for instance, tourism), but they are often rendered by small businesses that are usually difficult to tax. The dominant role of excises in these countries may be reinforced by historic associations. Among small countries, those that have inherited British taxing traditions derive the highest contributions from excise systems.[16]

Receipts from Individual Excise Items

The excise on hydrocarbon oils—historically a latecomer to the field—is clearly the most important single item in terms of revenue, contributing more than 10 per cent of total tax revenue in at least fifteen countries (Table 3:4). In Italy and Pakistan, the share exceeds 16 per cent. In contrast, excises on hydrocarbon oils contribute very little in petroleum-producing countries (although, of course, various taxes on the export of petroleum are very important).

Table 3.4. Revenue Importance of Selected Excise Goods, 1969–71 (in Per Cent of Total Tax Revenue)

Hydrocarbon Oils (≥ 10 Per Cent)		Tobacco Products (≥ 8 Per Cent)		Alcoholic Beverages (≥ 8 Per Cent)		Sugar (≥2 Per Cent)	
Italy	16.4	Ireland	12.0	Ireland	14.4	Uganda	5.8
Pakistan	16.2	Cyprus	11.3	Honduras	14.4	Kenya	3.7
India	14.6	Sri Lanka	11.1	Mauritius	12.5	Tanzania	3.3
Argentina	14.4	Tunisia	10.5	Guatemala	10.9	Ethiopia	3.1
Lebanon	13.5	China (Taiwan)	9.8	Dominican Rep.	10.7	Morocco	3.0
Kenya	12.5	Indonesia	9.7	El Salvador	10.1	India	2.8
Senegal	12.4	Mauritius	9.0	Nicaragua	9.7	Malaysia	2.7
Sierra Leone	12.1	Greece	8.7	Finland	8.2	Syria	2.7
Morocco	10.9	Argentina	8.7	Sri Lanka	8.1	Turkey	2.5
Greece	10.7	Thailand	8.6	Kenya	8.1	Greece	2.2
Malaysia	10.4	Sierra Leone	8.4	Panama	8.0	Korea	2.0
Ethiopia	10.4	Nicaragua	8.3				
France	10.3	Singapore	8.1				
Tanzania	10.1	Dominican Rep.	8.0				
Ireland	10.0						

Soft Drinks (≥ 0.5 Per Cent)		Cement (≥ 0.5 Per Cent)		Matches (≥ 0.2 Per Cent)		Salt (≥ 0.2 Per Cent)	
Nicaragua	2.1	China	2.0	Nicaragua	0.9	Ethiopia	2.0
Uruguay	1.4	Syria	1.8	Portugal	0.7	Syria	0.6
Guatemala	1.2	Pakistan	1.2	India	0.6	China (Taiwan)	0.5
Thailand	1.2	Israel	1.1	Nepal	0.6	Pakistan	0.3
Honduras	0.9	India	1.0	Dominican Rep.	0.4	Cyprus	0.2
Costa Rica	0.9	Lebanon	1.0	Kenya	0.2	Italy	0.2
Austria	0.9	Italy	0.9	Tanzania	0.2		
Argentina	0.7	Costa Rica	0.8	Uganda	0.2		
Kenya	0.6	Nicaragua	0.8	Italy	0.2		
China (Taiwan)	0.5						

Source: Table 3.3. Separate computations for cement, matches, and salt.

Small countries also collect less than average from this category, perhaps because travel by car is geographically restricted. In most countries, particularly industrial ones, the excise is largely collected on motor fuel (as gasoline or diesel fuel), but in developing countries a substantial part of the hydrocarbon excise may derive from diesel oil used for industrial or agricultural purposes, kerosene (a basic heating and cooking fuel), or fuel oil. In India, for example, 37 per cent of the hydrocarbon excise is collected on diesel fuel, 19 per cent on kerosene, and only 33 per cent on gasoline.[17]

Closely related to excises on motor fuel are other road user charges, such as: (1) special excises, sales or purchase taxes on motor vehicles, spare parts, or tires; (2) registration fees and charges on vehicles based on a variety of factors such as market value, weight, payload or engine capacity, age, square footage; (3) passenger and freight charges, tolls, and various other levies classified as excises on transportation services in this study. The emphasis accorded to different kinds of road user charges varies widely from country to country, depending on their objectives. Table 3:3 shows, for instance, that Cyprus, Malaysia, and Singapore collect 8 per cent or more of excise revenue on motor vehicles in the form of registration fees and licenses, a figure that is almost as high as the excise on hydrocarbon oils in these countries. Other countries, for instance Ghana, Syria, and Thailand, collect substantial import duties on motor vehicles; in Ghana the import purchase tax yields as much revenue as the license tax.[18] In the EEC, member countries collect on average 3 per cent of total tax revenue in the form of motor vehicle taxes (including the special excises on cars levied in lieu of the import duties previously chargeable). In several countries, special excises on tires, in addition to taxes on passenger and freight transport, make an important contribution to tax revenue as shown in Appendix C, Table 2.

The examples given above are limited to a few countries, partly because of the multitude of forms of excise taxation in this field and partly because data limitations do not permit statistical aggregation for all countries. But a cursory examination of the available data reinforces the view that the automotive field is a very important tax base with wide ramifications in terms of economic efficiency and equity (as the well-to-do in most countries are generally the heaviest users).

The traditional excises on tobacco products and alcoholic beverages vie for second place in importance, although they have less claim to equity. The tobacco excise share exceeds 8 per cent in fourteen countries, the alcohol excise in eleven countries. The primary purpose of these excises is revenue and they appear to fulfill that objective well. Small countries rely heavily on traditional excises. Table 3:4 also shows the contribution to tax revenue of five other common goods taxed through excises—sugar, soft drinks, cement, matches, and salt. The last two items are shown primarily because of their historical interest. The separate excise on sugar in particular is a significant source of revenue in more than half the countries included in Table 3:3.

The excise yields of nontraditional excise goods are generally small. Little revenue, for example, derives from excises on nonalcoholic beverages such as coffee, tea and cocoa, although the tea excise is of some importance on the Indian subcontinent; the coffee excise in Costa Rica, Italy, and Germany; and a local cocoa duty in Ghana. Excise receipts from textiles are most important in India and Pakistan, where they contribute approximately 5 per cent to tax revenue, but the item is also of some significance in China (Taiwan), East Africa, Ethiopia, and Korea. Other nontraditional excise goods included under miscellaneous nonfood items are soap (India, Jamaica, Kenya, Pakistan, Uganda), footwear (India, Jamaica, Sierra Leone), glass and chinaware (India, Mexico, Pakistan), household utensils (Jamaica, Nepal), medicines and pharmaceuticals (India, Portugal, and Scandinavia).

The contribution of luxury goods to total tax revenue is very small everywhere, exceeding 1 per cent only under the extended systems of China, Japan, and Korea. In these countries, most "luxury" excise revenue is collected on electrical appliances, television sets, and radios. This finding should not be interpreted, however, to mean that luxuries are not taxed heavily, as the definition of luxury goods adopted in this study is rather narrow. It could, for instance, be extended to the automotive field, most excisable services, and possibly most textiles. In addition, in many countries luxury goods are frequently subject to luxury sales tax rates and where, as in many developing countries, luxury goods are not produced locally, they may be subject to high import duties.

The provision of services suitable for taxation, particularly transportation, communication, and financial services, is in large measure a function of economic development, and by extension so is their possible contribution to revenue. In the financial field, insurance taxes are most prevalent; in high-income countries, receipts from this source average 1 per cent of tax revenue. Only a few countries tax banking activities separately: more than 1 per cent is collected under this head in Ecuador, Uruguay, and Turkey. Quite a few countries collect excises on foreign travel as a form of luxury consumption—either on air tickets, in the form of terminal fees, or as landing rights. In terms of revenue, transportation excises are very much a Latin-American phenomenon, but on the other hand, hydrocarbons and motor vehicles appear to be taxed more lightly there than elsewhere. Among other services, many countries tax the provision of electricity, gas, and water. Hotel taxes appear to be confined mainly to areas with tourist activities such as the Caribbean and East Africa.

Betting and gambling taxes, which include lottery profits, are most productive of revenue in Panama (12 per cent), the Dominican Republic (4 per cent), Cyprus (3 per cent), Uruguay (3 per cent), and Thailand (2 per cent). Not much information could be obtained on the revenue productivity of entertainment excises levied in the form of admission charges to cinemas, theatres, and sporting events, because the data were too scattered. In high-income countries, however, such taxes contribute between 0.1 per cent and 0.2 per cent to tax revenue. Many countries also collect some revenue from hunting, fishing, and dog licenses, but in no case does the yield exceed 0.1 per cent of tax revenue.

Regional Excise Patterns

Finally, the regional importance of excise systems is illustrated in Table 3:5. The regions are first ranked in order of the importance of their respective excise shares, and then in order of excise ratios. The ranking by excise shares roughly moves from the extended excise systems of the Indian subcontinent (where the excise share is on average 45 per cent), the Far East, Caribbean, and Central America, to the intermediate systems of Eastern Africa and the Mediterranean, and finally to the limited excise systems of Australasia, North America, Northern Europe, and South America (where the excise share is less than 14 per cent). However, the ranking changes markedly when excise revenues are measured in terms of gross national product; then, with a ratio of 6.39, Northern European countries collect more excise revenues than any other region, while South America has the lowest ratio of 2.56.

As in the case of the hydrocarbon excise, the excise shares of other traditional goods also suggest that receipts often tend to be lower in countries that are major producers of the taxed items: the tobacco excise share, for example, is lowest in North America, where more than one-fifth of the world's tobacco is grown, while the alcohol excise share is lowest in the Mediterranean area which produces more than half of all wine.[19] In Northern Europe the tobacco excise is exceptionally high, because governments wish to limit foreign exchange expenditures on unmanufactured tobacco. As usual, there is an exception that proves the rule: northern European countries brew almost one-third of all beer, but the alcohol excise ratio is higher in this region than anywhere else.[20] Historical influences may play a particularly strong role in this case: the protestant ethic permits people the taste of sumptuary goods, but lets

Table 3.5. Regional Excise Patterns, 1969-71[1]

	Total Excise Systems	Tobacco Products	Alcoholic Beverages	Hydrocarbon Oils	Subtotal Traditional Goods	Sugar, Soft Drinks, Other Foods	Textiles, Luxuries, Producer Goods	Services, Entertainment	Motor Vehicles	Non-classified Items
In Per Cent of Total Tax Revenue										
Indian Subcontinent (2)	44.6	6.2	4.2	15.4	24.1	4.2	10.8	2.3	2.9	0.6
Far East (3)	35.0	7.3	5.8	5.5	18.6	3.0	5.6	4.1	3.3	0.3
Caribbean and Central America (8)	29.2	5.1	9.9	6.3	20.7	1.8	—	4.4	2.2	2.8
Eastern Africa (6)	29.2	5.1	7.1	10.3	22.1	4.9	2.0	0.7	2.3	—
Mediterranean (6)	27.7	6.3	2.1	9.8	18.2	1.2	—	2.7	3.5	1.3
South East Asia (6)	27.5	8.5	5.2	7.7	20.6	1.7	—	...	...	0.9
Northern Europe (11)	22.5	5.0	5.2	6.4	16.6	0.7	—	1.3	3.2	0.7
Western Africa (3)	22.0	4.8	2.7	10.5	18.0	—	—	0.4	1.1	1.8
Middle East and North Africa (6)	20.4	6.3	—	8.0	14.6	2.4	—	...	1.7	...
South America (7)	18.2	5.1	3.5	6.7	14.9	—	—	1.8	1.0	0.7
Australasia and South Africa (3)	17.4	4.5	5.5	4.5	14.4	—	—	1.5	2.7	—
North America (2)	13.8	1.4	2.6	3.5	7.6	—	—	2.3	3.3	0.5
In Per Cent of Gross National Product										
Northern Europe (11)	6.39	1.42	1.53	1.75	4.70	0.24	—	0.38	0.94	0.18
Far East (3)	5.98	1.25	0.99	0.95	3.20	0.52	0.96	0.68	0.58	0.05
Indian Subcontinent (2)	5.40	0.75	0.52	1.86	2.92	0.51	1.31	0.28	0.35	0.08
Mediterranean (6)	5.02	1.10	0.38	1.84	3.33	0.22	—	0.49	0.61	0.24
Eastern Africa (6)	4.23	0.79	1.06	1.46	3.25	0.63	0.25	0.11	0.30	—
Australasia and South Africa (3)	3.95	1.98	1.20	1.06	3.24	—	—	0.39	0.60	—
South East Asia (6)	3.85	1.16	0.76	1.04	2.85	0.26	—	...	...	0.13
Caribbean and Central America (8)	3.68	0.66	1.23	0.74	2.57	0.22	—	0.67	0.29	0.31
North America (2)	3.61	0.37	0.69	0.93	1.98	—	—	0.62	0.89	0.10
Western Africa (3)	3.43	0.71	0.41	1.66	2.78	—	—	0.06	0.17	0.32
Middle East and North Africa (6)	3.38	1.11	—	1.26	2.42	0.42	—	...	0.23	...
South America (7)	2.56	0.76	0.48	0.92	2.11	—	—	0.26	0.14	0.08

Source: Appendix C.

— indicates that goods are not excisable, or that the number of countries within the region that tax such goods is very small; ... indicates that the excise shares and ratios in a region diverge so widely that an average would not have any meaning. Figures in brackets indicate the number of countries included in each regional average.

them pay dearly for it. Similarly, historical influences may account for the high tobacco taxes in Mediterranean countries as the excise was once viewed as a penalty on moral transgression.

Concluding Remarks

To summarize, excise systems, defined to include all selective taxes on goods and services, are a productive tax category. The relative reliance on excise taxation is somewhat greater in low-income than in high-income countries, but the difference is not very significant. However, when measured in terms of gross national product, high-income countries collect more in excises than do low-income countries. The yield of excises usually exceeds that of the sales tax, which in most developing countries is in any case really an excise-type levy on a few local manufactures and a supplementary import duty. Small countries tend to rely more heavily on excises than large ones, perhaps because of their narrow domestic manufacturing base for sales and income taxation.

The most widely and heavily taxed goods are tobacco, alcoholic beverages, and petroleum products. These items together contribute more than 70 per cent of all excise receipts, or 18 per cent of total tax revenue. When fuel taxes, motor vehicle taxes and other road user charges are considered jointly, the automotive field clearly emerges as the most important source of excise revenue. The consumption of all products associated with motoring has increased sharply in the post-war period, offering new sources of added revenues. Low-income countries rely relatively heavily on excises on goods—sugar, soft drinks, textiles, cement—but in high-income countries these items are usually included in the sales tax base, and excises on motor vehicles and services are the most important. Regionally, the extended excise systems of the Indian subcontinent and the Far East collect the largest proportion of total tax revenue in the form of excises, but collections in northern European countries are greater when expressed as a percentage of gross national product.

CHAPTER 4

INCIDENCE AND EQUITY
OF EXCISE TAXATION

The most basic criterion for tax policy and design is a fair distribution of the tax burden. Under the ability-to-pay principle this means that taxes should bear some relationship to people's capacity to pay them, that is, the amount of taxes should be the same for people in the same economic position (horizontal equity), but different for people in different positions (vertical equity). Horizontal equity may be associated with the concept of equal treatment before the law. Vertical equity, on the other hand, is related to the income redistribution function of the tax system that lessens differences in primary distribution caused by the market mechanism; it is associated with progressive taxation.[1]

Income, broadly defined to include anything that contributes to the ability to command goods and services for personal use, is usually considered the most appropriate measure of taxpaying ability, [2] but consumption (and property, or some combination) may be considered a valid alternative. Nicholas Kaldor has argued that consumption is a better tax base than income—that people should be taxed according to what they take out of the common pool rather than what they contribute.[3] However, since income is the most widely accepted measure of taxable ability, this concept is followed here.

At first sight, the excise base appears a poor index of taxpaying ability. Given the same income, it may be argued, excises discriminate on the basis of the consumption or use of particular goods or services, and thus the burden of excises depends upon consumption patterns. Hence, excises appear to flout the principle of horizontal equity.[4] A more serious indictment is that excises are regressive, that is, payments decline as a fraction of income as income rises. This is based on (1) the general assumption that the share of consumption in income falls as income increases (which is generally true), and on (2) the more specific assumption that the ratio of excise payments to consumption expenditures falls or does not rise enough to prevent a decline in the ratio of excise payments to income when moving up the income scale. This is not necessarily true as it does not allow for differences in consumption patterns and in excise design.

This chapter appraises the income redistribution function of excises, on the assumption that it is generally undesirable to make market-determined incomes more unequal through the tax system. The potential of excises in this area is examined, preceded by some theoretical observations on who might bear the excise burdens. Obviously a closely related issue is how excise structures are or should be designed to attain the desired policy objective. That is treated in the last part, following a discussion on the requirements for progressivity in excise taxation.

OBSERVATIONS ON THE THEORY OF EXCISE INCIDENCE

Like other taxes, the imposition of an excise affects economic choices and ultimately results in a redistribution of real income among households, whether they be consumers, owners of firms, or suppliers of labor services. Excises affect choices not only in relation to the taxed commodity but also in relation to commodities that are left tax free. The distributive effects are called the incidence of excises; they are primarily a matter of changes in relative commodity prices and factor rewards.

There are two ways of analyzing incidence. In the partial equilibrium setting, the analysis focuses primarily on the structure and adaptability of the market for the taxed commodity; demand schedules for products of tax-free industries and related factor supply schedules are assumed to remain unchanged. Modern incidence theory, on the other hand, attempts to account for all changes in real income. In a general equilibrium setting, the effects of a tax on households are examined both in their role as consumers of goods and services—the income-uses side of the budget—and that of suppliers of factor services—the income-sources side.[5]

The partial equilibrium approach studies the effects of an excise as a price phenomenon in which incidence analysis simply involves the application of general price theory to taxation.[6] In a profit-maximizing competitive world—and, except for extreme circumstances, in monopoly situations too—the direction and extent of an excise-induced price change then depend on the demand and supply elasticities of the taxed commodity. The general rule is that the more elastic the supply and the more inelastic the demand, the greater the amount of the excise borne by the consumer relative to the producer.[7] This appears logical, since with elastic supply the producer can readily leave the industry, and with inelastic demand the consumer is less able to turn to alternative goods. Generally, it is assumed that supply is the more elastic, particularly in the longer run, and therefore, a forward shifting of the tax to consumers is considered the most plausible outcome.[8]

The forward shifting of excises on sumptuary goods and necessities is readily apparent. It is less so in the case of luxury goods, but that it does occur would seem to be borne out by the results of a detailed study of price responses to excise reductions in the United States in 1965.[9] It was found in this study that retail price changes generally equaled the excise reduction, presumably because related price elasticities of demand were low and supply elasticities large in the relevant range of output of the taxed products. Thus prices of goods on which retail excises were eliminated (toilet articles, watches, rings, handbags, wallets, weekend cases, and silverware) fell by approximately the full amount of the previous excises. The same held for goods subject to manufacturer's excises (household appliances, radios, television sets, sporting goods, office machines, cars, car accessories), except that for the cheaper items the price changes were generally less than the full excise reduction.[10] The elimination of excises on admission charges and club dues was not reflected in lower prices, which seemed predictable, because in such cases the supply situation (that is, seating or membership capacity) is often inelastic in the short run.

In a more complete analysis, the impact of the excise on factor rewards and its effects on the demand and supply schedules of tax-free industries would have to be accounted for. If a differential approach is adopted (under which the excise replaces an equal-yield tax on all consumption) and full utilization of resources is assumed, then the excise-induced price increase of a good, say X, would lead to a decline in the output of X and factors employed in producing X would then move into the production of a tax-free good, say Y, where they would receive a relatively higher reward.[11] At the same time, as the price of X increases, the demand for Y would rise and consequently the output of Y. Assuming that both goods are produced under conditions of increasing costs, it is then conceivable that the excise burden of X might have to be shared by Y to an extent depending upon the elasticities of substitution of Y for X on the part of both producers and consumers. In addition to the effects resulting from the uses side, there may be effects from the sources side, because the altered product mix would lead to a fall in the return of factors specific to production in industry X, and an increase in the earnings of factors of particular importance to production in industry Y.

On the whole, however, complete forward shifting of excises is assumed to be the rule. Excise burdens are generally assumed to fall on consumers and distributed on the basis of consumption expenditures on excisable commodities. This assumption is made, as pointed out by Richard Musgrave, because: (1) the imposition of an excise drives a wedge between saving and consumption, and therefore the primary determinant of excise incidence arises on the income-uses side of household budgets; and (2) distributional effects on factor rewards and demand and supply schedules in tax-free industries are probably neutral, or may be disregarded in most cases because the size distribution of factor income arising in various industries remains largely unchanged by the imposition of excise duties.[12] Thus the working hypothesis under general and partial equilibrium analysis is the same and bears out the old maxim that consumers bear consumption taxes.

QUANTITATIVE FINDINGS ON EXCISE BURDEN DISTRIBUTION

Once it is assumed that excise burdens are distributed in relation to consumer expenditures on excisable commodities, changes in the ratio, or effective rate,[13] of excises paid to income received by households at different points in the income distribution, may be taken to indicate the nature of the incidence: a declining rate implies that an excise is regressive, a rising rate that it is progressive, and no change in the rate means a proportional incidence. The findings on the distribution of excise burdens in various tax incidence studies are summarized in Table 4:1. Obviously, traditional excises are the most important, but most studies also provide information pertaining to other excises. As elsewhere in this book, a distinction is made between the situation in low-income and in high-income countries.

The mathematics of incidence analysis may seem simple, but there are usually great conceptual and empirical difficulties in defining and measuring both the numerator and the denominator for various levels of income. These difficulties have been discussed at length in the professional literature and are only briefly alluded to here.[14] Most incidence studies use a more or less broad concept of annual income. The possible omission of income in kind may mean that effective tax rates are overstated in the lower range of the income distribution. In India, Lebanon, and Norway, consumption expenditures are taken as the denominator. Particularly for excises and other taxes on goods and services, the expenditure base has been rationalized as a better indicator of permanent income than actual annual income, because it allows for behavioral variations at different points in the life cycle.

Most studies draw on household budget surveys for consumption data on excisable commodities. These surveys, often undertaken for urban areas only, are normally conducted to collect information for cost-of-living indices; hence they tend to concentrate on expenditures for basic commodities such as foodstuffs and possibly traditional excise goods, rather than, say, on luxury items. Further difficulties are that people may not remember accurately expenditures on goods that consist of small amounts spread over relatively long periods of time, while some individuals may be reluctant to disclose large spendings on, say, alcoholic beverages.[15] More generally, differences in data sources, income definitions and assumptions on consumption patterns may systematically bias the results and make any comparison a hazardous undertaking. On the whole, however, some general patterns of excise incidence are worth noting, even after allowing for differences in methodology that are sometimes substantial.

Low-Income Countries

In the low-income countries shown in Table 4:1, the tobacco duty appears to be the most regressive of all traditional excises. Progressivity in the lower income range is imparted to the

Table 4.1. Tax Incidence Studies: Summary of Findings on Excise Burden Distribution
In Per Cent of Total Income or Expenditure

Author (Date of Publication), and Year of Estimate	Country, Monetary Unit, and Income Classes[1]					

Low-Income Countries

INDIA (rupees)

Ministry of Finance (1969); 1963–64	*Total*	*Under 50*	*51– 100*	*101– 150*	*151– 300*	*301– 500*	*Over 500*
State Excise on Motor Spirit	0.19	0.06	0.07	0.08	0.13	0.13	0.89
Motor Vehicle Tax	0.39	0.23	0.26	0.30	0.42	0.47	0.85
Entertainment Tax	0.15	0.05	0.09	0.11	0.16	0.26	0.34
Electricity Duty	0.16	0.09	0.11	0.13	0.16	0.23	0.26
State Excises	0.49	0.45	0.38	0.41	0.64	0.38	0.78
Central Excises							
Rural	3.95	2.76	3.01	3.29	4.33	4.89	7.47
Urban	7.70	4.87	5.01	5.72	6.43	7.06	16.10

PAKISTAN (rupees)

Azfar (1971); 1966–67	*Total*	*Under 100*	*100– 200*	*200– 400*	*400– 750*	*750– 1,250*	*Over 1,250*
Central Excises	3.04	1.46	2.28	3.02	4.12	6.10	5.47

PHILIPPINES (pesos)

Joint Legislative Executive Tax Commission (1964); 1960	*Total*	*Under 500*	*500– 999*	*1,000– 1,499*	*1,500– 1,999*	*2,000– 2,999*	*3,000– 3,999*
Tobacco Products	2.46	5.60	3.60	2.69	2.48	2.20	2.48
Alcoholic Beverages	0.52	0.58	0.44	0.44	0.50	0.49	0.85
Fuel and Oil	1.50	1.41	1.00	1.14	1.41	2.62	1.73
Motor Vehicle Tax (Business Use)	0.18	0.32	0.23	0.18	0.18	0.18	0.17
Motor Vehicle Tax (Common Carriers)	0.13	0.13	0.09	0.09	0.11	0.25	0.14
Public Utilities	0.09	0.06	0.04	0.07	0.10	0.11	0.12
Amusement	0.16	0.11	0.14	0.15	0.16	0.17	0.19

	4,000– 4,999	*5,000– 5,999*	*6,000– 6,999*	*7,000– 7,999*	*8,000– 8,999*	*9,000– 9,999*	*Over 10,000*
Tobacco Products	1.80	1.84	1.26	1.73	1.26	1.50	0.62
Alcoholic Beverages	0.75	0.96	0.40	0.63	0.43	0.62	0.27
Fuel and Oil	1.75	1.83	1.49	1.65	1.66	1.65	1.03
Motor Vehicle Tax (Business Use)	0.16	0.14	0.13	0.12	0.13	0.14	0.11
Motor Vehicle Tax (Common Carriers)	0.14	0.15	0.12	0.12	0.13	0.12	0.08
Public Utilities	0.12	0.12	0.11	0.14	0.12	0.13	0.07
Amusement	0.18	0.16	0.20	0.13	0.16	0.24	0.16

Table 4.1 (continued). Tax Incidence Studies: Summary of Findings on Excise Burden Distribution
In Per Cent of Total Income or Expenditure

Author (Date of Publication), and Year of Estimate		Country, Monetary Unit, and Income Classes[1]						

COLOMBIA (pesos)

McLure (1975); 1970 (Alternative A)	Total	Less than 6,000	6,000– 12,000	12,000– 24,000	24,000– 60,000	60,000– 120,000	120,000– 240,000	Over 240,000
Tobacco Products								
Rural	0.6	1.2	0.6	0.8	0.4	0.3	0.2	0.3
Urban	0.5	1.2	0.7	0.9	0.5	0.5	0.3	0.2
Alcoholic Beverages								
Rural	0.8	. . .	0.1	1.3	1.2	1.3	0.5	0.2
Urban	1.6	. . .	0.1	1.4	1.6	2.0	0.9	2.5
Gasoline								
Rural	0.5	0.7	1.2	0.1	0.2	0.2	0.2	0.2
Urban	0.3	0.2	0.2	0.2	0.2	0.4	0.4	0.3

GUATEMALA (quetzales)

Adler, Schlesinger, and Olson (1952); 1947–48

	Indigenous Farmer		Skilled Urban Worker	
	Heavy Consumption	Light Consumption	Heavy Consumption	Light Consumption
Family Income	1,200	1,200	1,200	1,200
Cigarette Excises	12	4	15	5
Alcoholic Beverages Excises	23	8	27	9
Entertainment Duties	. . .	. . .	6	2

LEBANON (Lebanese pounds)

De Wulf (1974); 1968	Under 6,000	6,001– 12,000	12,001– 18,000	18,001– 24,000	24,001– 30,000	Over 30,000
Tobacco Products	1.33	1.52	1.73	1.55	1.13	0.84
Domestic	(0.63)	(0.39)	(0.22)	(0.14)	(0.01)	(. . .)
Imports	(0.70)	(1.13)	(1.51)	(1.41)	(1.12)	(0.84)
Liquor	0.03	0.03	0.03	0.04	0.03	0.03
Inflammables	1.82	2.52	3.11	3.31	3.54	3.36
Salt	0.004	0.003	0.001	0.001	0.0001	0.0005
Cement	0.29	0.21	0.16	0.14	0.12	0.10
Entertainment	0.03	0.05	0.07	0.09	0.08	0.01

PANAMA (balboas)

McLure (1974); 1969 (Assumption A)	Total	Under 500	501– 1,000	1,0001– 1,500	1,501– 2,000	2,001– 2,500
Tobacco and Alcoholic Beverages	1.81	1.61	2.52	2.88	2.65	2.55
Gasoline and Oil	1.02	0.58	0.82	1.00	1.12	1.18
Automobiles and Accessories	0.56	—	—	0.22	0.40	0.56
Municipal Vehicle Taxes	0.15	—	—	0.05	0.10	0.15
Food	0.48	0.76	0.87	0.77	0.63	0.56

Author (Date of Publication), *and Year of Estimate*	*Country, Monetary Unit, and Income Classes*[1]					
Clothing	0.31	0.24	0.34	0.36	0.36	0.38
Furniture and Wood Products	0.06	0.03	0.06	0.07	0.06	0.07
Radios, TV, and Refrigerators	0.15	—	0.16	0.19	0.20	0.23
Jewelry, Perfume, and Crystal	0.07	—	—	—	—	—
	2,501– 3,600	*3,601– 6,000*	*6,001– 10,000*	*10,001– 20,000*	*20,001– 50,000*	*Over 50,000*
Tobacco and Alcoholic Beverages	2.25	1.55	1.25	0.87	0.51	0.23
Gasoline and Oil	1.28	1.30	1.19	1.04	0.73	0.41
Automobiles and Accessories	0.74	0.86	0.94	0.93	0.71	0.42
Municipal Vehicle Taxes	0.20	0.23	0.26	0.25	0.20	0.11
Food	0.49	0.41	0.31	0.24	0.13	0.06
Clothing	0.38	0.38	0.31	0.25	0.15	0.08
Furniture and Wood Products	0.07	0.08	0.07	0.05	0.04	0.02
Radios, TV, and Refrigerators	0.22	0.18	0.14	0.11	0.07	0.02
Jewelry, Perfume, and Crystal	0.01	0.03	0.16	0.31	0.35	0.05

High-Income Countries

ARGENTINA (thousand pesos)

Bobrowski and Goldberg (1970); 1965	*Total*	*Under 90*	*90– 130*	*130– 185*	*185– 275*	*275– 365*
Tobacco	0.05	0.02	0.05	0.06	0.06	0.07
Combustibles	0.26	0.71	0.44	0.31	0.22	0.24
Vehicles	0.26	—	—	0.02	0.05	0.07
	365– 500	*500– 650*	*650– 900*	*900– 1,400*	*Over 1,400*	
Tobacco	0.06	0.06	0.05	0.04	0.02	
Combustibles	0.20	0.24	0.31	0.27	0.22	
Vehicles	0.21	0.20	0.37	0.35	0.57	

GREECE (drachmas)

Karageorgas (1973); 1964	*Total*	*Under 15,000*	*15,000– 28,499*	*28,500– 54,999*	*55,000– 77,099*	*77,100– 119,999*	*Over 120,000*
Tobacco	2.02	5.78	4.96	3.66	2.31	1.44	0.94
Alcoholic Beverages	0.26	0.42	0.42	0.44	0.30	0.19	0.20
Crude Oil and Mazout	0.81	1.15	1.13	0.92	0.73	0.64	0.83
Gasoline	0.75	0.20	0.36	0.46	0.42	0.48	1.27
Kerosine	0.34	0.51	1.21	0.72	0.41	0.22	0.08
Sugar	0.63	0.36	1.60	1.21	0.81	0.44	0.28
Matches	0.10	0.52	0.27	0.17	0.11	0.06	0.04
Luxuries	0.16	0.09	0.10	0.11	0.11	0.13	0.24
Transport	0.63	0.26	0.31	0.35	0.35	0.35	1.12
Amusement	0.24	0.02	0.12	0.21	0.22	0.23	0.31

Table 4.1 (continued). Tax Incidence Studies: Summary of Findings on Excise Burden Distribution
In Per Cent of Total Income or Expenditure

Author (Date of Publication), and Year of Estimate	*Country, Monetary Unit, and Income Classes[1]*						

NORWAY (kroner)

Biørn (1975); 1967 (Income Compensation Corresponding to Removal of Excises)	*15,000*	*20,000*	*25,000*	*30,000*	*35,000*	*40,000*	*50,000*
	(Percentages of Total Consumption Expenditure)						
Tobacco							
Single	−1.18	−1.15	−1.13	−1.10	−1.07	. . .	. . .
Married	−1.54	−1.39	−1.29	−1.22	−1.17	−1.12	. . .
Married, 1 child under 16	. . .	−1.54	−1.39	−1.29	−1.22	−1.17	−1.09
Married, 2 children under 16	. . .	. . .	−1.29	−1.19	−1.13	−1.09	−1.04
Married, 3 children under 16	. . .	. . .	. . .	−1.06	−1.01	−0.98	−0.96
Alcohol							
Single	−0.70	−1.04	−1.35	−1.63	−1.88	. . .	. . .
Married	−0.77	−0.92	−1.12	−1.34	−1.55	−1.75	. . .
Married, 1 child under 16	. . .	−0.54	−0.68	−0.86	−1.06	−1.26	−1.64
Married, 2 children under 16	. . .	. . .	−0.68	−0.76	−0.88	−1.04	−1.36
Married, 3 children under 16	. . .	. . .	. . .	−0.48	−0.56	−0.68	−0.98

GERMANY (D-mark)

Roskamp (1963); 1950	*Under 2,400*		*2,400– 3,600*		*3,600– 4,800*	*4,800– 6,000*	*Over 6,000*
Tobacco	3.2		4.3		3.7	3.5	1.1

CANADA (thousand dollars)

Gillespie (1964); 1961 (Using "Broad Income" Concept)	*Total*	*Under 2.0*	*2.0– 2.9*	*3.0– 3.9*	*4.0– 4.9*	*5.0– 6.9*	*7.0– 9.9*	*Over 10.0*
Federal Excises	2.3	4.3	2.6	2.6	2.3	2.5	2.4	1.5

UNITED STATES (thousand dollars)

a. Calmus (1970); 1961	*Total*	*Under 1.0*	*1.0– 1.9*	*2.0– 2.9*	*3.0– 3.9*	*4.0– 4.9*
Excises Remaining						
Tobacco Products	0.56	0.59	0.70	0.83	0.89	0.78
Alcoholic Beverages	1.02	0.80	0.89	0.81	1.25	1.06
Highway Trust Fund	0.78	1.21	0.73	0.84	0.93	0.94
Excises Repealed						
Manufacturers	0.46	0.45	0.34	0.34	0.45	0.55
Retail	0.12	0.11	0.10	0.10	0.12	0.13
Communications	0.24	0.74	0.43	0.33	0.32	0.29
Admissions and Dues	0.04	0.04	0.02	0.04	0.04	0.04

Table 4.1 (concluded). Tax Incidence Studies: Summary of Findings on Excise Burden Distribution
In Per Cent of Total Income or Expenditure

Author (Date of Publication), and Year of Estimate	Country, Monetary Unit, and Income Classes[1]					
	5.0–5.9	6.0–7.4	7.5–9.9	10.0–14.9	Over 15.0	
Excises Remaining						
Tobacco Products	0.65	0.69	0.57	0.44	0.25	
Alcoholic Beverages	0.84	0.99	1.05	1.10	1.00	
Highway Trust Fund	0.93	0.91	0.83	0.72	0.47	
Excises Repealed						
Manufacturers	0.54	0.55	0.50	0.46	0.29	
Retail	0.11	0.13	0.12	0.12	0.12	
Communications	0.28	0.26	0.24	0.22	0.15	
Admissions and Dues	0.03	0.04	0.04	0.05	0.06	
b. Musgrave, Case, and Leonard (1974); 1968	Total	Under 4.0	4.0–5.7	5.7–7.9	7.9–10.4	10.4–12.5
Federal Excises	2.0	2.1	2.4	2.7	2.6	2.5
State and Local Excises	1.1	1.4	1.6	1.7	1.6	1.5
Motor Vehicle Licenses	0.3	0.4	0.4	0.5	0.4	0.4
	12.5–17.5	17.5–22.6	22.6–35.5	35.5–92.0	Over 92.0	
Federal Excises	2.3	1.8	0.9	0.8	0.6	
State and Local Excises	1.3	1.0	0.5	0.4	0.3	
Motor Vehicle Licenses	0.4	0.3	0.2	0.1	0.1	

Source: See Bibliography.

. . . indicates that data are not available; — means that the figure is zero or less than half the final digit shown.

[1] Income classes are in annual income, except for India and Pakistan—monthly expenditure; Norway—consumption expenditure; and Lebanon—annual expenditure.

Lebanese cigarette excise, however, because of the much higher tax content of imported cigarettes that are mainly consumed by the rich. Generally, the alcohol excise is less regressive and may even be proportionate over large ranges of income. The automotive excises exhibit substantial progressivity, the motor vehicle taxes more so than the fuel excises, which seems logical because the former permit greater differentiation according to patterns of use between low-income and high-income groups. Excise incidence of other goods and services varies widely. Duties on salt and matches appear decidedly regressive, but those on public utility services and entertainment are generally progressive, as is the foreign travel tax in Turkey.[16] Interestingly, the extended excise systems of India and Pakistan exhibit substantial progressivity on account of the heavy discrimination in excise design in favor of necessities and against semiluxury and luxury items. The progressive incidence of many excises in the Panamanian tax system is worth noting.

Of course, the effective excise rates depend crucially upon assumed or observed differences in consumption patterns. For instance, there is a presumption that patterns of expenditures on excisable goods, and by extension their excise content, are likely to differ substantially between highly monetized urban areas and essentially rural subsistence sectors of a developing economy. Rural families may purchase most of their goods from local small-scale producers whose output is either exempted or escapes taxation, while urban families are likely to buy more factory made or imported goods that tend to be taxed more effectively. Obviously, excise burden patterns will differ accordingly. For instance, the Indian study calculated that the incidence of commodity taxes was substantially larger in the case of urban families, rising from 11.1 per cent for the lowest expenditure groups to 24.6 per cent for the highest, compared to 5.8 per cent and 11.9 per cent, respectively, for rural households.

Recent incidence studies have given much greater recognition than past analyses to the importance of these inter-sectoral differences in consumption patterns, and it has been surmised that these differences might cause effective tax rates to exhibit progressivity. At least that was the conclusion of a study on the incidence of the Peruvian tax system, which on the whole was markedly progressive, rising from 5.2 per cent for the poorest quartile of the income distribution to 23.0 per cent for the top quartile.[17] This is partly attributed to the excise system and the large tax content of such highly income elastic goods as better quality cigarettes, imported alcoholic beverages, and electrical appliances. Because car owners generally belong to the upper 5 per cent of the income scale, automotive excises were also progressive. At the same time, the excise content of transportation expenses of the poor was small, because buses and trucks use low taxed diesel oil or low octane gasoline. More generally, it was noted that rural production and consumption remained largely outside the domain of the tax system; hence, effective tax rates should be low.

These differences in consumption patterns and commercial integration would always work in the desired direction if low-income families lived only in rural areas and high-income families in cities. Obviously that is not the case, and there is reason to believe that the urban poor are much less in a position to escape excise burdens than low-income rural families, because perforce they consume more processed and imported goods that fall within easier reach of the tax collector. Thus, Charles McLure concluded that overall effective tax rates of urban families were three to five percentage points higher than those of rural families, and that in several cases the urban rates were twice as high as those of the rural poor.[18] These differences are significant in view of the fact that low-income urban families pay on average some 10 per cent of their income or expenditures in the form of taxes. But in the rural versus urban excise setting, it may be argued that by moving to urban areas, the poor are in effect expressing a judgment that, the heavier excise burden notwithstanding, they are better off.

High-Income Countries

On the whole, there appears to be less potential for progressive excise taxation in high-income countries for three reasons: their greater degree of commercial integration; smaller variations in consumption patterns between rich and poor; and their more effective tax administration. The studies listed in Table 4:1 show that, taken together, traditional excises are moderately progressive in lower-income classes, then proportionate, and sharply regressive in higher-income ranges; progressivity, if it exists at all, appears to occur with automotive excises.[19] Excises on nontraditional goods and on services appear to exhibit the same type of incidence as in low-income countries; those on services are often progressive.[20]

Of substantial interest is the Norwegian study that treated the sumptuary excises separately. It found that the share of expenditures on tobacco decreased with rising total consumption expenditures, but that of alcoholic beverages increased. Expenditures on alcoholic beverages, however, declined markedly with increasing family size, which was not true for tobacco products; "this obviously reflects the fact that the expenditure elasticity for tobacco is fairly low for most income brackets and family sizes, whereas alcoholic beverages have most of the characteristics of 'luxury commodities.'" Interesting for its formulation is also the conclusion that "from a distributive point of view a reduction (increase) in taxes on alcoholic beverages appears to have an effect similar to a reduction (increase) in the progressivity of income tax combined with a reduction (increase) in general child allowances."[21]

There is an interesting U.S. study, which deals exclusively with the distribution of the excise burden on urban consumer units before and after the repeal of a large number of manufacturer's and retail excises on luxury items, as well as the incidence of remaining excises on sumptuary goods, automotive items, and a number of specific purpose levies.[22] According to the author, the repeal measures enacted in 1965 reduced the total excise burden on urban consumers from 3.38 per cent to 2.47 per cent of annual income. The distribution of the burden was broadly the same after as before the enactment, although excise reductions were considerably larger for the lowest income class (1.57 per cent) and considerably smaller for the highest income class (0.69 per cent). If tax policy is viewed as doing what is possible at the margin, a small measure of success might be ascribed to the changes.

In the same study, a regressivity index was computed for fifty-one individual excises. A zero value indicated proportionality, negative values regressivity, and positive values a progressive distribution. The values of the index for individual excise items ranged from a very regressive –37.1 for the excise on smoking tobacco, to a fairly progressive 14.2 for the tax on furs. Progressive excises that were repealed included, in order of their progressivity: club dues, musical instruments, phonograph records, cameras and films, jewelry, handbags and luggage, general admissions, and cabarets. Progressive excises that remained were distilled spirits, firearms, fishing equipment, and passenger automobiles. These findings are of some significance because they indicate that even in a high-income country excises on luxury items may fulfill a role supplementary to that of the income tax.

Some Further Comments

Summing up the findings of the tax incidence studies, it appears that the tobacco excise is regressive almost everywhere. The incidence of other excises varies. On the whole they do not appear to be very progressive in high-income countries. Excise systems in low-income countries, however, may exhibit moderate progressivity on account of the dualistic nature of the economies, class-differentiated consumption patterns, and excise structures that discriminate against nonessentials. However, results must often be considered as the quantification of sometimes doubtful assumptions; generally data have been used to suggest an hypothesis on excise burden distribution rather than to test a preexisting theory. Moreover, the definitions of income, the choices and assumptions regarding the allocation of consumption and tax data, and the assumptions on incidence, are debatable.

There are also a few other qualifications to be made. First, by taking average group incomes and consumption patterns, the income distribution approach adopted for most incidence studies in effect suppresses individual differences between families in the same income class. These inter-family variations in consumption patterns are highlighted under what is called the "typical household approach" to tax incidence, under which tax burdens are computed for families of given size, income, and consumption habits (rather than actual tax payments allocated to income classes). Thus, the Guatemalan study listed in Table 4:1 estimates that the excise burden of heavy consumers of cigarettes and alcoholic beverages may be three times larger than that of light consumers of the same items. This finding underscores the horizontal inequities of excise taxation.[23] However, the widespread acceptance of the sumptuary excises might be taken as an indication that society regards their incidence as equitable, even though it is contrary to principles accepted for most other taxes.[24]

Second, even excises on cigarettes and alcoholic beverages may exhibit progressivity, largely because home-made consumption of these items is perforce excluded from the tax base. But this implies that the excises will become less progressive as the monetization and market orientation of the economy proceeds. If progressivity is to be retained, therefore, excise structure and rates must be modified over time to reflect the changes in consumption patterns. This should be possible in most developing countries where other commodities with high income elasticities of demand become increasingly important in the market basket of the well-to-do.[25] In highly industrialized economies, however, the redistributive function of the tax system must primarily be fulfilled by a comprehensive, progressive income tax.

Third, it should probably be emphasized that the redistributive role of an excise system cannot be viewed in isolation, but must be examined in the context of the impact of the fiscal system as a whole. For instance, in industrial countries, regressivity in excise taxation may be acceptable, because there are compensating elements elsewhere in the tax system. In developing countries some progressivity in commodity taxation may be achieved through the import duty system.[26] Alternatively, relatively high effective rates at the lower end of the income scale may not be regarded as unfair when government expenditure policies are clearly biased in favor of the poor.[27] The prevalence of low effective rates, combined with an absence of low income-oriented education, health, and employment programs might be considered a poor alternative.

Fourth, there is the question at least with regard to developing countries whether a qualitative assessment of the impact of an excise system through deductive reasoning, observation in the market place, the examination of rate structures, is not at least as good an approach as the techniques which are used in the incidence studies. The point is that the application of tax incidence analysis, which appears of limited value anyway, should not be viewed as a goal by itself, but should lead to an assessment on which a reform of existing rate structures may be based. More narrowly formulated, given the context of a fixed budget in terms of size and composition, the concern should be focused on the situation at the margins: how to decrease the excise burden on the poor by increasing the burden on the well-to-do. Much of the remainder of this chapter is devoted to that end, but first an attempt is made to provide a tighter formulation of the requirements for greater progressivity in excise taxation.

REQUIREMENTS FOR PROGRESSIVITY IN EXCISE TAXATION

Engel's law of consumption specifies that the share of essential goods in total consumption, such as food, will fall as the level of income rises, while the share of nonessentials will increase.[28] This is a useful point of departure if an attempt is made to impart progressivity in excise tax design, because it means that if the base consists of nonessential commodities, excise payments might be an increasing percentage of income when moving up the scale. But the classification that would be required of goods and services into essentials and nonessentials, or necessities and luxuries has often been the subject of controversy. Much of the misunderstanding arose from the belief that any definition inevitably involved highly subjective social and moral considerations, testimony for which can be found in the legislative records of excises on cosmetics, perfumery, and jewelry.[29] In a somewhat cynical view, luxuries are goods and services that only the other person can afford. In another, necessities are defined as goods and services necessary for maintaining a reasonable standard of living. Generally, these definitions merely substitute one ambiguity for another.[30]

It has also been pointed out that the distinction between necessities and luxuries differs between village and city, and between countries, generations, and professions. In Europe, such common items as bread and sugar were at one time considered nonessential goods, and in the early nineteenth century, soap and bathrooms were regarded luxury items that corrupted the English nation. In India a refrigerator would widely be considered a luxury, but in Kuwait it may be viewed as a seminecessity. Some goods are valued differently even among countries at approximately the same level of economic development. Thus, while chicken is part of the menu of every family, until recently it was considered a luxury food in most European countries.[31]

At any one time, however, the cross-section income elasticity of demand for various commodities in individual countries appears to be a good criterion for distinguishing between necessities and luxuries, as it avoids subjective notions on what people "need" or do not "need." Luxuries for which expenditure rises proportionately faster than income are then items with income elasticities exceeding unity, necessities would have income elasticities smaller than unity but greater than zero, and commodities with negative income elasticities would be inferior. Thus, the first requirement for progressivity in excise taxation is that excisable commodities have an income elasticity greater than unity; by definition an ad valorem excise imposed on them would be progressive.[32] However, if the good in question is highly sensitive to price changes (which will happen when it is narrowly defined so that substitutes are available), an excise would restrict consumption and hence the effect of the progression would be limited. A subsidiary requirement, therefore, is that excisable commodities and close substitutes should have low price elasticities of demand (after the income effect of changes in price has been eliminated).[33]

A second requirement for a progressive excise system would be that expenditures on excisable commodities account for a large fraction of incomes in the middle and upper parts of the income scale, but that they should be a minor item in the budgets of low-income groups. For the progression to be appreciable, consumption by the higher-income class must be significant; among individual goods fountain pens do not satisfy this criterion, but motor vehicles do. The excise system should have a broad coverage of different kinds of semiluxury and luxury goods, and within each group care should be taken that substitutes are included in the excise base. Overall, this would also improve the horizontal equity of the excise system, as individuals within higher-income groups may have different tastes for luxury goods, but on the whole may spend similar amounts, for example on either cars or pleasure boats.

However, even if the second requirement is satisfied, it may well be necessary for revenue purposes that excise taxation extend fairly far into the lower-income ranges. This would not necessarily be incompatible with the first requirement of income elasticity, but to increase the progressive impact of the excise system, it should then be possible to break excisable commodities down into subgroups. Easy specification is the third requirement for attaining progressivity in excise taxation. It would permit the application of graduated rates that differ on the basis of the nature, quality, or price of excisable commodities, on the assumption that consumption patterns vary accordingly. Generally, higher-income groups buy higher-priced varieties of a commodity. Evidence for this may be found in various household budget surveys that note that the expenditure elasticity of demand for a particular product is generally higher than its quantity elasticity. If price is taken as the distinguishing criterion, then bracketed specific or ad valorem rates, discussed in Chapter 2, that increase proportionately faster than price would best ensure progressivity.

Of course, the key to the whole issue of progressive excise taxation—and the fourth requirement—is simplicity in administration, which may involve a trade-off against the third requirement on subspecification. Easy administration requires precise definitions of excisable goods in order to minimize the number of disputes and arbitrary assessments by tax officials, as well as the possibility of imposing enforceable controls or accounting checks on production, and a number of other factors discussed in Chapter 8. Excises on silver, gold, or jewelry and handicrafts often do not satisfy the criterion for administrative simplicity.

Finally, the support that taxation derives from prevailing social and moral views on what goods and services should be considered luxuries should not be lost on policymakers. Therefore, to increase the acceptability of progressive excises, a fifth requirement might be that the commodities in question should be widely regarded as signs of affluence; by implication their taxation would be viewed as an indication of governments' determination to strengthen economic equality.

DESIGN OF EXCISE RATE STRUCTURES

To what extent do excisable goods and services satisfy the criteria outlined above, particularly that on income elasticity? And how can greater progressivity be imparted to excise rate structures? Since the concern is primarily with minimizing regressive effects, the focus is first on excisable products that are known to figure prominently in the market basket of lower-income groups, to be followed by a survey of the excise taxation of luxury goods and services. Although data on income elasticities are generally not available, household budget surveys often do provide data on expenditure elasticities. The difference between the two elasticities should be small in lower-income and middle-income classes where little saving takes place. More important for the regressivity problem, if the expenditure elasticity for a particular product is less than unity, then the income elasticity should also be less than unity.

Reducing Regressivity

Prima facie, the regressivity of many excise systems can be attributed to the heavy excises on tobacco products and alcoholic beverages.[34] As shown in Table 4:2, expenditures on tobacco products comprise some 3 per cent of total household expenditures in most countries, and the expenditure elasticity generally lies between 0.5 and unity. Calculations for industrial countries indicate that price elasticities of demand for tobacco products also lie below unity.[35] Therefore, a uniform ad valorem excise on a package of cigarettes would take a larger portion out of the household budgets of the poor than of the rich, leaving the poor with little room to escape the excise either by reducing consumption or by switching to untaxed substitutes.[36] Regressivity is aggravated when the excise is imposed at the raw tobacco (import) stage as is done in the United Kingdom and other countries that follow British taxing traditions, because at this stage any rate differentiation based on consumer price—assuming that lower-priced articles loom larger in low-income budgets—is not possible. The regressive impact is also accentuated if uniform specific excises per unit of production rather than ad valorem levies are imposed, because the former also discriminate more against lower-priced items.

In many developing countries, however, the poor are probably saved from the potentially strongly regressive impact of the tobacco excise, because the excise is collected at the manufacturing stage, where differentiated rates may be applied based on the nature of the product and its price. Thus, in Indonesia a lower rate of excise is imposed on indigenous cigarettes made with black tobacco and cloves that are primarily consumed by lower-income classes. Similarly, on the Indian subcontinent, *biri* cigarettes attract a much lower rate than American-blend cigarettes.[37] Moreover, many low-income countries are primary producers of tobacco, and any cigarettes rolled on a cottage industry basis would either be exempted, or simply evade duty. On the plausible assumption that lower-income groups purchase cheaper cigarettes, some countries graduate excise rate schedules according to the retail price of cigarettes. Thus, in the Philippines the effective excise rate per pack of twenty of the cheapest brand of nonindigenous cigarettes is 12 per cent, as against 30 per cent for the expensive imported brands. Such rates may be levied in the form of bracketed specific or ad

Table 4.2. Selected Countries: Expenditures on Excisable Goods and Expenditure Elasticities According to Household Budget Surveys

Country[1] and Year(s) of Data	Tobacco Products — Percentage of Total Expenditure	Tobacco Products — Expenditure Elasticity	Alcoholic Beverages — Percentage of Total Expenditure	Alcoholic Beverages — Expenditure Elasticity	Sugar Products — Percentage of Total Expenditure	Sugar Products — Expenditure Elasticity	Tea, Coffee, Soft Drinks — Percentage of Total Expenditure	Tea, Coffee, Soft Drinks — Expenditure Elasticity	Clothing — Percentage of Total Expenditure	Clothing — Expenditure Elasticity
Pakistan (1963–64)	3	0.9	—	—	3	1.6	1[2]	1.8[2]	8	1.2
Kenya (1957–58)	3	0.8	4	2.3	4	0.4	1	2.2	6	1.8
Sri Lanka (1963)	2	1.2	4	0.7	7	0.6	2	0.9	10	1.4
Philippines (1965)	3	0.9	2	0.6	...	...	...	...	7	1.1
Tunisia (1965–68)	3	0.9	—	—	2	0.6	3[3]	0.7[3]	13	1.0
China (Taiwan) (1965–67)	3	0.8	1	0.9	...	...	1	1.3	5	1.3
Peru (1974)	...	...	1	0.7	2[4]	0.4[4]	2	0.9	...	...
Chile (1965)	1	0.8	2	1.1	2	0.6	1[5]	0.9[5]	13	1.1
Venezuela (1966)	1	0.5	1	1.0	1	0.5	1	0.6	6	1.0
Ireland (1965–66)	6	0.6	4	2.1	2	0.4	1[6]	1.6[6]	9	1.6
Japan (1968)	1	-0.4	2	0.3	2	0.6	1	0.6	11	1.5
Italy (1963–64)	2	0.7	4[7]	0.7[7]	1	0.7	1[8]	0.7[8]	10	1.3
United Kingdom (1962)	6	1.0	4	2.2	2	0.5	1[6]	1.0[6]	8	1.9
France (1966)	...	...	4	0.4	1	0.2	1[6]	0.4[6]	...	...
Denmark (1964–65)	5	0.6	3	1.6	1	0.1	2[8]	-0.1[8]	9	1.1
Switzerland (1961)	3[3]	1.1[3]	...	...	1	-0.3	2[8]	0.7[8]	10	1.8
Sweden (1958)	2	1.1	2	1.7	1	-0.7	1[6]	0.8[6]	9	1.0

Source: FAO, *Income Elasticities of Demand for Agricultural Products* (Rome, 1972). Coefficients are computed from cross-section data using double-logarithmic specifications. For the limitations to the comparability of the coefficients, see page 98 of the FAO study.

. . . indicate that the data are not available.   — means that the figure is zero or less than half the final digit shown.

[1] Ranked in order of per capita GNP shown in Appendix C, Table 1. Generally nationwide coverage, but metropolitan surveys for Peru, Chile, and Venezuela; surveys restricted to employees in the case of France, Denmark, and Switzerland.
[2] Tea only.
[3] Including alcoholic beverages.
[4] Including salt and condiments.
[5] Coffee only.
[6] Soft drinks only.
[7] Including soft drinks.
[8] Tea, coffee, and cocoa.

valorem rates, and through the use of constructive values much of the administrative simplicity associated with specific rates can be maintained.

From whatever figures are available, it would appear that the percentage of total expenditure on alcoholic beverages is similar to that on tobacco products; demand, however, appears more income elastic. The highest expenditure elasticities are found in Ireland and the United Kingdom owing to the extremely high duties. Again, rate differentiation may go a long way in reducing regressivity. First, product differentiation is feasible. Thus, among alcoholic beverages the income elasticity of beer is generally lower than that of wines and liquors (except in major wine producing and consuming countries around the Mediterranean, where wine is considered a necessity) and, therefore, excise rate schedules might discriminate in favor of beer and against other alcoholic beverages. Second, indigenous brews, mainly consumed in low-income rural areas, are often exempted—examples are opaque beer in Central Africa and palm wine in West Africa. In most low-income countries, expensive liquors (usually imported) are mainly consumed by high-income groups. High rates of excise are, therefore, justified on equity grounds.

Interestingly, the income elasticity of demand for sugar declines as economic development proceeds, and becomes negative in very high-income countries where sugar consumption has reached saturation levels. In low-income countries the regressive impact of the sugar excise can be greatly reduced by exempting or levying reduced rates on unrefined forms of sugar. In Indonesia, brown or red sugar mainly consumed by the poor is exempt and the incidence of the excise on white sugar that is bought by urban high-income groups is probably progressive. Similarly, in India and Pakistan, unrefined forms of sugar such as *gur*, *khandsari* or *rab* are taxed lightly or not at all, the heaviest excise being borne by refined sugar. As in Indonesia, excise incidence might then be progressive; the high expenditure elasticity for sugar in Pakistan would seem to point in that direction.

There are fairly large variations in expenditure elasticities of nonalcoholic beverages and the distribution of excise burdens is likely to vary accordingly. The expenditure elasticity of soft drinks generally lies around unity; thus an excise would probably be proportional. Presumably little can be done to increase progressivity for soft drinks, although in Indonesia a higher (sales tax) rate is charged on those manufactured in automated plants. As these drinks are presumably consumed by higher-income groups, some progressivity may be imparted by the rate structure. Expenditure elasticities on coffee and tea differ widely, but as indicated by revealed preferences, tea appears to be more of a necessity than coffee. An excise on coffee may well have a progressive incidence in many countries.

Increasing Progressivity

Table 4:2 also shows that in most countries people spend some 10 per cent of their household budgets on clothing which, with few exceptions, appears to be a fairly income elastic commodity. Few countries impose an excise on textiles (of those listed in the table only Pakistan, Kenya, China, and Italy), but those that do might find that the incidence would be progressive, particularly if the excise rate structure discriminates against the more expensive varieties. It is noteworthy that in India the excise rate is differentiated on the basis of the fineness of the fabric, on the assumption that coarser textiles are primarily bought by the poor. But this objective would not be achieved to the extent that coarse textures are also used in the manufacture of tapestry and furnishings, which are bought mainly be the well-to-do.[38]

Low-income countries that wish to correct for pretax income differentials through their excise systems should include in the base the goods listed as luxury items in Table 4:3. Electrical household appliances, television sets, phonographic and photographic equipment, and expensive sporting goods, taken together, are fairly important items in the household

Table 4.3. Excises on Luxury Goods in India, Japan and Korea
In Per Cent[1]

Kind of Goods	India[2]	Japan[3]	Korea[4]
Smoking Requisites, Lighters	Rp 3/lighter	20	40 (60)
Clocks, Watches	—	30 (10)	10
Cosmetics, Toilet Articles	30	10 (5)	20
Jewelry, Gold and Silver Products	—	15	30 (160, 200)
Fur Products	—	15	200
Carpets	15	10	—
Furniture	—	20	20 (40)
Electrical Appliances	25	15	65 (55)
Air-Conditioners, Refrigerators	75 (100)	20	65
Radios	Up to Rp 300	10	5
Television Sets (Including Tubes)	20	20 (15)	65 (45)
Photographic or Cinematographic Equipment	30 (20)	15	30 (50)
Phonographic Equipment, Musical Instruments	20 (10, 25, 30)	15 (5, 10)	55 (30
Slot Machines and Other Game Requisites	15	20	200
Golf and Billiard Requisites, Rifles	—	30	150
Motor Boats, Yachts	—	30 (10, 15)	200
Passenger Automobiles	20 (40)	30 (5, 10, 15)	20 (15, 40)

Sources: Japan, Ministry of Finance, *An Outline of Japanese Taxes 1975*; Japan Tax Association, *Asian Taxation 1974*; and Korea, Ministry of Finance, *Korean Taxation* (1975).
— indicates that excises are not listed separately.

[1]Rates between brackets are imposed on smaller units, parts, accessories, or higher priced varieties; all rates are levied at the manufacturing stage unless otherwise indicated.

[2]In India, luxury goods are subject to excise under an extended excise system that includes 128 commodity groups. Virtually all excisable goods are also subject to state sales taxes at varying rates.

[3]The Japanese excise system is called the commodity tax that in addition includes a 5 per cent levy on soft drinks, coffee, cocoa, and tea; duties on jewelry, fur products, and carpets are levied at the retail stage.

[4]The Korean excise system is also called the commodity tax. It resembles the Japanese tax, but covers also a large number of intermediate and finished products.

budgets of higher-income groups, with income elasticities of demand usually well in excess of unity. The demand for these durable consumer goods, however, tends to be relatively price elastic, but this drawback can be mitigated by a broad coverage of luxury goods.[39] Confining luxury excises to cosmetics and perfumery, as many countries do, precludes effective use of excises for redistributive purposes.

The income elasticity of demand for most services is generally greater than unity. Therefore, excises on travel, entertainment, admission charges, restaurants, hotels, and tourism, are likely to have a progressive incidence in most countries. Few statistics are available, but a study for New Zealand indicates that cultural activities, entertainment, transportation, and communication, have income elasticities clearly greater than one.[40] In another study, the income elasticity of meals taken outside homes in high-income countries is found to range from 1.2 in Canada to 2.7 in Switzerland.[41] However, the demand for most services is almost certainly more sensitive to price changes than that for luxury goods. Accordingly, the progressive impact of high excises on services should be more limited. On equity grounds, excises on foreign travel and club dues are probably to be favored most strongly.

The single most important vehicle for increasing the progressivity of excise systems, particularly in developing countries, is the motoring field. The demand for passenger cars and gasoline is usually highly income elastic, expenditures comprise a sizable part of household budgets, and related excise levies are easy to administer and meet socially with a high degree of acceptance. A detailed presentation of the equity function of motor vehicle taxes and related duties is given in Table 2 in Chapter 5.

In developing countries, almost any form of excise taxation of private motor vehicles may be expected to be an effective means of progressive taxation, as only high-income groups own them, but of the various road user charges shown in Table 5:2, excises directly related to the value of the vehicle, if properly designed, are likely to have the most progressive incidence. The choice might then be between an excise on new motor vehicles with a bracketed ad valorem duty rising with the value of the vehicle, or an annual license system with fees graduated in favor of cheaper and older vehicles.[42] License fees would probably be best, as their administration is easier (the incentive to evade the excise is smaller than in the case of a one-time levy) and, unlike an excise on new vehicles, increases in annual fees do not give rise to windfall profits on vehicles already on the road. In view of ownership patterns in developing countries, progressivity in excise taxation would also be imparted by high duties on gasoline. In industrial countries, it is sometimes argued that the situation may be different because the poor often purchase second-hand vehicles that are generally less efficient.[43] But it could also be pointed out that the large drop in car prices after initial use is a highly effective means of income redistribution.

CONCLUDING REMARKS

An important, if qualified, conclusion of this chapter is that although excises may not be an ideal index of taxpaying capacity, on the whole they appear to perform better in this respect than is generally believed. In many developing countries almost certainly some progressivity can be imparted through the heavy taxation of expensive cigarettes, liquors, refined sugar, expensive clothing, the luxury goods enumerated in Chapter 2, gasoline, passenger cars, foreign travel, hotel rooms, restaurant meals, admissions, and club dues. To be sure, progressivity is unlikely to reach those at the top of the income distribution, but in developing countries an income tax would not do that either. On equity grounds, there is much to be said for excise systems with a broad coverage of luxury and semiluxury goods, whether domestically produced or imported, although care should be taken that only major items are included in the base;[44] heavy excises on cosmetics, perfumes, beauty parlors, and dry cleaning establishments are often hardly worth the cost of collection.

It is fitting here to draw attention to the recommendations on excise tax reform of the Puerto Rican Tax Reform Commission, because they were primarily based on equity considerations.[45] Although the Commission found that the incidence of the existing excise system was already progressive up to family income levels of $10,000 (which includes nine-tenths of the island's families), it thought that the system's income redistribution function should be further emphasized, particularly since the system was administered so effectively.[46] The Commission recommended: (1) the conversion of the specific excises on traditional excise goods, tires, tubes, and cement to ad valorem excises; this would eliminate discrimination against lower-priced items bought by the poor; (2) the reduction of exemptions for consumer durables; (3) the imposition of higher duties on automobiles with a taxable price in excess of a specified pretax value and the conversion of the unit tax on low-priced automobiles to an ad valorem rate; and (4) an increase in the gasoline excise.

In high-income countries that have reasonably administered, global, progressive personal income taxes, the income redistribution role of excise systems is very limited, if it exists at all. There, most excise systems are basically limited, and any progressivity in the automotive and entertainment fields is usually offset by the regressive impact of excises on sumptuary goods. To a large extent this is probably a matter of choice. Given the existence of compensating elements elsewhere in the tax and expenditure fields, the excise system's merit lies primarily in its revenue function.[47] Nevertheless, a case for excises on luxury goods and services to supplement the role of the income tax remains. Consumer durables, in particular, might be taxed more heavily than they are under existing sales tax and excise systems; equity or political arguments for doing so seem to coincide with a justification on efficiency grounds, which are discussed in the next chapter.

CHAPTER 5

EXCISES AND ECONOMIC EFFICIENCY

Whereas the equity goal of taxation is concerned with a fair distribution of the tax burden, efficiency requires that a tax system should further, or hinder as little as possible, the optimum use of an economy's scarce resources. Because they are related to economic behavior, excises, like other taxes, influence the efficiency objective. That influence, which may be exercised deliberately or unintentionally, for better or for worse, is analyzed in this chapter.

First is an analysis of the state of the argument on allocative inefficiencies in consumption and production owing to the selective nature of excises. Next, the possible effects of excises on product mix and factor mix are examined, particularly as regards their implications for employment. The third section deals with the use of excises as proxies for price in highway finance, followed by their use as supplements to price in private markets to correct for external diseconomies in consumption or production. There may also be inefficiencies when the level of excise taxation differs between different tax jurisdictions, either in the national or the international setting. The concluding section considers some conflicts and trade-offs between the income redistribution and allocative roles of excises and points toward the need for the clear specification and coordination of objectives.

WELFARE ASPECTS OF EXCISE TAXATION[1]

The classic indictment against excises is that they impose a burden over and above the amount of the excise receipts. The argument, that can be neatly demonstrated with indifference curve analysis, is that a proportional income tax or a general sales tax levied at a uniform rate on all goods and services only has an income effect, but that an excise, being selective, in addition induces households to substitute nontaxed goods for taxed goods.[2] Because it may be assumed that the marginal unit of consumption of the nontaxed goods is less valuable to them than that of the taxed goods, households are thought to suffer a net loss in economic welfare—measured as the difference between the total loss of welfare resulting from the imposition of the excise, and the loss from a tax of equal yield that would not have interfered with economic choice. This differential burden owing to the substitution effect of the excise is referred to as the excess burden, or the dead loss of excise taxation.[3] According to Pareto's formulation of optimum conditions, the abolition of the excise and its replacement by a neutral tax would make some people better off without making anybody worse off.

However, over the years, it has been shown that a relaxation of the underlying assumptions—imperative if the theorem was to have any relevance to the real world—had such profound effects on the hypothesis, that little, if anything, remained of the supposed superiority of an income tax over an excise.[4]

The major theoretical rebuttal came in 1951 when I.M.D. Little proved that if the assumption of a completely inelastic labor supply was dropped, the distorting effects of an excise did not differ, qualitatively at least, from those of a proportional income tax.[5] Let there be three commodities, Little's argument went, of which one is untaxable leisure, in an economy in which labor is the only factor of production. In this situation, an excise on either one of the taxable commodities would distort two of the possible choices (between the taxed commodity and each of the two other commodities), while leaving the choice between the two untaxed commodities (one being leisure) undisturbed. But a proportional income tax (which under a no-savings assumption may be interpreted as an equal-rate excise on all commodities, except leisure) would also distort two of the possible choices (between leisure and each of the two taxed commodities), while leaving the choice between the two taxed commodities undisturbed.

In a major further contribution, Arnold Harberger elaborated on Little's proof and proceeded to make an efficiency comparison between an income tax and an excise based on quantitative measurement.[6] He found that the traditional preference for income taxation was still justified in the case of the United States, but pointed out that the conclusion did not necessarily have wider application, as each case had to be judged on its own merits. On the whole, the welfare cost of excise taxation is probably small. The total welfare cost of the U.S. tax system, for instance, has been estimated at some 3 per cent to 4 per cent of total tax revenues, of which about one-third is being accounted for by excises.[7]

Further modifications of the excess-burden theorem are required if the assumption of a fully competitive equilibrium is relaxed. Milton Friedman has contended that if monopolistic elements dominate the market, prevailing divergencies in substitution rates may call for an excise on a good produced in a parallel competitive market, in order to reduce the overall loss of welfare.[8] The traditional doctrine must also be modified if market failures are interpreted to include situations in which the production or consumption of certain goods gives rise to external economies or diseconomies not accounted for in market prices. In these cases private benefits or costs differ from social benefits or costs, and it may be argued that an excise (or subsidy) aimed at closing the gap may move the economy closer to optimum conditions.[9]

The general conclusion emerging from the debate on the welfare aspects of excise taxation is that in the real world, the choice between alternative forms of taxation is a second-best one; the optimum can only be attained subject to one or more constraints that themselves violate the conditions for Pareto-optimality. In this situation, an excise system that disturbs more optimum conditions is not necessarily inferior to an income or sales tax that disturbs fewer, because "if one of the Paretian optimum conditions cannot be fulfilled a second best optimum situation is achieved only by departing from all other optimum conditions."[10]

This conclusion appears to take the stigma of biased allocation out of excise taxation. Although each case still has to be considered on its own merits, the following guidelines can be formulated.

1. Since the excess burden of an excise is by definition inversely related to the elasticity of substitution of the taxed item, burdens on consumers of sumptuary products and necessities should be small, particularly if close substitutes are included in the base.[11] The demand for these goods is not very sensitive to price changes, and they are widely consumed—both factors that should work to reduce potential excess burdens. It is difficult to make a general statement for other goods and services in terms of the properties of individual demand functions. However, one can probably generalize about the conventional approach if the problem is restated in terms of the properties of the utility function as one of minimizing the total excess burden for all commodities in a multiple excise setting. Under this approach, A. B. Atkinson and J. E. Stiglitz conclude that "if direct additivity [of the utility function] is a reasonable assumption for broad commodity

groups, then the optimal structure of taxation from an efficiency viewpoint is one that taxes more heavily goods which have a low income elasticity of demand."[12]

2. The foregoing conclusion would suggest that on efficiency ground excises should be high for necessities, including sumptuary goods, and low for luxury goods—which implies a sharp conflict with the equity objective. But because it is not feasible to include leisure in any tax base, the hypothesis can be modified, and a second-best solution would be to tax goods and services that are complements to, or poorer-than-average substitutes for leisure.[13] These would probably include most luxuries such as jewelry, perfumes, furs, television sets, musical instruments, expensive sporting goods, pleasure boats, and virtually the whole range of entertainment and tourist-related services.

3. There is also a presumption, as pointed out in Chapter 1, that consumer burdens are largely "self-imposed": taxpayers may be aware of the wider range of options available under excise taxation, and they may well agree with the sumptuary purpose of high excises on tobacco products and alcoholic beverages, or the equity objective of the heavy taxation of luxury goods. Generally, these considerations are not applicable in the case of producer burdens, however, and there is therefore some basis for requiring policymakers to be primarily concerned with divergencies among rates of substitution in production. The imposition of an excise may pressure producers to reconsider the size of manufacturing establishments, for instance, or to adopt alternative production techniques, or yet to change the location of production.

4. Finally, an intriguing area is the use of excises with the "right" distorting effects aimed at improving the efficient use of resources. Under the broad definition of output as an aggregate welfare concept, this could include the use of excises to alter the factor mix in favor of labor. Here, excises would provide a correction to the price of capital, or encourage the adoption of labor-intensive production techniques. There appears to be a role too for the use of corrective excises where the production or consumption of a good involves important external diseconomies; congestion and pollution charges should be mentioned here, as well as excises on sumptuary products. There is the related question of dampening or altering the patterns of demand for energy through selective taxation, where excises can help the attainment of socially optimum prices for factors, goods and services.

EMPLOYMENT IMPLICATIONS OF EXCISE TAXATION

Textiles require more labor per unit of capital than fertilizers. Within the textile group, handloom weaving is a more labor-intensive mode of production than making cloth on automatic power looms. In this connection, it has been argued that if carefully designed, excises may induce changes in the composition of industrial output and techniques of production so as to increase aggregate employment. This is important for developing countries where capital is relatively scarce and labor abundant, for it has become clear that expansion of the manufacturing sector alone cannot absorb the increase in the labor force.[14] To be sure, a more labor-intensive production technique is not necessarily capital-saving, in other words, it need not have a low capital-output ratio; handpounding rice, for instance, uses only one-hundredth as much capital per man as machine milling, yet it yields only half as much output per unit of capital. Conversely, however, in India the capital-output ratio for cotton weaving in the handloom sector is only half as high as that in the powerloom sector.

Three approaches may be identified for the use of excise taxation to promote employment. First, excises may influence the output mix by favoring labor-intensive goods over capital-intensive goods, relying upon the consumer to substitute the former for the latter. Second, excises may influence the choice of technology, either directly by taxing capital goods, or indirectly by promoting the use of labor-intensive business forms or methods. A third approach would be to employ selective tax measures to induce firms to use existing capital stock more intensively, for instance through multiple-shift operations. Here the concern is with the first two approaches; the third is discussed in greater detail in the next chapter.

Output Composition

Clearly, the total labor cost of some products is higher relative to capital cost than that of others. Food, clothing, and shelter generally require more labor per unit of capital than electrical household appliances, television sets, air-conditioning units, or motor vehicles. The same is true of leather compared to plastic shoes, or of washing soap compared to detergents. Thus, broad distinctions between labor-intensive and capital-intensive goods are possible and differential taxation is feasible. Important backward and forward linkages may also be heeded. Cotton shirts require materials that may have been harvested by hand, and upon use the shirts may have to be handwashed and ironed, linkages which are absent in the case of drip-dry shirts made from synthetic fibers. In the extended excise systems of the Indian subcontinent excise rate schedules are often graduated accordingly.

The Indonesian cigarette industry is an interesting example of excise discrimination in favor of labor-intensive products. Basically, the industry manufactures two kinds of cigarettes: the machine-made types that use blends of partly imported light and bright tobaccos and are therefore referred to as white cigarettes, and the hand-made indigenous varieties, called *kretek* cigarettes, that use dark and heavy bodied leaf mixed with cloves. The white cigarettes are produced by twenty-two large and highly capital-intensive enterprises employing less than 5,000 persons in all, while the *kretek* cigarette industry, dominated by a similar number of large enterprises, employs some 100,000 persons.[15] The difference in labor-intensiveness of the respective production processes is obvious: in a *kretek* cigarette factory, one employee typically handrolls between 3,000 and 4,000 cigarettes a day and is backed up by other employees who handcut and pack the cigarettes, whereas a machine produces the same number in one to two minutes.

The Indonesian excise system favors hand-made cigarettes by taxing them at an effective rate of 20 per cent of the retail price, whereas the excise rate on machine-made cigarettes is close to 50 per cent. Prima facie, these rate differentials seem defensible in a country that has a high rate of unemployment. Interestingly, the tools that are used in the *kretek* cigarette industry—small wooden hand-operated rollers and blocks for packing cigarettes—are complementary to the use of labor, rather than substitutes for it.[16] However, differences in technology are not entirely predetermined, because *kretek* cigarettes can also be made on machines. Finally, consumption patterns between white and *kretek* cigarettes roughly coincide with patterns of income distribution between high-income and low-income groups, respectively.

Choice of Technique

Excises may be used to promote employment by another approach which encourages the adoption of more labor-intensive production techniques, regardless of the product that is being manufactured. Thus, it has been pointed out that factor proportions should be changed in favor of labor for handling, packaging and storing activities.[17] Here the selective taxation of certain capital goods with a strong labor-displacing effect such as conveyor belts, fork lifts, tractors, and certain types of construction equipment, might be indicated.[18] However, the choice of changing to manual operations may not exist in all industries and prescribing end-use exemptions in such cases might unduly complicate administration.

Another possible way the excise system could increase employment would be to use it to discriminate in favor of small-scale industries. These industries, defined to include all firms with twenty to fifty workers each, employ well over half the labor force in most developing countries, and there is evidence that they use more labor-intensive production methods than large-scale manufacturing establishments. Small-scale industries are particularly common where products are highly differentiated (as with textiles), where manufacturing operations can be easily separated and specialized (glassware, electric batteries, furniture, jewelry, ornaments), where raw materials are widely dispersed (board made from straw, wine, milk products), or where transport costs are high (bricks).[19] Favorable tax treatment of these and similar operations (which are often complementary rather than competitive to large-scale industries) may have a positive influence on employment.

Nowhere probably is the excise system used so intensively to promote small-scale industries as in India. As shown below, a wide variety of measures are used to protect and foster the development of village and small-scale firms in order to further employment.[20] In a few cases, preferential excise treatment is directly related to the size of the labor force or the absence of specified machinery, but in the majority, exemptions or the application of lower rates is made contingent upon the size of current or past output. In many cases, too, the excise liability is graduated, with successive slabs of output bearing a higher rate of tax. Employment may also be affected by tying the exemption to the form of economic organization (such as cooperatives); by attempting to provide backward linkages and make the exemption dependent upon the use of indigenous raw materials; or by providing forward linkages, such as exempting glass and copper used in the household manufacture of trinkets. The Indian scheme may indeed have affected the size of production units. According to reports, before preferential excise treatment was introduced, less than 10 per cent of the output of nonessential vegetable oils was produced by small firms, but subsequently the percentage rose rapidly to 50 per cent.[21] Whether this reduction in the size of production units has increased aggregate employment is difficult to gauge.

India: Excise Exemptions and Rate Differentiations[22]

A. *To promote small-scale industries*

   1. Exemptions based on the size of the input of labor and capital:
      a. Exemption if the total number of workers does not exceed a specified maximum: five workers in the case of glass and glassware, and electrical batteries; fifteen workers in the case of chinaware and porcelainware;
      b. Exemption if production is carried on without the aid of power (chocolates and confectionary) or if the number of machines does not exceed a specified number (cotton and silk fabrics).
   2. Exemptions
      a. Exemptions based on the size of current output:
         (1) Basic exemption for all producers, regardless of size of output: soap, processed cotton fabrics;
         (2) Basic exemption only if entire production does not exceed specified maxima: plywood, nitric and hydrochloric acids;
         (3) Lower rates for specified quantities for all producers: matches, bicycle tires and tubes, and vegetable nonessential oils;

(4) Basic exemption followed by a concessionary rate, but only if entire production does not exceed specified maximum: paints and varnishes;

(5) Basic exemption and graduated rates, regardless of size of output: strawboard.

b. Exemptions based on the size of past output:

(1) Preferential rates if production in each of the preceding twelve months did not exceed specified maxima: combustion engines, electric motors;

(2) Basic exemption related to production in each of the preceding twelve months: cosmetics, toilet preparations, nitric and hydrochloric acids;

(3) Basic exemption and preferential rates if production did not exceed specified maxima in any of the preceding three years: pulp board, grey board, mill board.

3. Exemptions related to the end-use of products:
   Glass for beads and bangles, copper strips, and foils for saris and trinkets.

4. Exemptions related to the form of organization:
   Cooperatives for cotton fabrics made on power looms.

5. Exemptions to promote the use of indigenous raw materials:
   Matches made from bamboo splints, plywood and insulating board made out of bagasse and straw, vegetable oil made from cotton seeds.

B. *To avoid taxation of successive stages of production:*

1. Partial exemption related to the use of duty-paid materials:
   Steel (pig-iron duty), iron and steel products (pig-iron and steel duty), aluminium manufactures (ingot duty), copper manufactures (copper ingot duty), motor vehicles (engine duty), refrigerators, air-conditioning appliances and machinery (electric motors and parts duty), footwear (component parts duty).

2. Partial exemption related to end-use of goods:
   Jute batching oil and soap used in jute industry, plywood for tea chests.

3. Exemption for the argicultural sector:
   Internal combustion engines for tractors in agriculture, tires for animal-drawn vehicles, coffee seeds used for sowing, raw naphtha ammonia and oxygen for fertilizer.

It is often argued that excises levied under extended systems may induce the vertical integration of business firms, owing to the taxation of successive stages of production and distribution. These excise-induced arrangements would be inefficient if they reduced specialization. However, since excises are imposed on physical units of production instead of on transactions, inputs and end-goods will both be taxed regardless of the form of economic organization, and vertical integration need not be encouraged. Perhaps for this reason, industry in India has not been as interested in a single-stage levy to eliminate cascade effects as in a single point of excise collection to facilitate compliance.[23]

In conclusion, it should be mentioned that caution must be recommended in using selective taxes to promote employment. For most goods, it might not be feasible to employ excises in this way, either because the rate differential is not large enough to have an appreciable effect, the production process cannot be clearly separated into labor-intensive and capital-intensive parts, or because the method is so complex and introduces so much administrative discretion that any beneficial effect is lost in red tape or collusive practices. There is also a presumption that small-scale industries are more labor-intensive than large. This is not because of the characteristics of the production function, but because their cost structures reflect scarcity prices more closely than those of large firms that are able to import capital goods and raw materials below shadow prices and have easier access to credit facilities and government subsidies. Equally important, wage legislation may be less effective in the small-industry sector, and wages therefore lower. If, as is probably true, most of the rigidities in the structure of production lie in the factor rather than the product market, then differential excise taxation may be of little help, and more general pricing policies affecting capital goods, wages, and the exchange rate may be called for.[24]

ROAD USER CHARGES AND TAXES

The various taxes, duties and license fees in the field of highway finance may be justified as charges for services rendered by the government. It is argued that since benefits derived by individual consumers are identifiable and measurable, "excise prices" should be set accordingly.[25] In this view, road services resemble goods produced in the private sector that are used optimally when their price, commonly referred to as the economic user charge, equals marginal social cost. And it is emphasized that the marginal cost should be the short-run concept, because once a road project is completed, this indicates the value of the resources in their best alternative use; road pricing policies based on long-run marginal cost would underestimate potential net benefits.[26]

The marginal cost consists of the variable maintenance cost of the road, paid for by the public road authority, and the congestion cost, which is borne by all users of the road. These costs, that can be expressed as an amount per vehicle/kilometer, will vary by type of road, type of vehicle, time of day or year, or weather conditions. Trucks and buses cause more damage to roads than do private cars. The variable maintenance costs of unpaved roads are significantly higher than those of paved roads, particularly in the rainy season in many developing countries. Similarly, congestion costs in urban centers are much higher than those on interurban or rural roads.[27]

The issue, therefore, is to find a set of economic user charges that adequately reflects the level and range of variable maintenance and congestion costs. This is not only very difficult, but there is also the problem that a user charge set at the level of marginal cost will not pay for the full cost of the service because road systems are generally characterized by decreasing average costs. Ideally, the deficit on account of the difference between cost and charge should be made up by taxes not related to road use so that optimal efficiency is not disturbed. But the pricing function of road user charges is often subordinated to their general revenue function, because taxes that equal marginal cost are difficult to design and collect, or because it is decided that the revenue derived from user charges in excess of marginal cost cannot be foregone. The inclination not to forego this revenue is likely to be strong, as the major automotive excises are easy tax handles and can be made progressive. The various highway-related excise bases that may be employed and the respective functions that they may fulfill are shown in Table 5:1.

Fuel taxes are a reasonable proxy for economic user charges as they reflect varying consumption per vehicle/kilometer. There is no way, however, for such taxes to differentiate adequately for type of road surface. This deficiency may be important in developing countries where the length of gravel and dirt roads far exceeds that of paved roads.[28] On the other hand, it may be argued that most motorized traffic uses the paved portion of a country's highway system anyway and that setting the economic user charge according to the variable maintenance cost of paved roads may be a fair approximation of marginal cost.[29] Fuel taxes may play some role as congestion charges if set higher in urban centers, but there are obvious limitations to the extent they can differ between areas, and a fuel tax is limited as a congestion

Table 5.1. Forms and Functions of Road User Charges and Taxes

Type of Excise	Price Function (Economic User Charge)		Equity Function	General Revenue Function
	Variable Maintenance Charge	Congestion Charge		
1. *Fuel Excises*				
a. Gasoline	Fair proxy as consumption varies per vehicle/kilometer, but cannot be used to differentiate between types of vehicles or types of road surfaces. Surcharge justified on higher octane ratings that increase vehicle/kilometer performance.	Supplementary role if excises set higher in urban centers, but differentiation by time of day does not possible and effect may be offset by encouraging use of vehicles with low power/weight ratios that increase congestion.	Incidence probably progressive in low-income countries in the case of private cars and taxis, but possibly regressive in high-income countries if poor are purchasers of old cars with low fuel efficiency.	Highly coveted source of general revenue. Very easy to collect as taxpaying firms (refineries or importers) large and few. Likelihood of evasion small, particularly if exemptions, for instance, to government agencies and diplomatic corps, not given.
b. Diesel Fuel	Same as gasoline, but excise per liter should be higher because diesel fuel is more efficient per vehicle/kilometer. Excise also higher on assumption that fuel primarily used by heavy vehicles that cause more damage to road system.	Unlike gasoline, surcharge not justified on assumption that diesel fuel consuming trucks primarily used in uncongested interurban transport and in buses that reduce congestion.	Incidence likely to be regressive if used in buses (transportation of low-income groups) and in trucks carrying low-value bulk goods produced and consumed by low-income groups.	Same as gasoline, but exceptions for commercial transport, agricultural, industrial, or heating purposes difficult to administer.
c. Lubricants	Related to use, but effect insignificant.	Not suitable.	Same as gasoline and diesel fuel, but effect insignificant.	Poor general revenue raiser, but easy to collect.
2. *Excises on Motor Vehicles and Parts*				
a. Motor Vehicles	Fair proxy, particularly in relation to unpaved roads; increases purchase price and thereby depreciation per vehicle/kilometer that results from use (not passage of time).	Largely unsuitable; may limit number of motor vehicles, but intensifies use. Some effect on congestion possible if excises discriminate against vehicles with low power/weight ratios.	Incidence possibly progressive in case of private cars, particularly if excise increases with value.	Good performance, but yield relatively unstable; no particular collection problems.

Table 5.1 (continued). Forms and Functions of Road User Charges and Taxes

Type of Excise	Price Function (Economic User Charge)			Equity Function	General Revenue Function
	Variable Maintenance Charge	Congestion Charge			
b. Tires, Tubes	Best proxy, particularly if differentiated by type of tire with higher excise on tires for heavier vehicles. High excise may prolong use and increase number of highway accidents.	Not suitable.		Incidence probably proportional.	Poor performance because tax base is small. Collection easy at point of manufacture or importation, but high excises may be incentive for contraband production or smuggling.
c. Spare Parts	Fair proxy to extent that replacement is the result of use (not time).	Not suitable.		Incidence probably regressive on assumption that old cars primarily used by poor.	Same as tires.
3. *License Fees*					
a. Weight	Fair proxy if differentiated on the basis of payload capacity in the case of trucks. Net weight is not a very satisfactory proxy in the case of private cars, because differences in weight are relatively small. License fees also not related to use.	Not suitable; raise fixed cost and intensify use.		Incidence probably regressive.	Generally stable and dependable source of revenue; collection relatively easy.
b. Power	Relatively poor proxy, unless based on power/weight ratio.	Negative effect if high fees increase number of vehicles with low power/weight ratios.		Same as license fees based on weight.	Same.
c. Value	Not suitable, particularly in the case of trucks.	Not suitable; same as license fees based on weight.		Incidence probably progressive, particularly if rates rise faster than pre-tax values.	Valuation of second-hand vehicles may be difficult.
4. *Weight-Distance Taxes*	Good proxy in case of trucks, particularly if levied on axle weight.	Not suitable.		Incidence probably regressive.	Poor performance; collection costs high since weigh stations and kilometer checks required.

Table 5.1 (concluded). Forms and Functions of Road User Charges and Taxes

Type of Excise	Price Function (Economic User Charge)			Equity Function	General Revenue Function
	Variable Maintenance Charge	Congestion Charge			
5. *Passenger Fares and Freight Charges*	Good proxy in case of buses and trucks; built-in differentiation by weight and distance possible.	Effect negative except on taxi fares and unless levied in combination with high congestion charges on private cars.		Same as weight-distance taxes.	Fair performance, but large number of taxpaying operators and compliance difficult to verify.
6. *Tolls*	Fair proxy if toll varies per vehicle/kilometer, but invariably subordinated by fuel charges.	Best proxy, but impractical.		Incidence probably regressive.	Poor to fair performance. Collection costs high because toll booths required and access must be limited.
7. *Parking Fees*	No suitable.	Good proxy if differentiated on the basis of time and location; can be operated in conjunction with restrictive licenses.		Incidence probably regressive.	Fair performance, but requires parking meters and policing.

surcharge since it cannot distinguish between peak and off-peak times of day. A congestion surcharge on fuel may also encourage the use of vehicles with low power/weight ratios, and these would generally increase congestion.

A much discussed issue is the widespread practice of taxing diesel fuel lower than gasoline. Out of forty-two developing countries, diesel fuel is taxed lower than gasoline in thirty-four countries, the same in seven, and higher in only one.[30] Among industrial countries, only Canada taxes diesel fuel higher. Although diesel fuel is only half as costly to produce as gasoline, it is argued that on efficiency grounds it ought to attract higher taxes because it delivers more kilometers per liter. Sometimes, though, differences in performance are compensated for in the form of higher license fees on diesel-powered vehicles, but these are not related to use. A relatively lower tax on diesel fuel may be justified when governments wish to promote commercial transport (for instance of rural crops), or use it to promote income distribution (since diesel is used by bus transportation, for instance). Moreover, the taxation of diesel fuel used for agricultural and industrial purposes might be the source of other inefficiencies; experience suggests that full or partial exemptions are difficult to administer.

While fuel taxes may be a fair proxy for the variable maintenance charge associated with the use of paved roads, excises (including sales taxes and import duties) on motor vehicles, tires, and spare parts are probably a much better proxy for distinguishing between types of road. In particular, tire excises come close to measuring the relative variable maintenance costs of different road surfaces,[31] but excises that increase the depreciable costs of a vehicle would also work in the right direction, because depreciation per vehicle/kilometer increases from paved to gravel to earth roads. On the other hand, these excises are largely unsuitable as congestion charges, and the absolute amount that can be imposed on tires, for instance, is obviously limited on the assumption that the incentive to engage in contraband production and smuggling increases the higher the duty. High excises would also induce longer use of vehicles which is likely to increase maintenance costs and the number of traffic accidents.

The various annual license fees in the motoring field are only fair proxies as economic user chargers, because they are not directly related to use. Fees based on weight or some form of weight/power ratio may reflect wear and tear on the road system, but they do not differentiate between types of road surfaces. License fees based on engine capacity may aggravate congestion by encouraging the use of low-powered vehicles. An unusual congestion license fee is found in the Bahamas where annual payments are based on the square footage of the vehicle.

Weight/distance taxes and in particular passenger fares and freight charges (as used in India and Korea and also in Austria and Germany) are probably inherently good proxies for variable maintenance charges, although they have administrative limitations (as explained in Chapter 8). Tolls and restricted licenses might be the best means to limit congestion, but so far they have been limited in their application because of the administrative costs and the inconvenience to the taxpayer. Parking fees differentiated on the basis of time and location are a good alternative, but they do not discourage through traffic.[32]

A highly innovative and unique traffic restraint scheme was introduced in Singapore in 1975 as part of a coordinated transport policy that includes better land-use plans, a mass transit system, a traffic control system, and a policy of restraining the rate of growth of car ownership through taxation.[33] The excise-pricing scheme that deals with traffic congestion consists essentially of (1) a system of easily obtainable area licenses valid for a day or a month and to be displayed in the restricted zone during designated hours; (2) a schedule of parking fees differentiated by area and favoring short-term as opposed to all-day parking; and (3) a park-and-ride scheme with special shuttle buses to carry commuters from fringe car parking areas into the restricted zone. To encourage higher vehicle occupancy and public transport, buses and car pools are exempted from the area license requirement; so are commercial vehicles and motor cycles. Special bus lanes, school buses to expand the peak-hour fleet, and the promotion of staggered work hours, are also part of the program to restrain and spread motorized traffic.

So far, the traffic restraint scheme in Singapore appears to have been successful. The volume of traffic entering the restricted zone during the hours that the special licenses must be displayed has been reduced by 40 per cent. The use of car pools has increased by 82 per cent, and bus patronage by 10 per cent to 15 per cent. Air pollution has also been reduced. Interestingly, the reduction in morning peak hour traffic did not carry over into the evening hour traffic on which no restrictions were imposed. Through traffic that had circumvented the restricted zone in the morning partly accounted for this, as well as a movement of cars into the restricted zone later in the day for use to return home, and the likelihood that morning bus passengers were picked up by car by members of their households in the evening. The park-and-ride scheme met with limited response and is being redesigned.

Ideally, a system of road user charges and taxes should be a two or three tier tariff reflecting the various possible objectives. Thus, the first tier might consist of appropriately differentiated fuel taxes and excises on motor vehicles and tires, and possibly some passenger fares and freight charges; together these would serve as a proxy for the variable maintenance charge and to some extent as a congestion charge. The second part might consist of heavy license fees, possibly differentiated by vehicle value, to cover the capital cost of a road building program and to attain equity goals. The third might be made up of restricted area licenses and appropriately differentiated parking fee schedules to reduce traffic congestion in urban areas. If carefully designed, both second and third tier taxes would probably impinge little on efficient resource allocation.

In conclusion, it may be noted that with the possible exception of Canada and the United States, the pricing function of road user charges and taxes has been completely overshadowed by their role as general revenue raisers. Probably because the automotive field is a near ideal tax handle, road user charges have generally been set far in excess of variable maintenance costs at least of paved roads. There may be good reasons for this, particularly on general revenue and equity grounds, but whatever the case, the pattern of economic user charges should still be an important concern. Roger Smith has pointed out that "many countries can design user charge systems which will improve resource allocation without reducing revenues below current levels, without increasing the inequity of the tax system, and in most cases without significantly increasing administrative costs."[34] Further efforts to improve the process of identifying objectives and their relationship to alternative forms of excise taxation seem clearly worthwhile.

EFFLUENT CHARGES AND ENERGY TAXES[35]

As has been suggested, urban roads are often congested because their use is underpriced, or at least inappropriately priced in terms of spatial and temporal location. As a result, the private costs of a journey differ from its social costs. An equally pertinent example of this form of allocative inefficiency is the zero-pricing of the waste-assimilating capacities of water and air. Because water and air are treated as free goods, the market system encourages their overuse, and in the process this generates social costs in the form of environmental damage (water and air pollution) which is not accounted for in consumer user charges or product prices.[36]

As in other economic matters, two principal approaches may be adopted in attempting to find a solution: (1) under the regulatory approach pollution standards are set and prohibitive fines enforced on emissions in excess of prescribed limits; (2) under the excise approach, a charge is imposed on every unit of pollution discharged into the water or the air and it is left to the market mechanism to find the least-cost solution for keeping the environment up to desired standards. A bureaucratic approach has thus far been favored in the United States, where regulatory agencies have set effluent discharge and emission standards, supplemented by subsidies for the construction of waste treatment plants, and tax exemptions, tax credits, and accelerated depreciation allowances in connection with the installation of pollution equipment. According to Allen Kneese and Charles Schultze, however, the scheme is cumbersome, corruptible and arbitrary and capricious in its impact.[37] Incentives introduced thus far have proved costly to operate and cannot accommodate the immense industrial diversity and accompanying variations in waste discharge and related environmental damage. There is, moreover, a real danger that implementing agencies become the captive of the industries they are intended to regulate. Similarly, direct and indirect subsidies are very rigid, as they are linked to particular technological processes that may not be the most efficient form of waste treatment as regards place, time, or production process, and by concentrating on the treatment of pollutants after they emerge, negate the potential of alternative production techniques that generate less pollution.

Supported by the results of various cost-benefit analyses, Kneese and Schultze instead argue persuasively for the excise approach, basically by imposing effluent charges on each unit of pollutant discharged into the air or water. In their view, this approach would be efficient because it would leave firms free to vary pollution reduction depending on the cost of the treatment. Each firm would try to find that point whereby, say, the cost of removing an additional pound of biological oxygen demand would equal the effluent charge.[38] The excise approach would leave firms free to innovate new and cheaper preventive techniques either before, during, or after the completion of the production process. Besides, the effluent charge would almost certainly be passed on to the consumer, who, being faced with a higher price for the polluter's product, would look for a relatively less expensive substitute. Several European countries (Czechoslovakia, France, Germany, the Netherlands, and the United Kingdom) have explored solutions to water pollution problems more or less along the lines of the excise approach.

In the case of air pollution, arguments similar to those mentioned above may be given in support of an excise on sulphur oxides. For automobile emissions a smog tax has been proposed, under which each automobile would receive a periodically adjustable smog code and on that basis be subject to a surcharge on gasoline purchases.[39] Purportedly, the advantages of the tax are that a driver would retain several options (similar to those of a restricted license system for congestion control): he may use the car, or avail himself of public transportation, move closer to his work, share the cost through a car pooling system, or buy a car with a less polluting engine. However, a smog tax may well raise formidable enforcement problems as it relies heavily on voluntary compliance.

Approximately three-fourths of all air pollution is caused by energy processes, indicating that environmental issues are closely intertwined with energy use. As a result of increases in oil prices more emphasis has been accorded recently to energy conservation measures. Excises on energy might reduce consumption and if applied selectively, modify energy demand patterns in favor of cleaner energy or less energy-intensive products or services. Obviously, the transportation sector is a prime candidate for the application of energy excises. As a conservation measure, a high excise on gasoline would probably be more efficient than an equal-yield excise on cars differentiated on the basis of power or engine capacity. In European countries, where pump prices are two to three times higher than in the United States, per capita gasoline consumption is only half as high after allowance is made for differences in income.[40] Additionally, high excises on private cars may promote public transportation which consumes only one-fourth as much fuel per person per kilometer. An excise on electricity and natural gas would be another way of curtailing energy consumption and pollution. Scandinavian countries have had substantial experience with electricity excises. A progressive incidence might be attained if rates on private use are graduated with higher rates on greater volume or on a larger electricity or gas bill.

Clearly, the use of excises to combat environmental damage and promote energy conservation is still in its infancy. The theoretical underpinnings of the excise approach have been seriously questioned, and it has been said that the complexities of applying corrective excises in any real world situation are so great that the charge-technique may fail to achieve its objective.[41] In practice, the excise approach may fail to check excessive pollution in cases where the marginal-damage function (defined as the incremental damage from a certain type of pollution at various levels of concentration in a region) is very steep, but the regulatory approach may be more expensive, because of its across-the-board application that does not allow for variations in pollution levels. Similarities between the charge and the control-technique are strong, of course, and this suggests that a mixed strategy may be best.

On the whole, pollution is typically a concern of high-income countries. A clean environment is a problem that comes with affluence; it is a "luxury good" with a high income elasticity of demand. Low-income countries usually have worries other than pollution and might use their comparative advantage in attaching a lower social value to a clean environment for employing polluting production processes that carry heavy excises in high-income countries. This is a case where the latter would further the efficiency of world resource allocation by applying border tax adjustments on the basis of the origin principle, that is, by not refunding pollution excises on domestically produced goods that are exported, nor levying such excises on foreign produced goods that are imported.[42]

EXCISES ON SUMPTUARY GOODS

The traditional argument for internalizing external diseconomies concerns the consumption of tobacco and alcohol. Smoking is a leading cause of many physiological diseases, and the cost of treatment not borne by the individual, including research-related expenditures and care for dependents, is substantial. Careless smoking is also an important cause of fires with known origin; in the United States it accounted for 7 per cent of estimated total building fire losses of known origin in 1973.[43] The social cost argument is even stronger in the case of alcohol consumption. For instance, in France one-third of all traffic accidents and 60 per cent of industrial accidents are blamed on alcohol, and one out of every three beds in the country's psychiatric hospitals is occupied by a victim of alcohol.[44] In the United States the economic cost of alcohol-related problems to the nation's economy in 1971 was estimated at $25 billion, or 2.5 per cent of gross national product, an extremely high figure compared to an alcohol excise contribution of only $8 billion in the same year.[45]

Although the traditional rationale for imposing sumptuary excises is well known, the cost of the external diseconomies is often underestimated. Opponents of high excises on tobacco products and alcoholic beverages argue that the regulatory purpose of the levies is not achieved because the products concerned have low price elasticities of demand; hence a reduction in consumption cannot be expected. However, price elasticities differ from zero and there is some evidence that extremely high excises are successful in driving down demand. In Sweden, where cigarettes cost about $1.50 per pack, cigarette consumption per adult is about one-third as high as in the United States, where cigarettes cost less than 50 cents. Norway also imposes a very high excise and adult consumption is only one-fifth as high as the American level.[46] Interestingly, the revenue intake from the tobacco excise is much higher in the Scandinavian countries than in the United States. The ratio of tobacco excise collections to gross national product is 1.2 in Sweden, 0.9 in Norway, and only 0.5 in the United States.[47]

Finally, it has been said that moderate consumers of tobacco and alcohol should not be penalized for the excesses of heavy users, but on the other hand it could be argued that moderate consumers also benefit from the intensive medical research programs partly induced by the effects of excessive consumption. Therefore, there may be a weak parallel with the benefit approach that is frequently expounded in connection with motor vehicle taxation. Much stronger is the position that condemns sumptuary excises on account of their regressive incidence; indeed, on this ground a moderation of the levy might be justified. Neither the benefit approach nor, as seen in Chapter 4, the regressivity argument has as much validity in developing countries as it does in the industrial world.

INTERNAL AND EXTERNAL COORDINATION

Excises may affect the location of production or distribution activities within a country if duties differ among, say, national, intermediate and local or municipal governments. In most countries the issue does not arise, simply because the right to tax goods traded country-wide is reserved to the national government. Sometimes differences in retail excises, for instance on traditional excise goods in the United States, will affect consumer purchase patterns and hence the location of distribution activities in border areas, but on the whole such cases are exceptional or their effect negligible. A few countries use their excise systems in a deliberate attempt to protect and promote regional industries; purportedly for this reason producers of art silk in North-West Pakistan, for instance, have been exempted from the national excise duty on this product.[48]

There are good reasons for centralizing the collection of excises, at least if they are collected at the manufacturing stage. Only the national government can coordinate such domestic excises with import duties on the same goods coming from abroad, or refund the excise on exports. When local governments levy excises at the manufacturing level, taxing possibilities in areas that are net consumers might be unduly restricted.[49] Moreover, decentralized excise collection would result in substanial duplication in administrative effort. Clearly, evasion would be difficult to control. Thus, in Colombia, where each region has its own liquor distillery, attempts to protect local revenue interests have led to cumbersome administrative procedures for levying excises on liquors shipped in from other regions, including the posting of excise officials along regional borders. The promotion of local liquor industries also distorts resource allocation as it protects inefficient distilleries from competition.[50] On the other hand, other excises, notably on admissions and possibly also on motor vehicle registration, are administered more efficiently by local governments.

More generally, decentralized or at least uncoordinated forms of excise taxation at the producer level may influence the location of industries within a country. Effects might be important in the case of traditional excise goods because of the greater variations in rates that would be possible. For nontraditional excise goods that are generally taxed lower, effects on industrial location may not be significant. At least in the United States, there are indications that state and local taxes as a whole do not loom large in decisions on industrial location because they are overshadowed by differentials in such major cost items as wages.[51] Country-wide efficiency may be affected when one taxing jurisdiction attempts to export the excise burden of its residents to other jurisdictions. Tax exporting may be successful if local industries enjoy an advantage with regard to factor supplies; the extreme case is a natural monopoly on the production of a good. An excess burden may then arise, because the opportunity to export the excise may induce the taxing jurisdiction to a relative overexpansion of its public sector.[52]

Much more important is the coordination of excises on domestically produced commodities and duties on imported goods. Here differences in taxation may affect resource allocation in two ways. First, if taxes on domestic goods are higher than those on imported products, the domestic industry would be unduly handicapped and resources would move into the production of untaxed goods or go abroad. In the second, more common case, if excises on imported goods are higher than those on similar domestic goods, the domestic industry would be unduly protected. As a result, resources would be drawn into the production of goods that could be produced less expensively elsewhere, and away from goods for which the country might have a comparative advantage, such as labor-intensive exportables.

To equalize competitive conditions between countries, border tax adjustments are commonly made to neutralize excise-induced price distortions between domestic and foreign goods. Thus, under the destination principle, compensating duties (generally incorporated in the import duty) are imposed at the import stage and any excise borne by domestic goods is rebated when goods are exported. Allocative efficiency should then be unaffected.[53] In most industrial countries compensating duties are indeed equivalent to the domestic excise, but in developing countries the duties are generally higher. It is believed that the effects of this protective differential has led to the establishment of uneconomic forms of import substitution.[54]

This points toward the necessity of coordinating domestic excises and tariffs; as a minimum unintended forms of import substitution could then be prevented. For this purpose, a functional distinction might be made between the excise imposed on domestic and imported goods, and the protective import duty levied to ensure that domestic industries have a chance to build up a competitive position. This can be achieved most easily by including imported goods that are subject to excises when produced domestically in the domestic excise base. At the import stage the excise should be levied on the duty-inclusive value of goods.[55] To be sure, incorporating the excise in the import duty would serve the same purpose, but distinct treatment focuses the attention of policymakers on the different role that each duty fulfills; possible confusion between ends and means may thus be prevented.

The EEC offers an interesting example of the coordination of national excise tax policies, if, in the interest of achieving a broader economic union, member countries wish to do away with border tax adjustments and formalities, but at the same time do not want to disturb competitive conditions.[56] The Benelux has proceeded farthest along the road of excise harmonization; treaties between Belgium, the Netherlands, and Luxembourg provide for a substantial degree of unification of tax bases and rates of the traditional excise goods, sugar, and some soft drinks. Differences in rates are not ruled out, however. Upward adjustments may be made unilaterally (presumably on the assumption that the resulting reduction in trade should limit such action) if they do not lead to the reintroduction of border controls. The consent of a joint ministerial committee is required if a country wants to reduce an excise below the agreed rate; the committee may refuse a request to that end if it rules that the reduction would disturb competitive conditions between the partner states.[57]

CONFLICTS AND TRADE-OFFS

There are important areas in which excises may both further a less unequal distribution of income and a more efficient allocation of resources even though their effect may be marginal. High excises on capital-intensive luxury goods, for instance, could affect the after-tax distribution of income favorably and also redirect resources into more labor-intensive modes of production. If they are properly coordinated with external duties, they should also result in a saving on foreign exchange expenditures and prevent the establishment of undesirable forms of import-substitution. Any increase in employment through differential taxation of products or technological processes may also be expected to improve the income position of the poor. As their demand for labor-intensive agricultural and other products is generally higher than that of the well-to-do, further employment linkages may ensue. The strongest case for excise discrimination can be made for goods that are simultaneously appropriate in the factor use sense and the consumption sense; Indonesian *kretek* cigarettes that are a labor-intensive product consumed by the poor, have already been cited as an example.

But the conflict between equity and employment comes sharply back into focus when a more even income distribution reduces the demand for labor-intensive services, which does seem to happen.[58] Neither is the case for high excises on luxury goods always as simple as it seems to be. For a large number of people in the middle-income ranges in developing countries—people who play a crucial role in economic development—the opportunity to purchase semiluxury or luxury products may act as a powerful incentive to work harder and save more. Meat, bicycles, toilet preparations, transistor radios, and musical instruments have been cited as incentive goods.[59] If high excises on these goods would have a substitution effect in favor of leisure that would outweigh the income effect, then the potentially favorable influence on production effort would reverse direction.[60] On the whole, however, this effect is probably less important than the strong income effect of heavy excises on tobacco products and alcoholic beverages. It may be argued that if these goods were not subject to excise, families at the lower end of the income distribution might have more to spend on high-protein foods and consequently be able to work harder. As Carl Shoup has pointed out, regressive excises may reduce gainful consumption, defined as "consumption of a type such that, in the event that it decreases, the output of the economy will decrease, either now or later, by more than the decrement in consumption."[61]

Thus, it may be difficult sailing between the equity and efficiency function of excise taxation. Intuitively, the choice might be made in favor of progressive excises—and the case for them remains strong—but efficiency trade-offs and revenue and feasibility considerations should not be ignored. In sorting out ends and means, Shoup advocates a goal-oriented solution: "defining units of measurement for ends, assigning a value to each end, and then selecting the means to achieve or approximate the ends . . ." because whatever the choices, there always remains "this overriding goal of consistent use of means in relation to specified ends."[62]

The weight that should be attached to each goal and the use that is made of each excise instrument depends on each country's social and economic policies. Often there may be more goals than instruments available, the effect of an instrument may not be fully predictable, or it may be used so intensively that it reverses direction.[63] But if the various goals and excise instruments are viewed together, broadly the prescription should be followed that internally the highest excises should be applied on luxury goods produced with capital-intensive technology, and the lowest on necessities or sumptuary goods made with labor-intensive production techniques. On the external side, the highest excise-cum-tariff should be levied on luxury goods that can also be produced domestically, and the lowest excise-cum-tariff on necessities that cannot be produced domestically. Additionally, in the automotive field, the highest excise should be levied on passenger cars owned by the well-to-do that contribute most to congestion and are heavy energy consumers, and the lowest on trucks and buses that are used in inter-urban transport or mass passenger transportation.

CHAPTER 6

PRESUMPTIVE EXCISE TAXATION

Difficulties are often encountered in taxing small producers, particularly under extended excise systems that cover virtually the whole range of industrial activity in a country. As will be seen in Chapter 8, conventional excise systems rely mainly on physical controls for compliance, and it would be very costly, of course, to extend these to every small manufacturing unit. As an alternative, small producers might be required to call for an excise official to check, assess, and allow clearance of excisable goods, but this would often be inequitable and would invite unauthorized shipment of goods when excise staff are not on the scene. Simply exempting small industrial units is often unsatisfactory too, because of the incentive offered to larger units to split up, and allocate their production among smaller establishments in order to avoid tax.[1]

Some countries, therefore, have instituted a form of excise taxation based on the output "presumed" to arise in manufacture from one or more production factors that can be more readily verified than output itself. One presumptive method used in India relates the excise liability to the number of machines in operation. This method has been applied to small textile, sugar, and battery plate producers employing not more than five workers. Producers then discharge their excise liability by paying a specified amount (usually monthly) for each machine installed. They are obliged, however, to maintain a record of the number of machines in operation and the number of shifts worked, since these form the basis for the excise assessment. Compliance control is limited to occasional visits by excise staff to verify that the number of machines and shifts actually worked do not exceed the number recorded.[2]

Presumptive excise taxation is often thought to represent an incentive to increase production, since it provides a reward for entrepreneurs whose output exceeds presumptive output. With a marginal tax rate of zero, the return on the incremental product would accrue fully to the entrepreneur himself. In this view, the penalty implicit in producing below capacity acts as a powerful incentive to increase production up to the point where actual production equals presumptive output. Thus, taxing productive capacity would induce firms to use their plant and equipment more fully. This could be an important consideration in developing countries, where underutilization of existing capital stock is a frequent phenomenon. In Pakistan, for instance, where capital is critically scarce, the use of industrial capacity is reported to be much less than in the capital-rich United States—a paradox of no small significance.[3]

Presumptive excise taxation, therefore, may serve two principal purposes: that of administrative simplification and convenience, and that of increased capacity utilization. This chapter examines the economic effects of levying excises on production factors or as lump sum levies, and considers which, if any, administrative benefits might derive from this form of excise taxation as an alternative to the conventional system. This is done mainly on the basis of the Pakistan experience, where presumptive excise taxation has been extended to whole industries, small as well as large manufacturing establishments. First, other schemes aimed at stimulating production are reviewed, and the conceptual and technical features of the Pakistan method are outlined. Next, the economic effects of the presumptive method are analyzed and attention is drawn to the main determinants of capacity utilization. The major findings are summarized in a concluding section.[4]

INCENTIVE SCHEMES TO STIMULATE PRODUCTION

Little attention has been given to the possibility of using taxes on production to promote a fuller utilization of existing capital stock.[5] Production incentives have been largely associated with agricultural taxes. Presumptive agricultural income taxes, for instance, based on standard land yields or on standard rates of return from the capital value of land have incentive aspects.[6] So do land taxes based on potential output or on the value of land determined as a function of potential output. On the whole, however, the incentive effect is only an incidental (if welcome) by-product of presumptive assessment methods, whose introduction reflects in most cases the difficulty of taxing the agricultural sector on the basis of actual yields and values.

Early incentive schemes relating to industrial production were designed to offset market imperfections, such as those which permitted monopolists to determine the price of their products and thereby earn excess profits by keeping their output below the socially optimum level. A notable example is the tax-and-bounty scheme designed by Joan Robinson, who suggested that monopolies should be encouraged to increase production to a competitive level through a subsidy equal to marginal cost of production less the marginal revenue corresponding to that output.[7] The excess profit (inclusive of the subsidy) would then be fully recouped through a lump-sum tax that would leave the post-bounty equilibrium undisturbed. However, she noted that the proposal would in fact be impractical because of the indefiniteness and variability of demand curves.

A more detailed incentive tax for production has been suggested by Klaus Knorr and William Baumol.[8] They argue that the rate of economic growth should be accelerated through a tax-and-rebate scheme involving the imposition of a flat rate penalty tax on each firm's value added, in conjunction with a tax rebate (or subsidy), dependent on the rate of growth of the value added to goods that the firm actually sells. A similar tax was experimented with in Canada in the early sixties, when an offset against taxable income was made available in the form of a tax credit for the sale of goods marketed in excess of the "sales base" (defined as average net sales in the three preceding years). Recently, the use of tax incentives for production has been recommended for developing countries by Vito Tanzi, who proposed a levy on potential value added, measured by deducting actual inputs from the full capacity output (determined through annual surveys) of manufacturing enterprises.[9]

These incentive taxes for production never left the drawing board, with the exception of the brief Canadian experiment. The latter, however, had uncertain economic and operational effects, with subsequent undesirable repercussions on business decisions, administrative efficiency, and effectiveness. Cumbersome antiavoidance provisions had to be devised to prevent noneligible integrated companies from splitting up. In addition, the levy discriminated against unincorporated businesses that were excluded from the benefits, and firms with sharply fluctuating sales were unintentionally favored over firms whose sales increased at the same rate each year. Moreover, price as well as volume increases were rewarded, although the former obviously did not contribute to higher output.[10]

CAPACITY TAXATION: PAKISTAN'S EXPERIENCE

The method of taxing small manufacturing units on a presumptive basis, developed in India during the fifties, was also adopted by Pakistan, where a more comprehensive version was designed in the sixties based on factory production capacity. By taxing capacity instead of actual production, the Government of Pakistan believed that the decline in average tax rates as production expanded would stimulate output. Furthermore, it considered that administrative procedures would be simplified to benefit both taxpayers and collectors, because the presumptive method did not require production controls and excise personnel could be withdrawn from factories, which would also remove a potential source of collusion and tax evasion.[11]

Initially, in five industries—cotton textiles, vegetable products (*ghee* and oil), sugar, cement, and soda ash—presumptive outputs were computed on an annual basis for each factory. These outputs, called production capacities, formed the basis for a fixed annual excise assessment, in principle payable irrespective of changes in actual production levels.[12] Production capacities, and hence tax liabilities, could be reduced by allowances for specified regions and adjusted with the installation of additional machinery or removal of old equipment. Abatements were granted if production had to be halted for reasons beyond a manufacturer's control or if widespread industrial setbacks occurred, and a refund scheme was in effect for exports. Because the excise liability was determined on the basis of production capacities, the presumptive levy was referred to as a "capacity tax"; this term is also used below.

Table 6.1. Pakistan: Sample Computation of Capacity Tax Liability, 1969/70

Kind of Cotton Fabric	Annual Production Capacity		Capacity Tax Rate (Paisa per Square Yard)[3]	Capacity Tax Liability (Rupees)[4]
	Square Yards[1]	Per Loom[2]		
Coarse	8,565,635	6,440	10	770,907
Medium	15,228,720	11,450	20	2,741,169
Fine	9,412,142	7,077	40	3,388,371
Superfine	8,699,745	6,541	70	5,480,839
Total Tax Liability				12,381,286
Monthly Installment				1,031,773
Tax Payment Per Shift (Abatement)				13,802

[1]Statutory Rules and Orders (S.R.O.), no. 61(R)/68, *Gazette of Pakistan*, April 22, 1968, p. 198.
[2]Capacity adjustment if loom is installed or removed.
[3]S.R.O. No. 120(I)/69, *Gazette of Pakistan*, June 28, 1969, p. 526.
[4]After reduction of capacities with the regional allowance for West Pakistan of 10 per cent; see S.R.O. no. 61(R)/68, rule 3(5).

The basic implementation of capacity taxation is illustrated in Table 6:1 for a Karachi-based cotton fabric mill assumed to be operating with 1,330 looms for 897 shifts (lasting eight hours each) annually.

Annual Production Capacities

Capacity may be defined as the rate of production that can be reasonably attained in the short run, given a fixed plant and equipment.[13] Basically, the Pakistan excise administration used three factors to determine annual production capacities: (1) estimates made by manufacturers themselves, (2) machine ratings, and (3) past production data. For sugar the percentage yield from cane, and for vegetable products output data of comparable factories were also used. More complicated rules were devised for cotton fabrics and yarn which, in addition, made reference to such factors as national average production, growth rates, and the hypothetical production of a profit-maximizing firm.

Machine ratings—that is, engineering estimates of potential output, were the most objective criterion and readily available for the standard type of equipment employed in the sugar, cement, and vegetable product industries. Data on manufacturers' estimates were derived from responses to industrial surveys or, more often, from requests for permission to import raw materials or capital goods. Since the import-licensing system was administered on a rated capacity basis, these requests probably overstated capacity. On the other hand, it is possible that past output data collected by the excise administration reflected underreporting by manufacturers; this would also be the case with output data of comparable factories. In some cases, therefore, a downward bias may have crept into the capacity estimates, offsetting the overstatements made in the import requests.

Considerable effort was put into the proper calculation of the annual production capacities of cotton fabric and yarn units. For that purpose, a Textile Industry Capacity Committee was appointed that undertook an intensive four-month survey of weaving and spinning activities in Pakistan by sending working groups (consisting of a textile technician and a cost accountant) to each mill.[14] The groups determined annual production capacities on the basis of the standard number of shifts per year and the average output for each spindle shift (in pounds) or loom shift (in linear yards). To determine shift production, standard efficiencies and machine utilization rates per spindle and loom were computed, the latter being reduced by allowances for maintenance, repair, and technical depreciation.

The Committee did not take into account any growth factor—defined in the capacity tax rules for the textile industry as "the past rate of improvement in production and likely increase in efficiency relating to improvement in technical, managerial, labour and financial factors of individual mills." This was because the recommended annual production capacities exceeded actual production in most cases.[15] Similarly, "the technically possible maximum production potential" of a unit aiming at "maximizing its profits before tax" was not taken into consideration, presumably because the output at which profits are maximized can hardly, if ever, be ascertained in practice.

After the capacities of each of the four taxable categories of cotton fabrics (coarse, medium, fine or superfine) had been determined, tax was assessed on the basis of square yardage, the rate depending on the fineness of the fabric. The tax liability was adjusted if an additional loom was installed or if a redundant machine dismantled and removed from the factory. Taxable capacity was then increased or reduced by the production capacity of the particular loom, computed by dividing the annual production capacity of the factory for each of the four categories of cotton fabrics by the number of looms.[16] Downward adjustments in the excise liability were made only if a loom was dismantled and removed, but not when it was temporarily shut down. On the other hand, the installation of new machinery resulted in an immediate increase in tax. The penalty for creating or operating with excess capacity was thus reinforced. However, once a firm operated at full capacity, the prospect of an upward tax revision might act as a deterrent to new investment.

Abatements and Export Rebates

To alleviate hardship, the capacity tax rules provided for two kinds of relief.[17] The first applied to industry-wide production failures: if, for reasons beyond the control of the factory's management (such as a cyclone or labor strike), actual production fell short of assessed capacity, abatement could be granted similar to the "disaster relief" provisions common in agricultural tax schemes. The provision was put into effect in 1967 when a number of sugar mills were seriously affected by a drought that had substantially reduced the sugar yield of cane. At the time relief was granted if actual production fell short of assessed capacity by 10 per cent or more.

Under the second relief provision, applicable to individual cases, abatement was given for any day or shift for which the factory had to be closed due to circumstances beyond the management's control, at a rate corresponding to the tax payable per day or shift. Normal cleaning or repair operations, as well as closures for a period of less than six days at a time, did not qualify for abatement, as they had already been taken into account in determining machine utilization rates. To safeguard revenue and presumably to limit abuse of these rules, the Government prescribed that abatement would not be allowed if actual production exceeded capacity output; and, if a shortfall arose in production, the abatement would not exceed the difference between the duty payable under the capacity tax and the tax that would have been due if the capacity tax had not been levied.

Although the abatement rules made the capacity tax more acceptable to the taxpayers, they still meant that actual production had to be ascertained; they did not remove the potential ambiguity between normal cleaning and repair activities and closures beyond the management's control. It would seem tempting to evade the six-day rule by resuming but not reporting production before the period expired. More important, there might be an incentive to postpone operations until the next six-day period, in order to qualify for abatement. Furthermore, factories might try to bunch production, particularly if they foresaw supply bottlenecks, and then halt operations, claiming circumstances beyond their control. In practice, the abatement provisions might favor firms with fluctuating production patterns over similar firms with output spread more evenly throughout the year, as the former would be in a better position to evade the rules. Finally, the abatements reduced the incentive effect of the tax—a general economic aspect, often noted in connection with presumptive agricultural taxes.

To achieve the Government's objective of freeing exports from tax, the administration allowed exporters a rebate on the capacity tax. This rule led to some of the more complex provisions of the capacity tax, because of the danger that the rebate would be too small if actual production (assuming it was all exported) fell short of assessed capacity; similarly, without explicit provisions to the contrary, too much would be rebated if exports exceeded that capacity. The desire to safeguard revenue made it necessary first, to relate the exportable product to the assessed capacity under which it had been produced, and second, to keep accounts for each factory, showing its capacity tax status and the rebates received. Rebates might have been given on the basis of a country-wide average tax rate per pound of yarn or yard of cloth, but this would have unduly favored firms eligible for other rebates (for example, those granted on a regional basis). An obviously undesirable effect was that if available credits had been exhausted, manufacturers might be inclined to suspend shipment of exportable products until the following year's capacities were notified. Moreover, a shift in the composition of a firm's production for export, for example from medium to fine fabrics, might become more difficult as capacity tax liabilities were based on historical production patterns.

Comparison of Excise and Capacity Tax Procedures

The technical analysis in the preceding section makes a comparison possible between conventional and presumptive excise procedures, as implemented in Pakistan, with respect to such basic processes as ascertaining the tax base, computing the tax liability, collecting and recovering the tax due, settling disputes, and ensuring the compliance and cooperation of taxpayers.

A presumptive excise obviates the need for the sometimes cumbersome production controls in effect under the conventional excise system. These controls, governed by complex provisions prescribing such matters as the design of buildings in which excisable commodities are produced or stored, and the movement of goods and personnel on factory premises, require the continuous presence of excise staff during working hours. They involve considerable interference in the day-to-day operations of most factories. On the other hand, the presumptive excise as levied in Pakistan, still required excise staff to verify closures for abatement purposes, and to ascertain actual production to prevent avoidance. That would not be necessary, of course, under the more limited scheme applied in India to small manufacturing units.

Compared to the precise assessment method under the conventional form of excise taxation, the determination of capacity remains an arbitrary exercise, no matter how much expertise and ingenuity are applied. Disagreements about the volume of actual production are factual, but those over the capacity of a plant involve judgmental factors making them more difficult to resolve. Presumably, a taxpayer's idea about the capacity of his factory changes as often as any of its determinants. The danger then becomes real, particularly if tax rates are high, that he will regard the assessment as inequitable and will subsequently request abatement, withhold his cooperation, or resort to litigation. Whereas taxpayers hardly ever went to court in Pakistan to dispute their liability for the excise tax, many taxpayers filed petitions under the capacity tax.

Under the conventional system of excise control, collections are safeguarded by the provision that goods cannot be cleared without payment of tax. The presumptive levy, on the other hand, permits the payment of an assessment in installments. This deprives the tax administration of an effective enforcement tool, even if replaced by high penalties for late payment, as was done in Pakistan. More generally, a presumptive levy seems less responsive to changes in income than conventional duties, because both the tax rate and the tax base remain the same as production expands, provided investment in new machinery does not lead to an immediate revision of the tax liability. From a comparison of tax collections before and after its imposition, Pakistan's capacity tax appears to have been a less income elastic source of revenue than the excise duties previously imposed.

Whether this should be considered a drawback depends on what happens to other taxes. If the capacity tax reduces the optimal capital stock-output ratio, allowing income to grow faster with a given investment budget, the base of other taxes would expand, with effects on revenue that might offset the lower income elasticity of the capacity tax. To increase tax collections, the tax base could be adjusted or the tax rate raised, but frequent adjustments of capacities work against the zero marginal rate effect of the tax. On the other hand, changes in the tax rate would not have that effect.[18] As a more general point, the capacity tax, like a presumptive income or land tax in the agricultural sector, does not sacrifice revenue like the usual tax incentive.

Tax evasion in the form of collusion between taxpayers and tax officials might not occur to the same extent under a presumptive levy as under a conventional excise. In Pakistan, particularly in the textile industry, the old excise method of control reportedly induced some manufacturers to use the cover of darkness for the unsupervised production of excisable commodities.[19] Although daily contact is avoided under a presumptive levy, the possibility of malpractice in the verification of abatements and the ascertainment of, say, the fineness of cotton fabrics as the basis for the export rebate, remains. Furthermore, underreporting of actual production does not affect the tax liability directly, but to the extent that past production data are one of the determinants in ascertaining capacity—and the Pakistan experience shows that they became increasingly the critical variable, perhaps because they were less open to taxpayer objection—underreporting is reflected in a lower estimate of capacity; in fact, it may be institutionalized in this way. Moreover, if past production data continue to play a crucial role in the determination of taxable capacities, the excise administration must verify their reliability, and that can only be done through thorough audit work.

Clearly, by its nature, the proper measurement of capacity is a very complicated exercise requiring expert accounting and engineering skills if it is not to become, like some methods of presumptive income taxation, "mainly a guessing game organized according to variable rules."[20] Even if machine ratings or peak forward projections from past and comparative production data provide useful approximations, some inherently arbitrary elements remain.

In Pakistan, virtually unavoidable ambiguities in capacity concepts proved difficult to reconcile with the taxpayers' ideas of fairness. This resulted in frequent recourse to litigation, pressures to set up committees to review capacities, increased correspondence and file work, and delays in tax collections. Most difficulties were ironed out in 1972, however, when new rules were promulgated.[21] In evaluating the Pakistan experience, the gains on the assessment side (particularly for the taxpayer) should be weighed against the increase in appellate and tax collection work. As under other taxes, however, no shortcuts appear to be available that would enable the excise administration to avoid the problems, first of proper initial assessment, and second, of adequate updating and verification.

ECONOMIC EFFECTS OF PRESUMPTIVE EXCISE TAXATION

The liability for the conventional excise varies with a firm's production volume, whereas in principle liability for the presumptive tax shows no such variation but is a fixed (lump-sum) levy. In other words, the conventional duty is part of a firm's variable costs, but the presumptive excise belongs to its overhead or fixed costs. Another, probably more realistic point of view, is that the presumptive excise resembles a property tax on plant and equipment based on physical characteristics. In Pakistan, the latter concept appeared to apply most aptly to cotton textile and vegetable product factories, where changes in the tax liability were a function of the number of machines in operation. For continuous integrated production processes, such as cement, soda ash and perhaps sugar, the lump-sum tax idea has relevancy.

Who Bears a Presumptive Excise?

Under partial equilibrium analysis,[22] a presumptive excise viewed as an addition to fixed costs does not have any effect on output and price in the short run. If a firm is in equilibrium before the tax is introduced, equating marginal cost and marginal revenue, this point should still determine the most profitable output (or least loss) after the tax is imposed. However, there would be long-run effects. In a competitive industry, the imposition of such a levy causes the average fixed and total cost curves to shift upward. Unable to cover total cost, marginal firms will be forced out of business and leave the industry; subsequently, the average revenue schedule of the remaining firms will shift upward. The size of the ultimate effect will depend on long-run supply and demand elasticities, but under the usual assumptions, price increases along with the scale of operation of the remaining firms; however, this need not affect their degree of capacity utilization. In the case of a monopolist, price and output do not change in the first instance, but over time capital would be shifted out of the monopolist's sector, if his profits net of the presumptive excise are less than the return that he can earn elsewhere (although this is unlikely if the monopolist still earns excess profits after the imposition of the presumptive excise). Finally, as a lump-sum levy, the income effects of the presumptive excise may possibly induce entrepreneurs to increase their efforts.[23]

A presumptive excise that is a function of the number of machines in operation, and is measured by their notional output, resembles a property tax on business assets. A firm's product would then be taxed indirectly through a tax on one of the production factors (machines), and the incidence of such an equal-yield levy on machinery would be like that of a regular excise on the product itself. As is well known, in a competitive world, the imposition of an excise duty has a contractionary effect on industry's output, while price increases to an extent, depending upon the elasticities of the supply and demand schedules. Under increasing cost conditions, the increase in price will be less than the increase in duty. Similarly, if demand is relatively elastic, price will increase less than if consumers are strongly attached to the product. To some extent, interfirm adjustments may differ under the presumptive excise because of divergent machine-to-production volume ratios. The same results would obtain for a monopolist, except that the adjustment would be effected through a change in the individual firm's marginal cost curve rather than the industry's supply schedule.

A firm's demand for machines—a derived demand depending on the call for its products and the supply of substituting factors of production—will also be affected. Machinery already installed, being a highly specialized factor of production, may have to absorb part of the new tax, and its value would fall accordingly; to that extent the owners of the machinery would have to bear the burden. They might try to shift part of the new tax backward but if much of the machinery is imported, that would probably be difficult; forward shifting is more likely. In any case, the effective cost of the taxed factor (machinery) will probably increase. Such an increase in factor cost may have a beneficial effect on capacity utilization, if it is assumed that excess capacity has been consciously built into capital stock. The increase in the price of capital will then induce firms to increase their desired level of capacity utilization rather than expand existing capital stock; therefore, with a given investment budget, resources will be freed for capital investment elsewhere or, probably more important, for increasing raw material supply. Another effect (in most cases beneficial) will be that the increase in the cost of the taxed production factor (machines) will induce firms to substitute labor for capital. However, if capacity utilization is adversely affected by underpricing of capital, a direct tax on industrial equipment would appear more appropriate than a presumptive excise, or when capital is imported, as it is in most developing countries, by appropriate corrections in the exchange rate and import duty tariff.[24]

However, the assumptions underlying the foregoing analysis may be unrealistic in view of prevailing market imperfections. The existence of excess profits and monopoly prices (inter alia resulting from a scarcity of imported inputs), in conjunction with licensing and other direct controls, may make the ultimate effect of a presumptive excise indeterminate.[25] If entry into an industry is limited or blocked because costs are high and credit facilities are largely in the hands of established firms, a presumptive excise viewed as a lump-sum levy may strengthen the oligopoly, because the increase in fixed costs makes entry even more difficult. On the other hand, it can also be argued that the presumptive excise makes production restrictions more costly and therefore forms an incentive for the individual firm to break the "agreement" among the oligopolists. Furthermore, imported raw material inelasticities may mean that a firm's marginal cost curve is kinked and intersected by the marginal revenue curve within the undefined range.[26] The imposition of the presumptive excise would then cause the marginal cost curve to shift upward, but the output associated with the equilibrium level of production does not change; neither does price. The presumptive excise would be paid out of profits with no salutary effect.[27]

Determinants of Capacity Utilization in Pakistan

Although the incentive to production was one of the main reasons for imposing the capacity tax in Pakistan, the industries to which it was applied were among those with the highest capacity utilization rates of the entire manufacturing sector. Cotton textiles, sugar, cement, and vegetable products all fell within the top one-third of a ranking computed by Gordon Winston.[28] Cotton textiles, Pakistan's largest industry by number of units and total turnover, had the second highest utilization rate, operating at 70 per cent of capacity (94 per cent if not adjusted for the number of shifts) in 1965/66, which was the year that the capacity tax was introduced.

These industries and others with high utilization rates had important characteristics in common that enabled them to utilize their resources more fully even in the absence of tax incentives. First, they were less dependent on imported raw materials than most other industries, and therefore not subject to the perennial foreign exchange constraints or the problems of a raw materials licensing system administered on a rated capacity basis, thereby inducing the creation of excess capacity. A second characteristic of these industries was that they did not face demand competition from imports to the same extent as industries with lower utilization rates.[29]

Other factors that were positively related to capacity utilization included large export volumes (inducing demand expansion), a larger than average firm size (enabling the exploitation of economies of scale), favorable capital/income ratios (reflecting profit-maximizing adjustments to prevailing cost patterns) and high rates of growth. Interestingly, competitive firms appeared to have higher utilization rates than industries with only a few firms that could substitute either inventory accumulation or excess capacity for price fluctuations when faced with changes in demand. Competition may also have prevented manufacturers from installing excess capacity by importing (overinvoiced) capital goods in excess of requirements, which was considered an easy, although illegal, means of transferring capital abroad.[30]

In conclusion, therefore, by using independence from raw material imports as a criterion for choice, the Government in effect applied the capacity tax to those industries that did not need any incentive. It may also be surmised that a number of other economic factors have such an important bearing upon the degree of capacity utilization that the effect, if any, of a tax incentive is comparatively very small. Finally, technological factors may play an important role. The trends and fluctuations in the utilization of textile mills in Pakistan, for example, could be partly explained by lack of textile engineering expertise, inefficient use of machinery, absence of proper maintenance and temperature controls, lack of standardization and specialization, and ineffective managerial supervision. More generally, this suggests that an improvement in industrial extension services will enable firms to do what the capacity tax is supposed to force them to do. Again, the agricultural parallel is striking.

CONCLUDING REMARKS

Two crucial assumptions underlie the effectiveness of an incentive to stimulate production. First, it is assumed that demand is strong enough to clear the market of the goods produced at capacity level operations. Second, the incentive is predicated on the belief that there will be an adequate flow of variable inputs—raw materials and intermediate goods—at current prices; if these cannot be procured in adequate quantities because of a limited foreign exchange budget or other factors, firms are not able to utilize existing capital stock fully, regardless of the incentive offered. The effectiveness of any tax device to stimulate production will be limited by the extent to which these two conditions are satisfied.

More generally, these assumptions affirm that the provision of a suitable macroeconomic framework is an essential requirement to promote industrial growth. Disincentives and imperfections which hinder an efficient functioning of the market mechanism should be removed before incentives to increase production are added to the tax policy arsenal. In the meantime, a presumptive excise in the form of a property tax on business assets could correct a relative underpricing of capital goods and thereby inhibit further unjustified expansion. However, as illustrated by the Pakistan case, such a measure is not as effective as direct recourse to the price of the scarcity factor (the exchange rate) itself, because it is not as comprehensive. Pakistan's complex and overvalued exchange and trade system, involving multiple currency practices and widespread restrictions, was overhauled in May 1972—accompanied by a substantial devaluation of the rupee and some import liberalization.[31] In the same year the tax holiday scheme was abolished, after having been suspended in the previous year. Over time, these measures should redress the imbalances caused by the relative underpricing of capital and should give the economy a chance to grow to capacity.

Of course, presumptive excise taxation will remain useful as an administrative tool for ascertaining the excise liability of small manufacturing units that cannot be covered by the conventional method of excise control, or expected to keep adequate records. In this context, levies on machinery or intermediate goods may serve as a proxy for actual production. Here, the presumptive excise can be compared with the *forfait* or *abonnement* system of assessment for the excise and sales taxes in France, Italy and other countries. Under this system, the tax liability that is agreed upon between the taxpayer and the tax official for one year usually also determines the liability for the two following years. In this respect, the Pakistan experience may serve as a useful lesson for other countries.

CHAPTER 7

FISCAL MONOPOLIES

In a large number of countries, the production or distribution of products such as tobacco, matches, alcohol, sugar, salt and occasionally some other goods or services is reserved by law to government. The manufacturing or selling enterprises are usually referred to as fiscal monopolies. The surpluses that they generate are economically similar to excises, and in this sense fiscal monopolies and excises may be considered alternative and comparable tax devices. Fiscal monopolies often fulfill important regulatory functions too, as sumptuary or price control agencies. Yet little is known about these important instruments of taxation.

This chapter explores the place of fiscal monopolies in taxation. It falls into three parts. The first deals with the rationale of fiscal monopolies, their form, and the stages of production and distribution they cover. The second presents a global overview of fiscal monopolies, and the third part discusses their revenue, certain managerial aspects, and the pricing policies pursued. Public monopolies such as public utilities are not covered; their function is not to raise revenue (in fact they often operate at a loss) but to provide essential services.[1] State marketing boards and agricultural price support agencies that may also be called public monopolies are not included either.[2]

RATIONALE AND FORMS OF FISCAL MONOPOLIES

Like excises, fiscal monopolies originated in the royal prerogatives, tax privileges, patents, and tax farming institutions of former times; their revenue potential was then paramount.[3] The salt monopoly, for instance, was a major source of government revenue for the Han dynasty in China, as well as for the European sovereign during the Middle Ages. Fiscal monopolies flourished notably in Europe during the mercantilist period, and they remained a favored tax device in those countries that continued a tradition of state intervention. From there, they spread to South America, the Middle East, North Africa, and elsewhere. On the other hand, ever since the famous debate of 1601 in the House of Commons, this form of taxation has been strongly criticized in England. They did continue to operate after the debate, but were abolished in 1689.[4]

Rationale of Fiscal Monopolies

More recently, the motives leading to the introduction of fiscal monopolies have diverged widely. In the case of tobacco products, revenue appears to have been an overriding objective. When Napoleon reestablished the French tobacco monopoly in 1810, he stated that tobacco, of all commodities, was the most taxable, and even today the statutory goal of the monopoly is the *maximation du rendement fiscal*.[5] In the nineteenth century, the fact that governments could determine prices of monopoly goods and by extension, revenue, was an important advantage over the arduous process of obtaining parliamentary approval for increases in tax rates—although a sumptuary purpose may also have played a role. This motive was certainly a key element in the monopolization of alcoholic products, notably in Scandinavia and the

Canadian provinces—where the production and distribution controls were further strength-ened by a system of personal permits—as well as in some American states following the repeal of prohibition in the thirties.

Another important objective of tobacco and alcohol monopolies is to stabilize the production and prices of the primary producers. This is the main rationale, for instance, of the alcohol monopoly in France, where the related excise is administered separately. On the other hand, the motive for monopolizing matches for instance, and in Sweden, tobacco, has been administrative.[6] Some fiscal monopolies, too, have been created as a form of security for the payment of foreign debt. In the Ottoman Empire, at the turn of the century, the proceeds from the tobacco monopoly were earmarked for Debt Administration.[7] Similarly, in Greece a management company of Greek state monopoly goods was created at the beginning of this century owing to Greek defaults on foreign loans.[8]

Functionally, therefore, the primary objectives of fiscal monopolies range from revenue earning to the regulation or support of a particular activity. In fact, these objectives may differ from one country to another with regard to the same product, and from one product to another within the same country. But objectives may change with time, and since these functional differences are in addition difficult to employ as a distinguishing criterion, the main categorization in this chapter is by product. For this reason the French alcohol monopoly, for instance, is considered a fiscal monopoly here, although its function is purely regulatory.

Forms of Fiscal Monopolies

Bräuer categorizes fiscal monopolies according to how far, and at which stage, they intervene in the production and distribution process of a particular product. Full monopolies include all, or virtually all, stages of production and distribution: from the growing or mining and processing of raw materials, through various stages of intermediate processing to the manufacture and sale of the final product. Partial monopolies, on the other hand, encompass only one or more stages of production: production monopolies; or one or more stages of distribution: wholesale and retail monopolies.[9]

The legal form of fiscal monopolies differs from country to country, although in most cases the influence of the Ministry of Finance on pricing policies is quite strong—in the revenue type because of the impact on government receipts, in the regulatory type because of the subsidies that may have to be paid out. Generally, three forms of economic organization operate: the departmental, corporate, or concessionary form, involving different degrees of financial and administrative autonomy.

In most Mediterranean countries fiscal monopolies are organized as an administrative department (as in Libya), or an autonomous government agency (as in France, Morocco, and Tunisia). Those alcohol monopolies whose main role is to ensure a just price to domestic producers (as in Austria, France, Germany, and Switzerland), are also organized as semipublic agencies. At least nominally, the second, or corporate form of organization would appear to allow a much greater degree of autonomy, but all shares are usually in government hands.[10] The tobacco monopolies in Algeria, Austria, Italy, Japan, and Thailand fall into this category. The third form, which is rare, occurs when the monopoly is conceded to one or more private enterprises. In Portugal, for example, two private enterprises share a monopoly concession for tobacco products, and in Lebanon a single corporation exploits the tobacco monopoly on behalf of the government.

These distinctions of fiscal monopolies by function (revenue or regulatory), kind (production or distribution), and form (departmental, corporate, or concessionary) are not mutually exclusive. Any combination is possible, although regulatory monopolies are not usually imposed at the production stage, nor are they likely to be organized as a corporation. But the various distinctions do often blend into each other, and the differences between publicly and privately operated monopolies may sometimes be minimal. There would appear, for example, to be little difference between the concessionary type of monopoly in Lebanon and Portugal, and the liquor tax systems in Burma, Nepal, and Thailand, although these are not considered fiscal monopolies here. In Thailand, for instance, exclusive marketing rights for the operation of distilleries in each province are conferred by ten-year contracts awarded to the producers bidding the highest monthly guaranteed production, which establishes the minimum tax payment.

Finally, some monopolies also manufacture products in competition with private enterprise. The *Fabrica Nacional de Licores* in Costa Rica has a monopoly for alcohol and distilled liquor, but also produces fruit wines, vinegar, and mineral water in competition with private producers. Similarly, in Turkey, the tobacco monopoly produces matches in competition with private enterprise. As government production is not a matter of legislative authority in these cases, these operations are not considered as fiscal monopolies in this study.

OVERVIEW OF FISCAL MONOPOLIES

Of 126 countries surveyed, 44, or 35 per cent, have monopolized the production or sale, or both, of one or more products. Alcohol and tobacco monopolies (along with related monopolies of matches, lighters, and cigarette paper for example) are the most common, followed by salt, sugar, and petroleum. Table 7:1 shows all monopolies by product, country, and region, lists the legal form of each monopoly, and the stages at which they are imposed, indicating where they are purely regulatory.

Monopolies of Tobacco, Matches, and Cigarette Paper

Tobacco monopolies are found in twenty-six countries, heavily concentrated in the Mediterranean and Middle Eastern area (the cradle of most of the world's fiscal monopolies), but they also occur in the Far East and Eastern Africa. Most tobacco monopolies extend to virtually all production and distribution stages and also have the exclusive right to import and export tobacco products. In Sweden, on the other hand, individual dealers are allowed to import tobacco products, but must pay excise and import duties to the monopoly. In Turkey and Lebanon, private exporters may buy directly from growers who deliver their products at the monopoly's depositories. Partial monopolies are found where tobacco is not grown or manufactured domestically, such as in Iceland. Even in the case of full monopolies, various arrangements often leave most of the initiative at the growing and retail stages to private businesses. In Lebanon and Turkey the primary concern is not the protection of the monopoly, but the quality of the tobacco. There are detailed regulations regarding the areas that may be cultivated, the type of seeds to be used, picking and handling methods, destruction of residue, and a host of other matters.

The French *Service d'Exploitation Industrielle des Tabacs et des Allumettes* (SEITA) has served as the organizational prototype for many other tobacco monopolies in the Middle East and Mediterranean area.[11] It was established in 1674 by Colbert, who is often called the father of mercantilism, and is a full monopoly, handling the purchase, manufacture, and sale (including retail) of all tobacco products and matches, including imported tobacco. Individual farmers are allowed to grow tobacco for themselves, but the monopoly supervises production through an allotment system that is established annually in consultation with the farmers' unions. Tobacco products can only be shipped under permit. Retailers are appointed by the

Table 7.1. Fiscal Monopolies of the World[1]

	Tobacco Products (26)	Matches (15)	Cigarette Paper (3)	Alcohol Products (22)	Salt (9)	Sugar (6)	Petroleum Products (8)	Other[2] (14)
Mediterranean								
Cyprus	—	—	—	Regulatory*	Production*	—	—	—
France	Production/ distribution*	Production/ wholesale*	—	Regulatory*	—	—	—	Gunpowder*
Greece[3]	Production/ wholesale*	Wholesale***	Wholesale**	—	Production/ wholesale**	—	Production/ wholesale**	Saccharine,* playing cards,** emery**
Italy	Production/ wholesale*	Wholesale*	—	—	—	—	—	—
Portugal	Regulatory***	Regulatory***	—	—	—	—	—	—
Spain	Production/ wholesale**	Production/ wholesale**	—	—	—	—	Production/ distribution**	—
Middle East and North Africa								
Afghanistan	Import/ wholesale*	—	—	—	—	Import/ wholesale*	Import/ wholesale*	—
Algeria	Production**	Production**	—	—	—	—	—	—
Iran	Production/ wholesale*	—	—	—	—	Production/ wholesale*	Production/ wholesale*	Tea, caviar*
Lebanon	Regulatory***	—	—	—	—	—	—	—
Libya	Import/ wholesale*	—	—	—	Import/ wholesale*	Import/ wholesale*	—	—
Morocco	Production/ wholesale*	—	—	—	—	—	—	—
Syria	Production*	—	—	—	Production/ wholesale*	Production/ wholesale*	—	Cement*
Tunisia	Production/ distribution*	Production/ distribution*	—	—	—	—	—	Playing cards,* gunpowder*[4]
Turkey	Production/ distribution*	—	—	Production/ distribution*	Production/ wholesale*	—	—	Tea,* coffee*
Africa								
Ethiopia	Production/ distribution*	Production/ distribution*	Production/ distribution*	—	—	—	—	—
Malagasy Republic	Production/ wholesale*	—	—	Wholesale*	—	—	—	—

Table 7.1 (continued). Fiscal Monopolies of the World[1]

	Tobacco Products (26)	Matches (15)	Cigarette Paper (3)	Alcohol Products (22)	Salt (9)	Sugar (6)	Petroleum Products (8)	Other[2] (15)
Somalia	Production/wholesale*	Production/wholesale*	—	—	—	—	—	—
Sudan	—	—	—	—	—	Production/wholesale*	—	—
Upper Volta	Regulatory***	—	—	—	—	—	—	—
Far East and South-East Asia								
China (Taiwan)	Production/distribution*	—	—	Production/distribution*	—	—	—	—
Japan	Production/distribution**	—	—	—	Regulatory*	—	—	Camphor*
Korea	Production/distribution*	—	—	—	—	—	—	Ginseng*
Sri Lanka	—	—	—	Wholesale*	Production/wholesale*	—	—	—
Thailand	Production/wholesale**	—	—	—	—	—	—	—
Northern Europe								
Austria	Production/distribution**	—	—	Production*	Import/wholesale*	—	—	—
Finland	—	—	—	Distribution**	—	—	—	—
Germany	—	Regulatory**	—	Production*	—	—	—	—
Iceland	Import/wholesale*	Import/wholesale*	—	Retail*	—	—	—	—
Norway	—	—	—	Production/distribution** Distribution**	—	—	—	—
Sweden	Production/wholesale**	—	—	—	—	—	—	—
Switzerland	—	—	—	Regulatory*	—	—	—	—
North America								
Canada	—	—	—	Retail (provinces)*	—	—	—	—

Table 7.1 (concluded). Fiscal Monopolies of the World[1]

	Tobacco Products (26)	Matches (15)	Cigarette Paper (3)	Alcohol Products (22)	Salt (9)	Sugar (6)	Petroleum Products (8)	Other[2] (15)
Mexico	—	—	—	—	—	—	Production/distribution**	—
United States	—	—	—	Retail (16 states)*	—	—	—	—
South America								
Bolivia	Production**	Production**	—	Production**	—	—	—	—
Brazil	—	—	—	—	—	—	Regulatory*	Emery**
Colombia	—	—	—	Production/distribution**	Production**	—	—	—
Costa Rica	—	—	—	Production**	—	—	—	—
Haiti[5]	Production/wholesale*	Production/wholesale*	—	Wholesale*	—	Wholesale*	Import/wholesale*	—
Nicaragua	—	Production**	—	Production*	—	—	—	—
Paraguay	—	—	—	Regulatory*	—	—	—	—
Uruguay	—	—	—	Production*	—	—	Production*	—
Venezuela	—	Regulatory***	Wholesale*	—	—	—	—	—

Sources: Government budgets, laws, decrees, and other documents; in some cases the source material was incomplete.

Asterisks are used to denote the legal form of the monopoly organization: * means that the monopoly is organized in the form of a government department or agency; ** that it is organized as a corporation; and *** that a monopoly concession has been granted to private enterprise. In some cases the information on the form of the monopoly had to be determined by inference, as precise data were not available. Figures in parentheses indicate the total number of each monopoly in the world. — indicates that monopolies are not found.

[1] Excluding state tobacco monopolies in the centrally planned economies of Albania, Bulgaria, China, Czechoslovakia, Hungary, Mongolia, Poland, Rumania, U.S.S.R., and Yugoslavia; the match monopolies in Bulgaria, Poland, Rumania, and Yugoslavia; the cigarette paper monopolies in Bulgaria and Rumania; the alcohol monopolies in Poland, Rumania, U.S.S.R., and Yugoslavia; and the salt monopolies in Czechoslovakia, Hungary, Poland, Rumania, and Yugoslavia. These monopolies were established before the economies of the respective countries were fully socialized and subsequently retained many of the characteristics of the fiscal monopolies discussed in this chapter.

[2] Government lotteries that are found in virtually all countries of the world are not included, although a good case can be made for classifying them as fiscal monopolies.

[3] Some monopoly products are manufactured by government departments (salt) or on a concessionary basis (matches), but the distribution and sale (except in the case of saccharine) is in the hands of EDEMED, the Management Company of Greek State Monopoly Goods.

[4] The gunpowder monopoly was abolished in 1954, but continues to be administered as before, as it has not been possible to find a private operator. See Jacques Magnet, *Les Finances Publiques Tunisiennes* (République Tunisienne: Ecole Nationale d'Administration, 1969), p. 142, fn. 1.

[5] By a series of laws and decrees, the role of the Haitian State Tobacco Monopoly was extended to many imported and domestically manufactured goods including sugar, cement, flour, soap, textiles, pork fat, alcoholic beverages, cosmetics, toothpaste, milk products, edible oils, electrical and mechanical appliances, tires, and tubes; for these products, however, the monopoly acts solely as a tax collecting agency.

monopoly and closely supervised in collaboration with the tax administration, and in addition to tobacco products, the monopoly's retailers are required to sell postage stamps and tax stamps.

The monopolies in other countries operate in much the same fashion. In Austria the tobacco monopoly also extends through the retail stage, retailers enjoy a geographical monopoly and are required to sell postage stamps and tax stamps—in addition to which they sell newspapers, souvenirs and various smokers' requisites to supplement their income. Retail licenses in Austria are granted solely to severely handicapped persons or to victims of the Nazi regime, and can thus be viewed as an instrument of social policy.[12] The Japanese tobacco monopoly, through a high-price, low-supply policy, restricts cultivation, thus increasing the availability of land for food production. However, recent declines in food production also reflect industry's competing demand for labor.[13]

Match monopolies are closely associated with tobacco monopolies and are usually administered by the same organization. They were established in many countries at the turn of the century. On the one hand, the product's inelastic demand features made it a coveted source of government revenue, while the health hazards involved with handling phosphorous products justified close government supervision and regulation. Production had previously often been organized on a cottage industry basis, and centralization substantially eased the administration of an excise. Finally, in many countries, monopolization prevented the takeover of the national match industry by the Swedish firm, *AB Svenska Tändsticks*.[14] Countries that already had tobacco monopolies found it convenient to extend similar rights to matches and substitutes such as lighters and flints. Combined monopolies in fact still exist in eleven countries, but in four where private tobacco industries already existed, separate match monopolies have been created.

Cigarette paper, since it is complementary in nature, can be regarded as a proxy for tobacco consumption; three countries have a monopoly for this product. In Greece and Venezuela it is operated in conjunction with a match monopoly, but in Ethiopia it is part of the tobacco and match monopolies.

Alcohol Monopolies

Of all the major monopolies, those for alcohol vary the most in function, kind, and form. Twenty-two countries have alcohol monopolies, covering primarily distilled spirits but sometimes other alcoholic beverages as well. Geographically, alcohol monopolies are mainly found in Northern Europe, North America, and some Latin American countries. Functionally, they range from the purely regulatory monopoly found in France whose only aim is to ensure a fair price to domestic producers—the excise is collected separately—to the full monopolies in China (Taiwan), and Turkey that include virtually all production and distribution stages.

These are the two extremes. Between lie variations: the simple administrative type of monopoly in Cyprus, which buys the crude spirits (Zivania) from producers and sells it at the duty inclusive price to domestic manufacturers of liquor; and the rectification monopolies with a regulatory function in Austria, Germany, and Switzerland, which produce distilled spirits and are the sole buyers from private distilleries. The monopolies sell the rectified alcohol to distributors, inclusive of an excise that varies with the use of the product for beverages, vinegar, cosmetics, medical, or industrial purposes. Similar monopolies are found in Bolivia, Colombia, Costa Rica, and Uruguay.

Alcohol distribution monopolies are primarily a Scandinavian and North American phenomenon. While the Finnish and Swedish monopolies extend to both the wholesale and retail stage, the monopolies in Iceland, the Canadian provinces, and sixteen American states cover only the retail stage. The monopolies operating at the distribution stage are usually confined to the sale of spirits; they may sell beer and wine but private outlets for these products are usually permitted as well—albeit subject to strict government regulations, often enforced by the monopoly. In Canada, for instance, the sale of beer and wine is controlled by the provincial liquor control boards.[15]

Outside Scandinavia, wholesale monopolies are found in the Malagasy Republic and Sri Lanka. In Sri Lanka the monopoly procures arrack from ten distilleries (of which one is state-owned) and sells this to licensed retailers at a profit subsequently transferred to the government. Retailers in toddy or arrack have a geographical monopoly, for which they must buy a license that is sold annually by tender to the highest bidder. Primary producers have to pay tapping fees at a fixed amount per tree, subject to a maximum of twenty trees.[16]

Other Fiscal Monopolies

Although salt monopolies are probably the oldest fiscal monopolies still in existence, they are a fading phenomenon; only nine are left. Their contribution to revenue is insignificant in most cases, except in Syria, where receipts exceed 0.5 per cent of total tax revenue. Virtually all are production monopolies, except in Austria where it is limited to the import stage. In Japan, the salt monopoly was originally a revenue device to help finance the Japanese-Russian war, and it is now used as a price control agency.

Sugar monopolies, of which there are six, are mainly found in the Middle East and Northern Africa. They are a mainstay of the government's revenue budget in the Sudan and Somalia, where they have provided as much as 15 per cent of total tax revenue. Eight countries have fiscal monopolies for petroleum products, but they are largely shown for historical reasons; many governments have a controlling interest in their countries' oil operations.

Other fiscal monopolies were created for a variety of reasons. The gunpowder monopolies in France and Tunisia are justified by the need to regulate the product. Monopolies for playing cards in Greece and Tunisia presumably exist on moral grounds. The Greek Government has become involved in a saccharine monopoly to protect the domestic sugar industry. In Japan, the camphor trade was monopolized to control prices when the country still produced half of the world's supply, but with the advent of synthetic products and the loss of Formosa, the largest producing region, the monopoly has lost most of its significance.

As in the case of excises, fiscal monopolies need not be confined to goods (although they usually are) but may also extend to services. There is widespread government monopolization of lottery operations, which have been accepted relatively easily, mostly as a revenue device, but also on regulatory grounds.[17] In the field of entertainment services, Dahomey has monopolized the distribution and showing of films.

EVALUATION OF FISCAL MONOPOLIES

It should be borne in mind in evaluating fiscal monopolies that the comparison with excises does not involve one between a centrally planned economy with state ownership of the means of production and a market economy with private enterprise. It does involve a comparison between government monopolized production and distribution of at most a few products, and the separate taxation of the same products manufactured and sold by privately owned but heavily regulated production and distribution units, both essentially operating within the framework of a market economy.[18] Every country has very strict controls on the production and distribution of such products as tobacco and alcohol. The implication, therefore, is that the differences between private and monopoly production of alcohol and tobacco products are often less than the differences between private production of these goods and any other unregulated form of business.

Countries with fiscal monopolies for tobacco and alcohol, and those with private licensing systems are probably more alike in their production than in their distribution activities, since both seek to stabilize the prices of primary producers. In the United States, for instance, the Department of Agriculture, after consulting associations of tobacco growers, sets marketing quotas and establishes price support arrangements similar in effect to those prevailing under the French tobacco monopoly. The licensing of retail outlets also enables strict supervision to be exercised in nonmonopoly countries at the point of sale to final consumers, although there the emphasis is on revenue and sumptuary control rather than on price stabilization. In monopoly countries, on the other hand, the retail licensing system may be used to restrict the number of retailers.

Revenue Considerations

One of the intriguing aspects of fiscal monopolies is their revenue potential since, after all, many monopolies were instituted with the purpose of augmenting government income. Taking all government revenues into consideration—profits, excises, sales, and other taxes —fiscal monopolies should contribute more to the fisc than a privately owned industry taxed through an excise, unless the latter is a private monopolist whose profits are taxed at a 100 per cent rate. In practice, however, an examination of the revenue data presents a very different picture.

Table 7:2 shows the revenues for virtually all countries with either tobacco or alcohol monopolies, or both. Tobacco monopoly yields range from slightly more than 1 per cent of total tax revenue in Ethiopia, only a fraction of what neighboring countries such as Kenya and Tanzania collect in the form of excises (6 per cent and 7 per cent, respectively), to almost 10 per cent in China (Taiwan), which is high by any standard, although still not as high as the 11 per cent share in total taxes of the Ceylonese tobacco excise. Sri Lanka's alcohol monopoly contributes as much as 8 per cent to tax revenue, but Mauritius, for instance, which has not monopolized the distribution of alcohol, collects 12 per cent of tax revenue from this source. Similarly, relatively large amounts of tax are collected by the Scandinavian alcohol monopolies, but none comes anywhere near the Irish alcohol excise which contributes 36 per cent of tax revenue, or 4 per cent of gross national product.[19]

It is clear from these data that there is as much variation in the yield of fiscal monopolies as there is in the yield of excises. These intercountry comparisons are somewhat misleading, as they do not allow for differences in tax rates (prices) and tax bases (consumption), nor for the influence of income. Little work has been done on this subject. Partial data indicate that tobacco revenues are probably lower in countries which have monopolies, after allowing for differences in per capita income. However, per capita consumption of tobacco is clearly also lower in these countries, perhaps partly because the number of retail outlets is smaller and less advertising is done. At the same time, that part of the tobacco retail price transferred to the treasury in the form of excises or profits is larger in monopoly countries than elsewhere.[20] This is most evident in the case of the Chinese wine and tobacco monopoly, which contributes more to government revenue than the tobacco and alcohol excises in Singapore, for example, although retail prices of the excisable goods are lower on Taiwan.[21]

Table 7:2 shows, interestingly enough, that practically all countries with alcohol monopolies, and more than half those with tobacco monopolies, also levy excises or sales taxes on monopoly products. In northern European countries particularly, excise and sales tax revenues and monopoly profits are kept strictly separate; in most of these countries

the profit element is comparatively small. Canada and those American states that operate fiscal monopolies have markup systems, although provinces or states that have retail
sales taxes usually also apply these to monopolized liquor sales. Under some other tobacco
and alcohol monopolies, for example in Japan and to a large extent in Costa Rica, the "tax
rates" are merely devices for distributing the monopoly's revenue.[22] In the case of sugar and
salt or other small monopolies, separate excises are usually not imposed, nor does the
monopoly always have separate financial accounts. Economically, the separation of excises
and profits is an anomaly because the monopoly's pricing policies determine the tax intake.
Institutionally, however, the imposition of separate excises may make sense, because their
yield is inherently more amenable to treasury control than are profit transfers. This is
particularly so when the monopoly is also involved with price subsidy operations. Finally, if
desired, the separation of excise and profit elements may facilitate a shift in emphasis from the
revenue to the regulatory function of fiscal monopolies.[23]

Management Aspects

The debate on the relative merits of fiscal monopolies often centers on operational
efficiency. Proponents of tobacco monopolies, for instance, have pointed out that substantial
economies of scale are effected when production and sales activities are combined. Distribution costs will be reduced, it is argued, because the wholesale function can be eliminated.
Moreover, absence of competition can reduce advertising costs, and since the number of
brands and retail outlets would be fewer (the latter with higher turnovers), trade margins
might be reduced. In some monopoly countries, retail costs run between 8 per cent and 10 per
cent of price, but costs are typically twice as high in private enterprise countries. It has been
pointed out that the monopolization of the Swedish tobacco industry, for instance, resulted in
a decrease in distribution costs, although not in production costs.[24] Concentration might also
enable monopolies to undertake more research.

In practice, as in the case of revenue, the evidence is conflicting. The French tobacco
monopoly has been thought of as a sophisticated and profitable enterprise with low overhead
costs, good research facilities, and efficient production and marketing operations.[25] On the
other hand, the Greek salt monopoly, at least until 1964, was apparently run in a distinctly
nineteenth century fashion: commercial accounts were not kept, there were little or no
improvements in production facilities and no modern business decisionmaking techniques.[26]
Similar comments have been made about some of the Colombian liquor-production monopolies. Since almost every region has its own monopoly, the enterprises are small and inefficiently
run, a situation compounded by interregional tariff walls and smuggling problems.

It has also been suggested that fiscal monopolies ease tax administration because they act
as evasion-proof tax collectors. There may be some historic justification for this, as seen
above, but incentives to evade tax remain equally strong. Tobacco growers, for instance,
would still attempt to divert part of their production elsewhere if paid a higher price.
Bootlegging would also remain as profitable as under an excise, and smuggling from abroad is
not likely to be curtailed through the monopolization of distribution channels.

There are in fact indications that the monopolization of the production and distribution
of alcohol and tobacco products may have harmed revenue in some countries. The Para-
guayan alcohol monopoly, for instance, has a legal obligation to transfer its collections to the
tax office every fortnight but apparently has not done so since 1947.[27] Similarly, the Turkish
tobacco monopoly has used its tax collections to finance growing stocks.[28] There is concern
that governments would be tempted to transfer more funds out of a monopoly than it could
stand, which would not only break the golden eggs, but probably kill the goose as well. The

Table 7.2. Revenue Importance of Tobacco and Alcohol Monopolies, 1969–71

	Tobacco Revenues as Per Cent of		Alcohol Revenues as Per Cent of	
	Total Tax Revenue	GNP	Total Tax Revenue	GNP
Mediterranean				
Cyprus	11.3	1.50	2.9**	0.39
Greece	8.7[1]	1.51	3.3	0.58
Italy	7.1*	1.36	1.3	0.24
Portugal	5.2**	0.89	1.1	0.19
France	2.8**	0.60	2.9**	0.63
Spain	. . .**	. . .	. . .	. . .
Middle East and North Africa				
Tunisia	10.5**[2]	2.29	—	—
Turkey[3]	9.5**	1.86	. . .**	. . .
Morocco	6.3*	1.06	—	—
Syria	5.1*	0.76	0.6	0.09
Lebanon	4.8*	0.47	0.4	0.04
Iran	1.5*	0.25	0.9	0.16
Algeria	. . .**	. . .	—	—
Libya	. . .**	. . .	—	—
Afghanistan	. . .**	. . .	—	—
Africa				
Somalia	13.0*	. . .	1.3	. . .
Upper Volta	6.0**	0.62	2.0	0.21
Malagasy Republic	3.6**	0.54	. . .**	. . .
Ethiopia	1.3**	0.12	5.6	0.50
Far East and South-East Asia				
Sri Lanka	11.1	1.94	8.1*	1.42
China[4] (Taiwan)	9.8*	1.75	6.5*	1.16
Thailand	8.6**	1.07	4.1	0.51
Korea	7.6*	1.16	5.5	0.85
Japan	4.6*	0.85	5.3	0.97
Northern Europe				
Finland	4.3	1.28	8.2**	2.43
Sweden	3.5**	1.17	6.0**	2.01
Germany	4.9	1.14	3.8**	0.89
Norway	3.0	0.92	5.2**	1.59
Austria	3.9**	1.05	2.4**	0.65
Switzerland	3.9	0.71	1.8**	0.34
Iceland	. . .**	. . .	. . .**	. . .

immediate postwar experience in Italy however, would not seem to confirm this fear; the Italian Government in fact reduced its share in gross receipts so that more funds could be set aside for the repair and reconstruction of the monopoly's plant and equipment.[29]

　　Are fiscal monopolies inherently less inclined to introduce new technologies, avail themselves of export opportunities, or meet the demands of the domestic market, as has been suggested? Sometimes the organizational form has been thought to be inflexible and the criticism has been met by granting the monopoly greater autonomy, by giving it, among other things, a corporate identity.[30] It has also been argued that consumers' welfare would be

Table 7.2 (concluded). Revenue Importance of Tobacco and Alcohol Monopolies, 1969–71

	Tobacco Revenues as Per Cent of		Alcohol Revenues as Per Cent of	
	Total Tax Revenue	GNP	Total Tax Revenue	GNP
North America				
United States	2.2	0.52	3.2*[5]	0.77
Canada	0.7	0.21	2.1*[6]	0.61
South America				
Nicaragua	8.3[7]	0.73	9.7**	0.87
Uruguay	6.9	0.86	4.1**	0.51
Bolivia	4.4[7]	0.36	6.2	0.51
Paraguay	4.0	0.42	5.1**[8]	0.53
Colombia	4.0	0.47	4.5**	0.52
Costa Rica	3.4	0.46	7.4**	1.01
Venezuela	2.5[1]	0.56	3.5	0.77
Haiti	. . .**	. . .	. . .**	. . .

Source: Appendix C.

. . .indicates that data are not available; —means that revenues are virtually nil; *monopoly revenues; **countries that also levy excises or sales taxes on monopoly products.

[1]Monopoly of matches and cigarette paper only.
[2]Includes monopoly revenues from gunpowder and playing cards.
[3]Revenues from tobacco and alcohol cannot be separated.
[4]Profits of tobacco and wine monopoly allocated as follows: tobacco products, 60 per cent; alcoholic beverages, 40 per cent.
[5]Sixteen states operate packaged-liquor retail stores.
[6]All provinces have monopolized the retail trade in liquor; Quebec and Prince Edward Island also have a special tax on the purchase of liquor; most provinces levying a general retail tax apply it to the price of alcoholic beverages.
[7]Match monopoly only.
[8]Including excises on soft drinks.

better served by private business which could offer a greater variety of brands, while in monopoly countries production does not adapt to demand. However, in private enterprise countries consumer tastes may be the result of deliberate manipulation by saturation advertising, which creates demand. In addition, overall consumer welfare should presumably include a consideration of health and other effects, and increased consumption of tobacco or alcohol resulting from "meeting consumer demands" may be a mixed blessing.

A valid point is whether fiscal monopolies can operate efficiently on the international scene. The issue has received particular attention in the EEC in connection with the provisions in the Rome Treaty regarding the establishment and maintenance of competitive conditions.[31] Virtually all monopolies extend to the import stage, and the major objection is against their natural tendency to discriminate against foreign brands. There may be some truth to this assertion, but in many countries without fiscal monopolies, trade and customs departments, often at the instigation of local producers, are equally capable of pursuing restrictive practices. There seems to be no reason why fiscal monopolies in one country (particularly those at the retail stage) cannot coexist with private licensing systems in a neighboring country, provided both adhere strictly to the destination principle, according to which imports are taxed to the same extent as domestic products, and refunds on exports are not greater than the tax actually borne. Presumably, however, this would involve a separation of the monopoly and the tax function of the government enterprise.

This section would not be complete without a reference to the interesting results of Julian Simon's recent study on fiscal monopolies in the United States.[32] When he compared the efficiency of state-operated retail liquor monopolies with private retail outlets in other states, Simon found that the monopoly states obtain greater revenues at lower costs, even though retail prices are comparably lower. He found four possible explanations for this. First, monopoly states have used their monopsonistic purchasing power collectively to extract from national liquor producers a price no higher than the lowest price for wholesalers in private licensing states. Second, monopoly states may have lower operating costs because they have fewer off-premise outlets that, in addition, operate fewer hours of the day. Third, lower profit margins in monopoly states may account for some of the difference. Fourth, various restrictive practices in private licensing states may make it difficult for efficient operators to enter the trade. However, as Simon points out, these findings may not have wider applicability.

Pricing Policies

The fiscal impact of monopolies is basically reflected in two areas. First, as a sole buyer of raw materials and intermediate or finished products, at a price which is lower or higher than that applying under competitive conditions, the monopoly is in effect either taxing the preceding stage or subsidizing its output. Second, by selling its products above or below the level at which the market would be cleared under competitive conditions, the monopoly either taxes or subsidizes the buyers of its product. Economically, the effects of these taxes or subsidies (which can also be considered negative taxes) are similar to those of excises, and need not be discussed further. Attention is focused, instead, on some institutional aspects.

A common policy of the major fiscal monopolies—of tobacco products and alcohol—regarding the monopsonistic side of their operations is to subsidize the output of primary producers, often by setting the price of raw tobacco or raw alcohol above competitive levels. This reflects deliberate government policy to support the farming population, often for social reasons, although it also clearly represents a tax on consumers or other factors of production. In this respect fiscal monopolies resemble agricultural price support agencies. This is also their role in the forced acquisition of stocks. In Turkey, for instance, as part of the tobacco monopoly's objective "to safeguard the value of the work of the producers," all growers are assured an outlet for their whole output. Consequently, the monopoly has had to built up considerable stocks in the face of a slack in world demand. To finance these, it had to resort to central bank credit (to which it has direct access) and has delayed the payment of its tax liabilities to the Treasury.[33]

Most fiscal monopolies presumably set their prices at a level that just clears the market of available supply. An alternative would be to set selling prices below that level, but demand would then exceed supply and the monopoly would have to adopt rationing, with the result, for instance, that smokers would be subsidized at the expense of nonsmokers. That arrangement would not be efficient, quite apart from being at variance with the revenue objective of fiscal monopolies.[34] Another alternative would be for monopolies to reduce supply and experiment with higher prices to maximize revenue, but for social and political reasons it is unlikely that most governments would be inclined to follow that course of action.

Another aspect of the pricing policies of fiscal monopolies concerns the objective of geographic price uniformity. The philosophy is that people in remote areas should not be charged a higher price than those in cities, even though distribution costs to the former may be substantially higher. In the absence of a fiscal monopoly, the same effect may be roughly achieved, of course, with a subsidy or surcharge. An example is the price equalization surcharge on petroleum products in Pakistan that aims at establishing the same price for the whole country, even though distribution costs are lower in the south. But the underlying assumption that people in remote areas are poorer than those in the main consumption centers may be fallacious. Moreover, price uniformity may have undesirable allocative effects, particularly for products such as kerosene that have a high price elasticity of demand, because the administered price does not reflect relative costs vis-à-vis substitutes such as charcoal.

There is another facet of distributive justice that should be mentioned in connection with the pricing policies of fiscal monopolies. Particularly in developing countries with sharp class-differentiated consumption patterns, some progressivity may be achieved if nonessential rather than essential goods are taxed. Even for the same product, a progressive element may be built into the rate structure if brands consumed by low-income groups are taxed more lightly than those bought by high-income groups; beer and liqueurs, or Indonesian *kretek* and American-type cigarettes, are examples.[35] Although such an effect could probably also be achieved through a set of progressive excises, the pricing mechanism of fiscal monopolies can obviously reflect government policies more accurately in this respect.[36] The same is true for demand management policies, or the tax burden distribution between producers and consumers. For these reasons, the pricing policies of fiscal monopolies have sometimes been characterized as institutionalized tax policy.[37]

Concluding Observations

Although fiscal monopolies and excises have been viewed as alternative tax devices in this chapter, the two do pose a fundamental choice between state and private ownership of production units. Moreover, once the choice has been made, it is extremely difficult to reverse. Normally, private enterprises cannot be taken over without compensation that at worst, if paid, may wipe out whatever extra profits the government expects, or at best impair the liquidity position of the new monopoly so that tax payments suffer in the process.[38] The social aspects of throwing numerous small producers out of business can of course be equally serious.

Depending upon the kind of monopoly, it may also be difficult to return a fiscal monopoly to the private sector in view of the monopoly's status in the government's bureaucracy, the rights acquired by management and employees, and the stabilization agreements entered into with primary producers. However, Ecuador (liquor) and Peru (tobacco) are recent examples of countries where monopoly operations have been successfully transferred to the private sector. Presumably, no serious problems would be encountered if governments were to relinquish possession of minor monopolies such as salt. Ecuador and Lebanon did so recently.

The question of monopoly versus private enterprise production has been considered at some length in Japan by a board of inquiry instituted to review tobacco monopoly operations.[39] Although the board found that the monopoly's pricing policies for raw materials, and its production plans, research, and cost accounting methods were deficient, it favored its continuation because the probable increase in advertising and sales costs involved in a change could harm revenue and tax evasion might be encouraged. The board also expressed concern over the potentially disruptive effects on farmers with whom the monopoly maintains stabilization agreements.

CHAPTER 8

EXCISE ADMINISTRATION

That tax administration is the key to effective tax policy is universally acclaimed, but in practice virtually ignored in the literature on tax.[1] There is a widespread preoccupation with what should be done rather than with how to do it: with the more dramatic policy changes and refinements rather than with the duller but indispensable mechanics of tax implementation.[2] Excises are no exception to this rule. If the wisdom gained from practical experience is committed to paper at all, it is usually buried deep in departmental reports.[3]

The emphasis on policy is understandable—tax policy, after all, can be subject to theoretical and rigorous analysis. Tax administration, on the other hand, is an art, something that depends on actions and intuition, but is difficult to harness conceptually and commit to paper. Nevertheless, it is useful to analyze basic administrative processes—in the case of this book, the issues arising in connection with the assessment, collection, and enforcement of various excises—and, subsequently, to point out the broad operational aspects that a policymaker must consider in choosing a particular type of taxation.

The essence of excise administration can be reduced to two principal problems: (1) to ensure that all excisable commodities are cleared for dispatch through or under the control of excise staff; and (2) to ensure that the correct amount of duty is collected on the commodities cleared. The first part of this chapter reviews the essential features of excise control: licensing, bonding, supervision of production, checks, and clearances. The second highlights some problems of assessment: the definition and classification of excisable commodities, the merits of specific versus ad valorem rates of tax, the application of exemptions, and the treatment of small-scale producers. The third and fourth sections attempt to single out some operational aspects peculiar to the excise taxation of services and motor vehicles. The brief concluding remarks turn up the feasibility of the various excises discussed. It should be noted that the arguments deal with the technical features of excise operations—the assessment, collection, and enforcement of the duties specified in the taxing statutes—and not with their responsibility, direction, and control, since these are hardly peculiar to an excise department, but are found wherever fiscal institutions are at work. Because administrative problems are obviously more acute under extended excise systems, a good deal of attention is given to the experience in India.

FEATURES OF EXCISE CONTROL

The administrative processes of excise taxation normally rely on quantitative measurements for assessment purposes, with compliance usually ensured through physical controls. These features are an integral part of the make-up of most excise systems, including the extended types that are operated on the Indian subcontinent and in the Far East. The outward sign of physical control is often the stamp or banderol on cigarette packages, liquor bottles, sugar bags, or other excisable goods, the officially numbered ticket to entertainment events, or the license plate or window sticker on motor vehicles.

The physical presence of the excise authority at the site of production is almost always considered essential for control in the case of sumptuary goods, but in many countries this may also be true for most nontraditional excise goods. Excise staff are then stationed on factory premises to check, examine, or take samples of excisable goods for inspection or testing in departmental laboratories. In a real sense, the excise collector becomes the gatekeeper of the factory; without his permission, nobody can enter and nothing can be shipped in or out.[4] Official checks may be supplemented or replaced by metering devices permanently affixed to machinery and equipment. In some cases, delivery records may be relied upon to verify compliance with the law; in others an agent, rather than being on permanent duty, may clear production upon request.

Registration and Licensing

Before excise controls can be operated, the authorities must be aware of the channels used by excisable goods. The excise department must know who is plying the trade and how—this refers primarily to the manufacturers from whom the duties are usually collected, but sometimes also involves traders in supplementary checks, or in checks that the taxed product reaches the consumer in an unadulterated state. A close watch may also have to be kept on exempt users of excisable commodities, if the weight of the duty is such that even minor diversions into illicit channels must be prevented. Before any excisable products are manufactured, therefore, the producers and dealers must be registered with the excise authorities. Production or trade without a license should be automatically illegal—in effect, the license lifts the legislative prohibition against production—and liable to prosecution and severe penalties, regardless of the amount of tax that has been evaded.

Integral to most licensing procedures is the submission of detailed information on the location and construction of factories, the number and capacity of plants and equipment, the nature of the production process, and other data relevant for enforcement purposes. In the case of sumptuary goods, which are heavily taxed and subject to strict quality controls, production can usually not be commenced without the approval of the excise authorities.[5]

A second condition for obtaining a license is normally the provision of financial security to guarantee the payment of the excise. Usually, the size of the bond varies with the productive capacity of the factory (based on the amount of duty for a fortnight's production, for example), or with the floor area of the warehouse where excisable goods are stored. Sometimes, only a cash deposit is acceptable; in other cases, a bank guarantee or personal surety is sufficient. Bonding is particularly important when physical controls are relaxed or dispensed with, or when excise payment is deferred until it is assumed that the manufacturer has recovered the amount from his customers. But even after a license has been issued, an annual renewal with a concurrent review of the data may be required.[6]

Although licenses are hard to obtain, they are not expensive. Normally, the fee covers the cost of registration, the initial survey, and the approval of the premises. As the cost of the survey will vary with the size of the premises, fees are often graduated accordingly. Further refinements of the license fee scale are unnecessary; after all, the main purpose is to regulate the activity itself rather than its scale.

Apparently, few problems are encountered with licensing procedures. If a license is required for each separately taxed item, this sometimes appears to involve some unnecessary duplication of work.[7] Of course, regardless of legal requirements, unlicensed production, particularly of alcohol, is a perennial headache for most excise administrators. In the United States, for instance, it is estimated that one out of every eight bottles of liquor consumed represents illicit moonshine production: some 17,000 stills of varying sizes are confiscated annually.[8] Usually, the penalties are severe and include imprisonment, fines, and forfeiture of all equipment which has produced the contraband.

Supervision and Measurement of Production

The data gathered during the licensing process provide the framework for measuring excisable quantities and applying physical controls with checks attuned to the peculiarities of each production process.[9] Control will be centered at the point in the production process where the liability to tax falls. Armed with a Sikes' hydrometer, a saccharometer, a polariscope, scales, and weights, or other measuring devices that often have to be provided by the taxpayer, the excise official or, under his instructions, the manufacturer, will intervene directly at this point and ascertain the quantity, volume, weight, strength, or length of the excisable commodity. Measurement may be quite simple—installing a bottle counter in soft drink factories or a metering device on yarn spindles. Raw tobacco may simply be weighed and cigarettes counted. In other instances, however, a more intricate form of measurement is prescribed. The excise on alcohol is often determined by reference to the strength of the product, while in some countries that on beer is calculated on the basis of the number of hectoliter degrees of wort.[10]

These direct measurements are usually supported by various indirect forms of control. Thus, excise laws commonly require that taxpayers must keep detailed records of quantities of raw materials, intermediate goods, and finished products, often on forms prescribed by the excise department. These records must show opening stocks, intake, discharge, or clearance of goods, and closing stocks. Periodically, excise officials will take stock of the products at hand and check the findings against the records. For many products there is a direct quantitative relationship between intake of raw materials and the amount of finished product, and this can be used to crosscheck various sources of information. Producers of alcoholic beverages must also keep a brewing or distillation book in which the technical details of the entire fermentation or distillation process are recorded.

After production is completed, excisable commodities are usually moved to a stockroom or warehouse; in the case of distilled spirits, storage for at least two or three years may be a legal requirement. Storage in bonded warehouses takes place under prescribed conditions and supervision of excise staff; when staff is stationed on the premises, the warehouse is probably the most jealously guarded part of the plant. Supervision is particularly strict when the doors of the warehouse are opened and goods cleared for consumption or shipment elsewhere, because it is usually at this point that the excise becomes payable. The excise collector may then make a physical count, check the outcome against the warehouse's records, and, if necessary, take samples for laboratory tests to determine the precise nature of the product.

The excise collector has been described in all his functions: as the policeman who keeps a close watch on and checks goods and persons that enter or leave the premises; as the engineer familiar with the location and construction of plant and equipment; as the chemist who verifies the composition of excisable products; and as the storekeeper who keeps a record of what comes in and goes out of the factory or warehouse.[11] This is the situation under most excise systems, although in industrial countries greater reliance is placed upon written records and periodic returns for assessment purposes.[12] Control over some commodities, such as petroleum products, is almost always exercised through checks upon accounts. The use of physical controls is most pronounced on the Indian subcontinent; elsewhere enforcement, particularly of excises on luxury goods, relies to a greater extent on accounting checks.

Understandably, under extended systems the requirement of physical supervision of production and dispatch of excisable commodities has strained administrative resources.

Excise administrations on the Indian subcontinent have experimented with so-called self-clearance procedures, under which some manufacturers are permitted to assess themselves on the basis of quantities cleared for sale, with excise staff periodically checking the delivery records.[13] Control is, however, limited to a verification of quantities; financial transactions are not examined.

PROBLEMS OF EXCISE ASSESSMENT

As has been seen, the computation of excise liability starts with a quantitative measurement of the designated units of the excisable commodity. But before measurement these units must first be defined, and afterwards a rate applied to convert them into tax liabilities expressed in monetary terms. Most excises are usually conceived of as consumption taxes, and methods must be designed, therefore, to exempt commodities not used for consumption purposes. Exemptions as well as differentiated rate structures may also be used, mainly under the extended excise systems, to pursue specified economic and distributive policies, and these bring corresponding problems of control. A final difficulty is to find effective methods of taxing, or exempting, cottage industries and small-scale producers.

Definition and Classification

James Crombie's dictum that definition is the essence of any taxation upon goods, certainly applies to excises.[14] Commodities to be taxed must be meticulously defined in the law. This is relatively easy for homogeneous goods that are only used for one purpose. Most products, however, differ widely in quality, composition, price, essentiality, application, or use, and bases should be developed to classify them in one way or another.

Forms of classification

For excise duty purposes, goods and services can be classified as follows:

(1) *On the basis of the nature, plant, or animal origin of the commodity*

The most straightforward example of this type of classification is the chemical formula: alcohol is ethyl alcohol, but not methyl or propyl alcohol; salt is sodium chloride; sugar is sucrose, but not fructose, lactose, or glucose. Tobacco, tea, coffee, and cereals all derive from clearly identifiable plants; similarly, there can be no mistake about the animal origin of butter, meat, and fish.

(2) *By reference to the contents of the commodity*

On the Indian subcontinent, yarn is distinguished by reference to the number of counts per pound; cotton fabrics are classified on the basis of the fabric weave into superfine, fine, medium, and coarse; matches into those made of bamboo splints and those of soft woods. Footwear may be classified according to whether it is primarily made of plastic, rubber, leather, or textile materials.

(3) *According to the designation or use of the commodity*

Paper can be used for cigarette tissue, packing and wrapping, printing and writing, or for the preparation of paper board. Various appliances, musical, and photographic instruments may be used either for household, industrial, scientific, educational, or recreational purposes, with excise rates that differ accordingly. A preferential rate may apply to the industrial or institutional use of electricity, gas, and water.

(4) *By reference to the nature of the production process*

Beer is made of wort, obtained by dissolving sugar or molasses in water, or by extracting the soluble portion of malt or corn in the process of brewing. Cotton textiles may be classified into grey, bleached, shrink-proofed, or organdie-processed fabrics, or into dyed, printed, mercerised, or chemically processed materials. Under extended excise systems, the output of establishments that do not use power or mechanical aids is frequently taxed at a lower rate.

(5) *On the basis of capacity, or size of plant and equipment*

Motor vehicles are often taxed on the basis of engine displacement, brake horsepower, size, gross weight, or seating capacity. Other excise rate structures may be graduated according to the size of plant or, within the same plant, according to production segments. Sometimes industrial machinery is taxed on a capacity basis as a proxy for production itself.

(6) *On the basis of the value of the commodity*

Cheaper brands of cigarettes, tea, or coffee, "with a retail price not higher than . . ." may be taxed at a lower rate of excise. Passenger cars are often taxed on the basis of their value, either instead of, or in addition to, an assessment according to capacity or weight.

(7) *According to the way that goods are packaged or sold in bulk*

In India, tea is taxed lower when sold in loose form, and the excise on patent medicines and pharmaceuticals depends almost entirely on the format, design, colors, and label of the container, rather than on the nature of the ingredients.

Sometimes the precise classification of a product depends on several criteria: soap in India is classified into toilet, household, laundry, and other. Partial exemptions are contingent upon the nature of the chemical compounds, the size of the container, the design of the label, or the product's capacity to absorb other liquids that would convert it into polishing, solvent, or textile cleansing soap. There are further subclassifications depending upon the use of mechanical power, and the size of the production establishment, and there was one relating to the weight of the soap bar.[15]

Problems with classifications

Several difficulties arise in applying a complex excise rate schedule; often the various terms and qualifying clauses are interpreted as they are applied. Classifications according to the designation, use or content of commodities are particularly troublesome; a host of different meanings may be attributed to "primarily used in" or "primarily consisting of." Extensive follow-up control or laboratory work may be required, and this often delays the settlement of the liability. Anomalies abound, and the potential for litigation is enormous. Situations arise where, for instance, tea that is sold loose from an open-ended carton is classified as "nonpackaged tea," but as "packaged tea" if there is a label on the carton showing the name of the manufacturer and the grade of the tea.

The use of a complex classification system obviously means a substantial increase in the workload of an excise administration, and not only because of the greater chances of misclassification and subsequent litigation. Refinements have to be made in the control mechanism that involve a greater degree of interference with production and trading activities, without any offsetting benefit to the fisc. Some classifications which may appear at first sight quite acceptable, may in practice cause endless difficulties. In India, the textile industry has complained that rulings for classifying various types of yarn, twists, or threads, are inadequate, and that there are no standard rules for exempting waste yarn and samples, or authorized tolerances for measuring length.[16] In doubtful cases, decisions are taken on an ad hoc basis. A zealous excise collector may then apply the higher of two rates, the taxpayer will appeal, and so it goes on.

Finally, in the anomalies arising from the application of a complex system, underlying policy goals may well be defeated. Thus, the distributional objective of taxing coarse cotton fabrics less because they are worn primarily by the poor is not achieved to the extent that such fabrics are also used in furnishings and tapestry mainly bought by the more well-to-do. The point here is that a classification cannot be adapted to the wide differences in consumption and production patterns which often obtain for the same product. In addition, rate differentiations can impose constraints on innovation, produce undesirable changes in production patterns, and can indirectly subsidize inefficient methods of production.

Specific versus Ad Valorem Rates

The excise rate may be either specific—expressed as a fixed amount per excisable unit—or ad valorem—expressed as a percentage of the unit's value. Combinations of specific and ad valorem rates are also used. In a situation of stable prices, the two rates yield the same amount of revenue, but when prices increase the ad valorem rate is obviously more productive, unless the specific rate is continuously adjusted to the prices. As this is usually not the case, ad valorem rates are generally favored in tax literature.

Specific rates are clearly easier to apply, because the value of excisable commodities does not have to be ascertained, and undervaluation can therefore not occur. This is particularly important for traditional excise goods or luxury items which are taxed at rates that are a multiple of pretax values. In these cases, ad valorem rates would also aggravate price increases. If a commodity is taxed at, say, 300 per cent ad valorem, a rise in its pretax value of 20 per cent would translate into an overall increase four times the corresponding amount.[17]

On the other hand, specific rates discriminate against cheaper brands of a particular product (usually bought by low-income groups), and encourage the use of higher priced raw materials.[18] Of course, this could be a desirable side effect if quality controls (such as in the case of alcohol) are a concurrent objective of the levy. A disadvantage of specific rates is that when they are adjusted they must take into account the treatment of stocks-in-trade assessed under previous rates but not yet sold to consumers. Additional assessments (floor-stock taxes) involve considerable administrative effort, but may be necessary either to ensure equal treatment or to forestall the destabilizing effects that the anticipation of rate adjustments may have on production.[19]

For ad valorem excise taxation, some constructive value of the excisable commodity is usually taken for assessment purposes. This may be the wholesale or the retail price, or if these cannot be ascertained, the production costs. The ad valorem rate of the cigarette excise, for instance, is often based on the retail price. This presents few problems in a small economy where the price of cigarettes is generally uniform throughout the country (and printed on the banderol), but in large countries with fragmented market structures retail prices may differ widely from one area to another.[20] For most other goods that are less homogeneous than cigarettes, the application of a uniform constructive value would be too discriminatory. In most cases, therefore, valuation experts are posted in each excise office; they are price and cost specialists familiar with the marketing and trading arrangements for each product, and accordingly able to ascertain its excisable value as defined in the law, such as "the wholesale value in the nearest market."

But the application of ad valorem rates is not without problems. Particularly in developing countries, it is often extremely difficult to establish market values for the output of small-scale industries that have widely differing cost structures, selling prices, marketing, and trading arrangements. Legal provisions such as "fair market value at arm's length" or valuation on the basis of "like kind and quality" are hardly helpful. In the case of larger manufacturers, the common interest of sellers and buyers complicates the valuation process. Consideration must also be given to aspects such as volume and trade discounts, packing and selling expenses, insurance, and freight charges, all of which may be included in the wholesale price of one manufacturer but not in that of another.[21] In some countries the list prices of selected manufacturers are taken as the constructive value for the whole industry, but obviously this solution is only feasible for a limited number of products.[22] The point is that valuation, unlike measurement, is often more a matter of argument than of fact, making disputes much more difficult to solve. Valuation for excise purposes resembles property tax procedures in this respect: no one is content until the value of his product has been reduced to that of the lowest in the sector.

Under the constructive type of valuation, the need to compute the number of excisable units for assessment purposes remains, and it is arguable that in administrative terms the application of ad valorem rates does not affect the enforcement aspects of the excise. If assessment is based on the invoice value, however, the picture changes fundamentally. Physical measurement, other than as a supplementary control measure, would then become unnecessary. Assessment and compliance control that are based on the producer's actual selling price would make the excise identical to a manufacturer's sales tax that imposes tax on turnover.

Exemptions and Rate Concessions

Kinds of exemptions

Under most excise systems, various exemptions affecting their administration are in use. These include:

(1) Exemptions for exports.

(2) Exemptions for products used for industrial, agricultural, scientific, or medicinal purposes (exemptions by end-use). Among traditional excise goods, these include tobacco products used in the preparation of insecticides; alcohol utilized in the production of varnishes, for medications or in hospitals; petroleum products employed in the manufacture of paints or for agricultural purposes. Under extended excise systems, tires for animal-drawn vehicles, or, for example, engines for tractors, are exempted.

(3) Exemptions related to particular persons or institutions. The most obvious examples are tobacco and alcohol products for members of the diplomatic corps, but many countries also exempt gasoline and other petroleum products used by the armed forces, the Red Cross, charitable institutions or for heating purposes in hospitals or homes for the aged.

(4) Exemptions as production incentives for cottage and small-scale industries. In many countries some differentiation in rates exists on the basis of output capacity, but on the Indian subcontinent the excise system is used extensively to promote the development of village and small-scale industries, in an effort to stimulate fuller employment, the economic development of rural areas, and to encourage a more equitable distribution of income.

(5) Exemptions to mitigate the cumulative effects of taxing successive stages of production. An example is sugar used in the brewing of beer. Cumulative effects may be a problem under extended excise systems that cover raw materials and intermediate goods, in addition to finished products.

Administrative problems caused by exemptions

Of all exemptions, those relating to exports are probably the easiest to administer, as the producer is often integrated forward to the export stage, and goods can be shipped under permit directly from the factory or a bonded warehouse. The end-use type of exemption, on the other hand, is more difficult to control and its application is commonly governed by strict regulations. Industrial users of alcohol are frequently licensed in the same way as producers, and are subject to tight supervision, including physical controls. Where possible, alcohol is methylated, and thereby rendered unfit for human consumption, converting the exemption by end-use into the more readily administered exemption by type of good. To make the control of end-use easier, an excise is sometimes imposed on industrial users. Some countries, for example, tax vinegar that is made from wort, or perfumery, cosmetics, and varnishes that have an alcohol base.

Much more unusual are the exemptions for small manufacturers (particularly popular in India) that are designed to stimulate production. As discussed in Chapter 5, the Indian exemptions and graduated rate schedules are primarily related to present or past volumes of production, but some are based on the number of workers, the mode of production, the end-use of the product, the juridical form of the enterprise, or the area in which the excisable commodity is manufactured. The attendant complications are enormous, as may be gauged, for instance, from the administrative ramifications that result from dividing the small-scale sector for matches into medium, small, and smaller production units, with further distinctions depending upon the use of bamboo instead of soft wood, or of mechanical aids to mix chemicals or cut labels, resulting in eleven different rates of excise for a commodity that yields a negligible amount of revenue.

These exemptions have been severely criticized in India.[23] Exemptions based on the volume of past or present production mean that the output has to be determined, without any benefit for the fisc. In India again, for instance, excise control has to be exercised over all soap factories with installed capacities exceeding half the exemption limit, even though most of them are not liable for excise. There may also be a strong incentive toward fragmentation of production activities. The Government has sought to counter this, by, inter alia, refusing licenses to producers with proprietary interests in other factories manufacturing the same product, but apparently to no avail. And of course, the additional administrative checks that the excise department has to impose distract from its revenue raising function.

Finally, there can be difficulties taxing successive stages of production. Administratively, extended excise systems may be a considerable nuisance to taxpayers and tax officials. In India, products made from duty-paid raw materials, or products used exclusively in subsequent (taxable) production processes, such as metal products, motor vehicles, appliances, and machinery, are partially exempted to meet this problem. There are also ad hoc solutions, including the in-bond movement of raw materials and intermediate goods, and the provision of credit for the tax paid at previous production stages. But these measures have to be dovetailed with the various physical controls, and hence are never comprehensive; they often cause additional discontent. Finally, it should probably be noted that the cumulative effects of extended excise systems are different from those caused by multipoint sales taxes; excise levies would appear to discriminate less among forms of economic organization, as the type of product rather than the transaction is taxed.

On the whole, the administrative problems arising from complex exemption schedules are similar to those mentioned in connection with definitions and classifications. Almost every exemption involves difficult control problems and brings in its train the possibility of misapplication, taxpayer dissatisfaction, and litigation. Manufacturers have to give more time to tax matters than they want to, or is commensurate with their other functions, while tax officials have to deal with cases that may be only of nuisance value in terms of revenue. As Crombie points out, it should always be possible to find a reason for freeing a particular product from excise, and an administrative device for effecting the exemption, but once exceptions are made it becomes impossible to draw the line.[24] The administration then becomes involved with numerous nonfiscal activities and has to rely increasingly on discretionary rules and practices, which inevitably result in more unequal treatment of equals and increase the chances of abuse.

Small Producers

The treatment of small manufacturers is not an administrative concern in most industrial countries, because the excise systems are basically limited, and industrial production of traditional excise goods is typically large-scale. This is partly a result of the high excise duties and extremely strict production standards.[25] However, this is not the case in most developing countries. In Indonesia, *kretek* cigarettes may be hand-rolled by small-scale producers, in eastern African countries opaque beer and in western Africa palm wine are both home-brewed. Other excise goods such as sugar, soap, soft drinks, shoes, and textiles are often also produced by small-scale industries. Some effective way must be found either to tax or exempt these producers.

As regards exemptions, using the number of workers as a criterion for defining small and large producers is probably as good a yardstick as any. The absence of electric power or mechanical aids is another criterion that is workable, as is the number of machines installed. But an exemption based on the size of output is much less satisfactory, because determining output for exemption is presumably as difficult as determining it for assessment, unless the exemption is broad enough to exclude all but the largest producers.[26]

The direct taxation of small producers obviously involves great administrative costs, and these can be near prohibitive. One way to get around the problem is to tax small producers indirectly through their inputs, provided of course that these are produced on a relatively large scale: examples are leather instead of shoes and caustic soda instead of soap.[27] Another solution, tried out on the Indian subcontinent, is to tax small-scale producers on the basis of output capacity as a proxy for actual output. This has usually taken the form of a duty on machinery. The administrative implications of this form of presumptive excise taxation have been discussed in Chapter 6.

SELECTIVE TAXES ON SERVICES

Operationally, the administration of selective taxes on services is sufficiently different from excises on goods to warrant separate treatment. Services differ from goods: they are intangible and typically rendered by retail-type establishments that cannot be as well-defined as manufacturing units, and many services may also be provided on a casual basis. Even under sales taxes, services are usually taxed selectively, that is, they are specifically enumerated in the law.[28] This is because a large number are considered unsuitable for taxation on social grounds (such as medical and educational services), or because they are rendered primarily to business establishments (as are most professional services). A list approach is also followed to keep most personal and repair services outside the tax because they are often difficult to reach. A tax department may administer the following excises on services.

(1) *Public utility services*

No particular administrative problems need arise in connection with the excise taxation of public utility services of gas, electricity, telephone, or telegraph communication. Controls can be built into the utility's billing and metering procedures, and it is not too complicated to exempt or apply differential excises on electric power or gas for industrial users. It is, however, difficult to distinguish effectively between the use of telephone and telegraph services for domestic or commercial purposes, and these are best taxed regardless of use; the only justifiable exemption is for coin-operated public telephones.

(2) *Hotel, motel, restaurant services*

Here compliance control, particularly of small units, is difficult as it has to rely on audit-type procedures. The excise, specified in percentage terms, is best imposed on the total hotel bill, including meals, beverages, and other services. For hotel services, enforcement is helped by records of guests which must also be maintained for regulatory purposes. Excise rates may be differentiated by classifying establishments into luxury, first class, and other categories. If it is thought desirable to distinguish between permanent accommodation (which might be exempted as taxation would be unfair to persons living permanently in hotels or boarding houses) and transient accommodation, this can be done by limiting the excise to persons staying, say, thirty days or less. For the small operator, an exemption by size of establishment may be provided. On equity grounds, an exemption may also be made for small restaurants catering to workmen or low-income families, or providing meals on a carry-out basis. Meals-on-wheels types of catering services for low-income earners can also be exempted without difficulty.

(3) *Personal services*

Services of laundries, dry cleaning establishments, barbers, beauty parlours, photo finishing and photographic firms are difficult to tax, because of their retail nature, even though no special definitional issues need arise. The same is true of repair services of tailors, watchmakers, radio, television and appliance shops, and garages. Often personal services and repair services are one-man operations without records. In the case of repairs it may be difficult to distinguish either in law or from the records between the repair element and the installation of new equipment.

(4) *Financial services and contracting*

Many countries levy selective taxes on insurance contracts or premia and some on banking services or real property contracts. Most of these excises may involve serious problems of interpretation and litigation, as it is often difficult to separate taxable and nontaxable activities or even to ascertain the tax base. In many countries, small building contractors are also difficult to reach.

(5) *Foreign travel*

An interesting and administratively feasible proposal for a three-tier foreign travel tax has recently been made in Colombia.[29] The tax would consist of a flat 5 per cent ad valorem charge on airline tickets, as well as a presumptive per diem tax on the time spent abroad in order to avoid the complications of applying the tax to foreign exchange expenditures. To simplify administration and to free short business visits from tax, it is proposed to apply a basic exemption to trips of up to six days. The travel of public officials would be included and the tax would be computed by reference to visa dates entered in passports.

(6) *Gambling, sweepstakes, lotteries*

In many countries, large-scale betting operations are a fiscal monopoly fully supervised by the government. In others, however, bets may also be accepted by private firms. When these are large, for instance in the case of totalizators or football pools, excise controls can be built into a firm's internal controls over employees. Evasion by small businesses that organize bingo halls, gaming clubs, and off-course bookmaking activities, or greyhound races and cockfights, may be widespread.[30] No difficulties should arise with the levy of an excise on gaming tables or slot machines.

(7) *Entertainment services, clubs*

Excise controls on a large variety of entertainment services are generally exercised through the issue of preprinted numbered tickets. Rates can be differentiated on a functional basis, with lower excises applied to soccer matches and films, for instance, than to cabarets and night clubs. Taxes on clubs should be levied on a gross receipts basis to include meals, beverages, and membership fees. Exemptions for small clubs may be defined in terms of gross receipts or on the basis of the club's assets, which could be easier.

EXCISES IN THE MOTORING FIELD

The operational performance of various road user charges and taxes has been broadly set out in Table 1 of Chapter 5. Some are imposed at the production stage with control and assessment aspects similar to those of excises on other goods, but others are applied in the form of periodic license fees that require different administrative procedures. Of all excises, those on motor fuel are probably the easiest to administer. The revenue can be collected at the refineries or upon importation into countries without refining facilities. Often the excise is a simple specific levy, the same whether applied to diesel or gasoline, whatever the octane rating. But as with other excises, administrative difficulties arise with the exemptions that are conditional upon the end-use of the fuel. Exemptions freeing gasoline for specified government agencies, or diesel fuel for agricultural or industrial purposes, may be difficult to control. To make the administration of an exemption or of differential excises easier, coloring techniques may be applied. However, enforcing this may be costly—as shown, for instance, by the Canadian experience with the coloration of untaxed heating oil to prevent illicit use by motor vehicles.[31]

Excises on new motor vehicles, tires and spare parts should also be relatively easy to administer as typically the taxpaying manufacturers are large and few in number. Differentiation by end-use (tires for tractors, trucks, or cars) is relatively easy. High excises, however, may be a strong incentive to contraband production or smuggling. Annual vehicle license fees appear to be more costly to administer than, say, excises on new vehicles because a new license has to be issued to every vehicle owner each year. On the other hand, the incentive to evade an equal-yield excise, and the chance of being successful, is greater. Administratively, there should be little difficulty in establishing the bases for the various license fees. For this purpose, official lists can be used that provide the assessor with the weight, power (cubic capacity), or the value for each make and type of vehicle.

Other road user charges are difficult and costly to administer. Weight/distance taxes levied in the United States, for instance, are based on daily records of distances traveled and monthly reports submitted by vehicle operators. Moreover, the tax authorities must build and man weigh stations to ascertain the tax base and collect mileage information from users. Collection costs of this method of charging road users are on average twenty-five times higher than those for the fuel excise,[32] but control over compliance is still extremely difficult and the excise has been referred to as a tax on honesty. The same could also be said of the passenger and freight taxes levied in Korea and some Indian states, because it is inherently difficult to verify the number of passengers or amount of freight carried. Tolls can largely be made evasion-proof, but are extremely expensive to administer, since toll booths must be installed and the access to highways limited. Costs may, however, be relatively smaller for tolls on bridges and tunnels.

Virtually all conventional road user charges and taxes are unsuitable to control congestion. Fuel excises differentiated according to location may have some merit, but zones may be difficult to establish equitably. In terms of administrative feasibility, the parking fee probably comes closest to reflecting the social cost of traffic density, although it bears little relation to congestion on the road. The fee system is fairly costly, however, as parking meters may have to be installed, while substantial policing is certainly required of parking places and lots. Licenses restricting access to congested areas by time of day that can be purchased from gasoline stations should also be feasible, although border problems associated with zoning or contour methods of defining restricted areas may be difficult to handle. The various mechanical and electronic systems of charging road users that have been proposed have not been put into practice so far.[33]

CONCLUDING REMARKS

Because they are relatively easy to administer, excise systems with coverage limited to homogeneous items with few substitutes—traditional excise goods, sugar, soap (caustic soda), cement, yarn—compare favorably to other taxes. They have a readily identifiable tax base, simple rate structure, and low collection costs. The really difficult administrative problems arise when the excise method is extended to a wide range of products involving complex classifications and exemptions based on content, designation, or end-use.[34] Under many extended excise systems, too much attention has to be paid to too many trifling sources of revenue, a luxury that a tax system not based on voluntary compliance cannot really afford. The Indian and Pakistan excise systems, for instance, may have a broader coverage than is commensurate with their administrative resources. In this connection, the Indian Central Excise Reorganisation Committee pointedly remarks that "a scheme that requires every manufacturer to file a formal application for clearance of each consignment with a detailed description of its contents, and provides for its examination, test-check and assessment to duty by excise officials and thereafter a formal permission to move the goods is not only formidable in its scope but is impractical in its execution."[35]

Similar comments can be made about the administration of excises on services. While the services rendered by public utilities, government controlled betting operations, or the entertainment sector may be relatively easy to tax, compliance control is difficult with hotel and restaurant services and virtually impossible in the case of most personal services. Numerous one-man operated service establishments without records of any kind are as difficult to reach as cottage-type manufacturing establishments. In most countries, too, the administration of fuel excises and motor vehicle licenses should be manageable, but certainly developing countries should stay clear of the more sophisticated congestion charges.

Of course, administratively, the best excises are those that can be "boxed in" at bottlenecks, be it at large manufacturing plants or at ports. Excise controls can be most easily installed when processes are automated, as in refineries, or when they can be linked to internal checking procedures over employees as at cigarette factories—procedures that may themselves have become more urgent by the amount of the excise. A high excise may also induce taxpayers to cooperate with the tax authorities to bring the competition within the net. In other instances, the continuous visibility of the act of consumption facilitates compliance control; motor vehicle license fees are the most obvious example.

In conclusion, although many excises do appear rudimentary in design and cumbersome to operate, on the whole their effective administration is relatively easy. Taxpayer cooperation is generally not needed for assessment purposes, and there are consequently almost no collection problems. At the same time, the physical control aspects of the levy provide great leverage to excise officials to interfere with the free functioning of business and trade. Therefore, they might be especially advised: "To give every *Facility, Despatch*, and *Accommodation* to merchants, traders and others that the Faithful Discharge of the Duties of such Officers and Persons will permit."[36]

CHAPTER 9

THE ROLE OF EXCISE TAXATION: AN APPRAISAL

There is a close interaction between a country's tax system on the one hand, and the economic, social and political environment in which it operates on the other. As economic development proceeds, the nature of the tax base changes, and in all probability so do views on the role of taxation and its efficacy as a tool for implementing social and economic policies.[1] With a given institutional background, a crucial question in the evaluation of any tax is also whether other forms of taxation would lead to greater equity and fewer distortions in resource use. Here economic efficiency should involve not only the direct and specific influences of taxation, but should also focus on its indirect, differential effects on the rate of economic growth and on stability.

POLITICAL AND SOCIAL FACTORS

Apparently institutional factors are important in shaping popular attitudes toward taxation. For instance, why is it that the tobacco excise, although probably the most regressive element in any tax system, may nevertheless be regarded as a fairer levy than the income tax?[2] Fiscal psychology, or the study of fiscal illusions, seeks to find an answer to this kind of question.[3] Specifically, this relatively new discipline explores the interaction between the ruling or governing elite of a country and its subjects by drawing attention to the conscious or unconscious efforts by governments to reduce people's awareness of the taxes they pay, on the assumption that a reduction in tax tensions should facilitate the transfer of resources to the public sector.

An excise or similar tax becomes less visible if it is absorbed into the price of the commodity on which it is imposed. When goods are sold on a tax-inclusive basis, the payment of an excise may be less painful to purchasers than when it is invoiced separately; purchasers may then be unaware of the amount of the excise or even of its existence. Probably few people in any of the EEC countries know that the amount of tax payable on any of the traditional excise goods may represent as much as 70 per cent of the respective retail prices.[4] Even if taxpayers are aware of the excise obligation, it is argued that this form of taxation is good, because it permits a perfect application of the principles that taxpayers should be able to discharge their liabilities in installments and be fully current at all times.[5]

Of course, the use of state enterprises as a vehicle of taxation is a near classic way of obscuring the real cost of government, because public approval for increases in tax rates may not even be necessary. The illusions that are generated in this case apply not only to the selling activities of fiscal monopolies, but also to their procurement operations, because special arrangements with raw material suppliers may represent additional hidden elements of tax-cum-subsidy schemes. Amilcare Puviani has also pointed out that resistance to a tax may be lowered if the tax is an old one or if the obligation is tied to some favorable or pleasurable event that makes it appear less onerous; here the alcohol excise comes to mind.

Probably even more important for the acceptability of various excises is the belief that they serve the public welfare or protect the individual. Several excises may be viewed as the successors to the sumptuary laws of former times that were designed explicitly to restrain extravagance through the minute regulation of private expenditure, particularly on food, clothing and furniture. Over time, however, outright condemnation on social or moral grounds was replaced by the heavy taxation of the articles previously considered inadmissable, but the underlying philosophy remained the same.[6] Tobacco and alcoholic beverages are still referred to as sumptuary products, but duties on admissions, gambling and luxury items are sometimes also defended as restraining undesirable consumption habits.[7] With the recent publication of tobacco's potentially damaging effects, the tobacco excise may regain some of its former status as a penal duty. Even though the voices of the moralists have recently become somewhat muted, the related notion that tobacco products and alcoholic beverages are not necessities is still widespread, although the idea that their consumption can easily be foregone is often illusory in the case of an item as strongly addictive as nicotine.

Whatever the illusions, whether rooted in social customs and beliefs or created by the tax authority for its own advantage, they may have considerably reduced people's sensitivity to various excises and enabled governments to exploit them more intensively than most other taxes. Of course, the existence of tax illusions is not confined to excises; it may be surmised, for instance, that the implementation of various income tax withholding schemes has greatly reduced taxpayers' resistance to this form of taxation. This diversion into the field of fiscal psychology should not be interpreted to mean that tax payments should be made as painful as possible (that might generate an illusion that would be too pessimistic), but the absence of any conscious sense of transfer is not the appropriate way in most cases for conveying the cost of government to the taxpayer. For this reason, excises may be less acceptable than other taxes.

The psychological factors and political realities mentioned above may partially explain the rather extensive reliance on excise forms of taxation during much of recent history. But there are several other cultural and administrative factors that favor their use, particularly in the early stages of economic development. Excise taxation would appear to be especially relevant in an environment that is broadly the opposite to that described by Richard Goode as conducive to the successful use of income taxation as a major source of revenue.[8] Following Goode's exposition, the factors that favor excise taxation are listed below.

1. In a predominantly subsistence economy with little commercial integration, most consumption items are home-produced, or local artisans provide whatever is needed —furniture, clothes and utensils; even these products are generally made to order and sold directly to the consumer. Large segments of the population purchase only a limited number of regionally or nationally traded products that can be taxed: cigarettes, matches, sugar, tea, coffee, trinkets, and a few others. Production units of any significance are island-like enterprises with few established forward linkages. In this situation, a broad-based sales tax is not necessary and an income tax not feasible, but selective taxes would appear to suffice for revenue purposes.

2. In a subsistence economy, where a majority of the population is illiterate, the excise method of assessment is better understood and therefore probably regarded as fairer. There are no complicated forms to fill in, nor the temptation or opportunity to make a false return; audit is unnecessary and there are no collection arrears. Broad-based sales and income taxes require a level of literacy that is usually not found among craftsmen and cottage-type industries. Income or turnover concepts, even when they are explained in instructions that accompany tax returns, cannot be comprehended easily. That is often true also in the case of larger establishments that have grown out of cottage industries.

3. In such economies physical forms of control should be easier to apply and more effective than checks upon written records, because books of account are hardly kept at all or not reliably and honestly maintained. The notion that ledgers might be kept to serve some other interest than that of the taxpayer is absent in the small family-type establishment. Usually transactions are settled against cash and not recorded. That situation is difficult to change if the tax administration has no allies in the form of stockholders, parent companies, insurance agents, or other third parties.

4. In most developing countries the tradition of voluntary compliance that is a basic ingredient for the successful application of income and sales taxes does not exist. Most people define their interests narrowly and do not include among them paying taxes to a remote authority. They regard taxes as confiscatory in nature and will only pay those which are inescapable. Excises are at an advantage here, because physically controlled taxes are less easy to evade than paper-controlled levies. Perhaps paradoxically, the successful administration of excises is more likely to improve taxpayer morale than more sophisticated levies that break down in implementation.

5. Selective taxes do not require broad-based political support, but merely an excise-type of control of designated segments of industrial activity. Returns do not have to be filed by the majority of the population and, in contrast with sales and income taxes, most people are therefore hardly aware of the taxes that are being paid. This should be in the interest of the authorities and accord with the desire of the populace to see the tax gatherer as little as possible.

6. Finally, an honest and efficient administration is easier to achieve with excises than under sales and income taxes, because the tax base is simpler, enforcement less complicated and internal control of the tax administration easier to accomplish. Counting goods or establishing their weight, strength or other physical characteristics requires fewer skills (although more hands) and is less subject to manipulation by tax officials than intricate valuation principles or the handling of non-arms-length transactions. For lack of adequate records, the determination of sales and income tax liabilities is often a matter of judgment, and this additional margin for a personal rather than a professional decision is more likely to lead to dishonest practices.

The greater prevalence of excise taxation in countries in the early stages of development is understandable, therefore. The first modern industries in these countries are usually either processing plants for local agricultural products or import-substituting industries for goods for which a large domestic market exists. In either case, such enterprises afford an obvious and relatively accessible tax base because the products concerned are generally homogeneous and uniformly priced. There are also helpful administrative similarities with the customs service with which the excise office is usually associated. As in the case of customs, an excise administration applies quantitative checks, the taxpayer plays a passive role, and only minimal records need to be maintained. Tax training needs are also small compared to those for sophisticated forms of sales and income taxation and the liability to the tax is usually readily understood by the taxpayer.

As the economies of low-income countries expand and diversify, there is a presumption that governments will be inclined to build on the administratively tested excise system to make up for the decline in import duty receipts that generally accompanies the process of import substitution, and to meet revenue demands that usually grow faster than the economy. There is also the view that tax structure is likely to follow rather than lead economic and social changes. The excise systems in developing countries might thus be expected to cover a fairly wide range of goods, as well as some services for which the demand rises with income.

Motor vehicle taxes should also be widely imposed, although initially the tax base would be rather limited. Excise systems in these countries, therefore, are likely to be of the intermediate or extended type, and since many of the excisable products are mass consumption items and hence potentially productive of revenue, the systems should play an important role in the tax structures. Here excise systems are given a wide definition to include excise-type forms of sales taxation that are not comprehensively defined, nor broad-based in practice, nor for that matter do they rely on voluntary compliance, or enforcement through checks upon written records.[9]

However, as economies grow more complex, large excise systems become more cumbersome. At a higher level of economic development, the inherently fragmented nature of excise coverage may not serve revenue needs adequately and may have undesirable economic effects. The free functioning of business and trade might be impeded, for example, because enforcement relies to a great extent on physical controls. With increased sophistication in taxpayers' accounting methods, governments presumably also have to modernize their assessing and collection methods, which may involve a shift of audit and enforcement techniques to books of account. For these reasons, a broad-based sales tax is probably a better alternative for high-income countries, as it is technically better adjusted to business needs, potentially capable of yielding greater revenue and conceptually superior in design. Although excises would not necessarily be abolished in these countries, their revenue role could be expected to be confined to traditional excise goods, motor vehicles, and entertainment services, commodities that are usually subject to much higher rates of tax than prevail under a general sales tax. As public administration becomes more efficient, however, more excises of the regulatory type will probably be used in an attempt to modify or reduce the demand for certain products.

COMPARISON WITH OTHER TAXES

The sales tax is the major alternative and indeed the logical successor to an excise system; a comparison between the two forms of taxation is, therefore, especially appropriate. A personal expenditure tax with exemptions and rate graduations, collected on the basis of individual returns, would be another alternative, but it is not considered here because of its administrative complexity and because it is not being applied in any country at present.[10] Import duties, defined as the amount payable over and above the domestic tax on goods coming from abroad, differ functionally from excises, but there are important similarities in their administration that should be mentioned. The excise, sales tax, expenditure tax, and the import duty are all consumption taxes. The two major alternatives to consumption that are recognized as a basis of taxation are income and wealth. The income tax will be included in the comparison, but no reference is made to wealth and property taxes, because they do not play an important role in the revenue structure of most countries and call for a totally different set of administrative skills. Finally, the comparison is only relevant with broad accounts-based sales and income taxes. The difference between excises and income and sales taxes that are narrowly defined and in effect administered on some presumptive excise basis is not fundamental, but one of name only.

Progressivity and Efficiency

When there are no major constraints on administrative capacity, a personal income tax is always to be preferred over consumption-based taxes on equity grounds; it is more certain to be progressive, usually broader in coverage, and more adaptable to the individual circumstances of taxpayers. In this setting, too, the choice between excise and sales taxation cannot be validly posed. Each fulfills a different role: the sales tax is primarily a revenue raiser and excises, in addition, fulfill regulatory functions. Both taxes are equally feasible and, given certain assumptions, the quality of the incidence should not differ.[11] In these circumstances, the income redistribution role of consumption-based taxes may probably be related to the scope of a country's social security system. If that scope is limited, then an attempt might be made to achieve as much progressivity in tax design as possible, basically through the exemption of necessities and the higher taxation of luxuries. If a country has a highly developed income transfer system, however, it might be argued that even necessities should attract the standard rate of sales tax, because the transfer system can adequately compensate for the relatively greater degree of regressivity which this may entail.[12]

Whether rate graduation should be practised through sales taxation or through the imposition of separate excises depends largely on the kind of sales tax in a country. The desired effect can be achieved through a retail sales tax or through a set of excises collected from retailers, or through a value-added tax using the tax credit method if the differentiated rates are levied only at the retail stage.[13] On the whole, however, differentiated sales tax rates or separate excises at the retail stage are difficult to administer, because of the diversity of products handled, the small size of many outlets, and the lack of adequate records. If a country levies a value-added tax or a retail sales tax, an argument can then be made for a set of separate excises on luxury goods collected at the manufacturing stage, where specialization is greater, establishments larger, and records better. But effective rates would differ from desired rates because of differences in trading margins and the location of distribution functions. This disadvantage must be weighed against the greater administrative feasibility of the manufacturers sales tax.

The case for the superiority of the income tax on equity grounds becomes less clear when administrative capacity is limited. In developing countries, most people who should be taxed are self-employed and income accrues mainly in kind or from capital sources, forms that are difficult to tax satisfactorily even in industrial countries. Moreover, in the absence of a tradition of voluntary compliance and appropriate accounting procedures, an income tax, as Richard Bird notes, is "neither global in coverage (since many forms of income escape effective taxation), nor (for that reason) particularly progressive nor, indeed, really on personal income."[14] Indeed, sometimes income is assessed on the basis of the most readily available external indicators of wealth, including housing, cars, servants, television sets, or other manifestations of spending power that are used as proxies in estimating income. As in the case of the excise taxation of luxuries, behind all this lies, of course, the assumption that some goods are better than others as indicators of taxpaying ability. A factor that should also be taken into consideration is that the potential redistributive impact of the income tax is perforce very small in developing countries. In Pakistan, for instance, income tax is paid only by about 1 per cent of all families, and the minimum exemption limit—which must be set high for administrative reasons—effectively excludes from income tax liability approximately 95 per cent of the population. In contrast, 80 per cent of the population over eighteen in Canada is covered by income tax.

These and other factors in developing countries have led Luc De Wulf to conclude that "personal income tax, generally considered the most effective means of taxing the rich, is relatively unimportant in most developing countries. The often more adequate administration of indirect taxes, the frequent existence of rate differentiation for various goods, and the widely different consumption patterns of different subgroups of the tax-paying population have resulted in a progressive incidence pattern for indirect taxes in many countries." The implication, therefore, is that "generalizations about taxes in developed countries, where direct taxes are found to be progressive (up to a certain level) and indirect taxes proportional or regressive, are thus not relevant for analyzing most developing countries, where these results are, most commonly, reversed."[15]

The efficiency comparison of excise systems should be with sales taxes, not with income taxes. In an industrial economy, efficiency appears to dictate a broad-based sales tax that interferes as little as possible with economic behavior.[16] In developing countries the choice is not so clear. Under most sales taxes it is difficult to exclude inputs from the tax, and cumulative effects may occur even under sales taxes that ostensibly avoid these effects in design, because experience indicates that credits or exemptions are not extended in practice. In this setting, excises may be more efficient, precisely because they are selective; for this reason they may also involve less undue interference with business and trade.[17] Care can be taken that no tax is levied on goods destined for export, a factor that is especially relevant in economies with many smallholders and processors of rubber, tea, coffee, spices, copra, palm oil, and other agricultural export products. Rebates or drawbacks at the export stage are simply not possible for lack of documentary evidence. In the international setting, there is probably little to choose between sales and excise taxes, provided proper coordination takes place. This is generally achieved in industrial countries, but in the developing world sales taxes on imported goods are invariably higher than the domestic levy, and this should lead to the same kind of inefficiencies that have been noted for excises in Chapter 5.

Economic Growth

The influence of taxation on economic growth turns largely on the consumption-saving choice and the work-leisure choice. The reward for saving may be greater under excise taxation than under a progressive tax on income that includes interest and profits in its base; saving is penalized more heavily here on the assumption that the share of interest and profits in income rises with the size of income. It may also be argued that the greater regressivity of excise taxation compared to an income tax will switch the burden of taxation from higher- to lower-income groups; total saving might then be greater if the former have higher marginal propensities to save than the latter. This differential effect is presumably absent in the case of excises on income elastic luxury commodities.[18]

However, there is much slippage between a particular individual's saving and total productive investment (defined to have a discounted value greater than its cost). An increase in private saving may merely mean that more gold and silver ornaments are bought as a better hedge against an uncertain future in place of an expansion of an individual's business.[19] A lighter tax burden on higher-income groups may merely mean that more imported luxury goods are bought. The excise bias against consumption may also have a depressing effect on investment as a function of expected consumer demand. Although there is some basis in theory that a switch from income to excise taxation would influence the consumption-saving choice in favor of saving, the extent of the change is unknown. In fact, there is no empirical evidence to support the contention that the switch would increase private saving.[20]

Government may play a role in restraining certain types of consumption in order to free resources for productive investment. Here investment may be broadly defined to include not only private plant and equipment, but also human capital formation in which government may play a crucial role. Excises on commodities like sumptuary goods with low price elasticities of demand should restrain consumption of untaxed goods in the same, if more erratic, fashion as a general sales tax. Of course, an increase in government saving may be at the expense of private saving. There is no guarantee that aggregate saving would increase through an increase in taxation. More generally, the means to bring about an increase in government saving are largely independent of the structure of the tax system.

Finally, a reduction in real disposable income of the poor through excise taxation may enfeeble them so much that their working or learning abilities would be further impaired. Probably the only thing, therefore, that can be said is that if any savings squeeze is decided upon, it should be supported by a consumption twist: revenues from the taxation of luxuries, cars, housing, and probably clothing should be diverted to increased expenditures on education, health, and food for the poor.[21]

Closely connected to the issue of economic growth is the effect of excises on people's willingness to work. It has been contended that excises on commodities that are insensitive to price would increase work effort compared to an income tax, because the latter makes the substitution of leisure for income attractive at the margin. In the case of luxury goods and services that are complementary to the enjoyment of leisure it may also be argued, however, that their taxation would increase the price of leisure and induce greater effort. Again the evidence is inconclusive. At least in industrial countries, empirical research seems to indicate that alternative forms of taxation have approximately equivalent effects on incentives to work.

In conclusion, there is no clear-cut case for favoring one form of taxation over another in order to promote economic growth.[22] But there is a presumption that if micro-effects are carefully heeded—distortions in production and disincentives on work effort avoided, unintended forms of import substitution prevented, and greater equivalence achieved between marginal social costs and benefits—then this should influence the rate of economic growth favorably, and hopefully also welfare, broadly defined to include employment promotion and income distribution.[23]

The Issue of Economic Stability

Taxes may dampen inflationary pressures if they reduce money demand relative to the supply of goods and services, valued at stable prices. The relativity of the effect is crucial: anti-inflationary effects are stronger if spending is reduced more and production that is demand absorbing less. The impact of an increase in excises on price-insensitive commodities is spread immediately throughout the economy; hence, the argument goes, they have peculiar anti-inflationary properties. On the other hand, it has been contended that these goods are commonly included in wage-indices and that an increase in their price would lead to compensating wage demands—something that supposedly would not happen under an income tax.

Goode has pointed out that there is no reason to believe that unions would not demand an increase in wages following an income tax-induced reduction in real take-home pay of their members; therefore, he does not believe that the major taxes differ significantly in their anti-inflationary effects.[24] Others, however, reason that the tax-wage effect is likely to be significant and conclude that consumption tax hikes are probably more inflationary than income tax increases.[25] The underlying considerations have led some European countries in the past to decrease excises and raise income taxes, because this would lead to an immediate reduction in the price level and dampen wage demands.[26] It is also argued that the effect may be positive if the emphasis is on demand-shifting excises rather than on demand-absorbing excises. Inflationary pressures may then be reduced, because demand is shifted from commodities with inelastic supply to others whose supply is more elastic. At least this was one of the reasons why Canada and the United States introduced a number of excises on luxury goods during the last world war.[27]

Closely related is the issue of the countercyclical effects of taxes. Taxes are said to have automatic stabilizing properties if they withdraw excessive purchasing power from the economy during the upswing of the business cycle, but reduce the government's claim on resources during the downswing. Generally, the stabilizing influence of excises and sales taxes is claimed to be weaker than that of an income tax, because consumption changes less than income. However, this is not true of all consumption goods to the same extent. Notably the demand for durable goods might be strongly affected if confronted by high selective taxes of a predictable duration. Recently, William Branson has again contended that a set of variable, reversible excises on durable consumer goods and business fixed investment, that is, postponable expenditures, would have a powerful intertemporal price effect that would make it more effective than an income tax as a short-run stabilization tool.[28] An essential element of the proposal is that the excise is predictable so that consumers and businessmen will take advantage of the tax differential by varying the timing of their purchases of durables. The longer the life-span of a good, the more effective the excise would be, because the intertemporal price elasticity of demand would be greater. Branson points out that the excise would work best on business plant and equipment that have a more certain demand response than consumer durables, but the longer period between order and delivery means that it cannot be turned on and off as promptly as an excise on consumer durables.

On the whole, the evidence on the use of taxes as economic regulators is inconclusive. Moreover, the effects of taxes as anti-inflationary and countercyclical tools depend crucially on the assumption that fluctuations in aggregate demand are the primary cause of economic instability. When this is not the case, even the directional implications of the prescription fail. Moreover, the kind of fine tuning discussed here is extremely difficult, if not impossible, to implement and monitor in industrial countries. It is perforce of very doubtful relevance in developing countries where realistic choices between alternative fiscal instruments are limited. In these countries, the tax system should primarily be evaluated on its ability to maintain the level of real government receipts in times of inflation. The performance of excise taxation in this respect has been discussed in Chapter 3.

Finally, excises like customs duties may have a bearing on the maintenance of a given exchange rate. Tobacco-importing countries have often justified high excises on the ground that they restrain domestic consumption and thereby help maintain external equilibrium. Balance of payments implications may also loom large in considering the excise taxation of hydrocarbon oils, cars, and luxury items that are imported. The receipt side of a country's trade balance may be favorably influenced by high excises that curtail domestic consumption and increase the exportable surplus. Duties on tea and coffee have been justified in this way in India, where penal excises have also been levied on exporters of cotton fabrics and sugar if prescribed quotas were not met.

Administration and Compliance

The administration of excises is very similar to customs operations, with the difference that instead of crossing international boundaries, goods enter the domestic market from premises closely guarded by excise staff. In a sense, then, factories in which excisable goods are being produced may be considered "extraterritorial," because nothing is admitted into the rest of the country without the permission of the excise staff. In some countries, such as France, this situation is explicitly recognized.[29] The role of excise officers is similar to that of customs staff: both canalize the flow of goods, verify and examine contents, classify, appraise values, undertake laboratory tests if necessary, check quantities and values against accompanying records, and do not release goods without payment of duty, or until bond has been provided. The problems of the customs house—misclassification, proper valuation, underreporting of magnitudes—are frequently also those of an excise administration.

In this capacity, excise and customs personnel are policemen, appraisers, and chemists, but not accountants or auditors. They may be familiar with the records of a warehousekeeper, but they would not feel at home with balance sheets, and profit and loss statements. This is in sharp contrast with sales taxes that rely on examinations of books of account and other documentary evidence to verify compliance with the law. To ascertain taxable turnover, sales tax auditors are concerned with financial flows and transactions, with debtors (sales) and creditors (purchases), and with cash and bank statements, but not with physical properties and quantities. A sales tax auditor is an expert in analyzing the flow of funds, in detecting the underreporting of sales, and in making net worth statements, but he is not acquainted with the technicalities of production processes and warehousing. In terms of ensuring compliance, therefore, a sales tax is much more akin to a business income tax, under which the proper computation of turnover is also the key to the examination of a taxpayer's return.

It is useful to emphasize the fundamental differences between tax systems (such as excises and customs duties) that rely on quantitative checks,[30] and those (such as sales and income taxes) that depend on accounting controls for enforcement purposes. In implementing the law, sales and income taxes basically rely on the voluntary filing of self-assessed returns by taxpayers. For these taxes to be effective, moreover, taxpayers must be willing and able to maintain proper accounts, while the tax administration must have enough trained and experienced auditors to examine the records proficiently.[31] Excises and customs duties, on the other hand, do not need taxpayer cooperation for assessment, and there are almost no collection problems. The reverse of the coin is, of course, that these duties offer a greater opportunity for exercising leverage, and this may in fact lead to undue interference with taxpayers' activities. But this may not be a great problem because the tax base is so obvious.

On the whole, excises emerge as an especially certain form of taxation. There is little room for arbitrary decisions and interpretations by the tax authorities. This contrasts with sales taxes that have provisions on valuation and non-arms-length transactions (very prevalent in developing countries) that may put the taxpayer at the mercy of the tax assessor. Income taxes, too, have underlying concepts that are difficult to define and apply in developing countries. To be sure, definitions and classifications in the excise field are not without problems either. Various discontinuities may occur, but these are almost always factual, as opposed to the more conceptual nature of the tax base under sales and especially income taxes, that may create numerous disputes between the tax administration and the tax-paying community—disputes with no outlet if the appellate system is deficient. The sterile pursuit of abstract perfectionism may be compared here with the greater certainty under excise laws that, properly designed, offer both taxpayers and tax officials a better understanding and appreciation of their obligations.[32] Finally, as defined here, the fundamental differences in compliance and enforcement techniques mean that a switch from the excise to the sales tax method requires an entirely different type of administration; it represents a quantum jump in administrative sophistication.

SUMMARY AND CONCLUSION

In view of the attention that has been given to general taxes on goods and services in recent years, it may have served a useful purpose to switch the limelight to more selective forms of taxation. In this book, these taxes have been grouped together under the category "excise systems." Excises are discriminatory in intent, and the tax liability is often computed on the basis of the number of units produced or services rendered. Revenue considerations loom large in the case of traditional excises on tobacco products, alcoholic beverages, and petroleum products, but these and other selective taxes are also imposed for sumptuary or regulatory reasons, or as proxies for price in the marketplace. Furthermore, progressivity and benefit-received goals may be pursued; employment promotion and stabilization may also be identified as objectives to which excise taxation can contribute. Specific justifications for excise levies may further their acceptability and serve to reduce tax tensions.

Taking stock of the use that is made of selective taxes, it appears that excise systems may usefully be divided into limited, intermediate and extended systems, depending upon the number of goods and services included in the base. A world-wide survey shows that the coverage of excise systems is not necessarily confined to traditional excise goods and the motoring and entertainment fields, but that at least two out of five countries tax a wider range of commodities. An ideal set of excises does not exist, but an intermediate system probably fulfills most needs fairly satisfactorily. In developing countries the base of such a system might include traditional excise goods, motor vehicles and a number of luxury goods and services. In industrial countries, the scope would be approximately the same, with a more limited coverage of luxury items and with a greater significance attached to effluent charges and energy taxes.

Excise systems contribute on average 25 per cent to governments' tax revenues, but sometimes as much as 50 per cent and hardly ever less than 10 per cent. This is almost always much more than receipts from sales taxes. Particularly in developing countries, sales taxes appear to be narrowly based in practice, and more akin to excises, or really in the nature of supplementary import duties. The characteristics of commodities most suitable for excise taxation in terms of revenue are large sales volume, few producers, inelastic demand, ready definability, and no close substitutes. On average, 70 per cent of excise receipts derives from the three traditional excise goods, and probably another 15 per cent to 20 per cent from the next seven items.

Excises are not necessarily inelastic in response to changes in income as has often been contended. In fact, in some countries physical forms of control may ensure the real value of government receipts better under inflationary conditions than accounts-based sales taxes. Of course, this presumes that specific rates are adjusted to maintain the ad valorem position. In general, more use might be made of ad valorem rates applied to constructive values (appraised retail values, for instance) so as to retain the administrative simplicity of the excise method of control and to steer clear of any discrimination against forward-integrated producers. Such ad valorem rates would also eliminate regressive effects of specific rates that distort consumer choices regarding low-priced items.

Regressive excises are acceptable if revenues cannot be raised by other means and if they finance badly needed public services for the poor. In any case, the widely held belief that most excises are regressive is, except for tobacco products, not supported by the incidence surveys that have been made. In countries that lack a substantial degree of commercial integration and in which consumption patterns differ between the poor and the rich, excise incidence may even exhibit some progressivity. It has also been observed that the poor probably buy nontaxable early-stage goods and spend little on excisable products whose price reflects expensive marketing services.[33] Relatively the heaviest excise burdens seem to be borne by the urban poor.

The income redistribution function of excises, or any other form of taxation, is inherently limited, but more can be done in excise design to expand it. In developing countries progressive commodity taxation is called for because income taxes do not always seem to fulfill the equity function satisfactorily. In industrial countries that use value-added forms of sales taxation, a separate set of excises on luxury items may be useful if differentially higher burdens are desired. Such excises may meet with a relatively high degree of acceptance because they leave consumers with more options than broad-based income and sales taxes.

The case against excise taxation on the basis of allocative inefficiencies in consumption has probably been overstated in the past, and inefficiencies in production may be less in developing countries than under other taxes if feasibility considerations are taken into account. Excises may promote economic growth precisely because they are selective, thus avoiding the cumulative effects of sales taxes. Selective taxation of labor-displacing capital equipment and capital-intensive products may have a favorable effect on employment, but the evidence is inconclusive. The taxation of capital goods may partially correct distortions in factor prices, as indicated by the Pakistan experience, but usually more general adjustments in pricing arrangements are called for.

On the whole, the use of excise systems for nonfiscal purposes, unless broadly stated, greatly complicates administration. It is not unlikely that the benefit, if any, of intricate schemes of exemptions and concessions to encourage particular industries and regions, or related to other special goals, is out of proportion to its cost and may jeopardize the revenue function of the excise system. Generally, excises are not finely calibrated instruments capable of achieving social and economic policy objectives. Here, as with the scope of the excise system, the problem consists of knowing how, not when to stop.

In industrial countries, the use of selective taxes to combat pollution is, in principle, superior to a regulatory approach. There are technical problems in designing suitable excises, however, and the technology for measuring pollution is probably still inadequate; further research in these is needed. That is also the case with the design of workable and acceptable congestion charges, although a promising beginning has been made in Singapore. Furthermore, a better appreciation of the functions of variable and invariate road user charges appears warranted. More might also be done on the selective taxation of energy to reduce or modify demand patterns. Greater coordination of excises and external tariffs seems desirable in developing countries; at least unintended forms of import substitution would then be prevented.

In a large number of countries, the production or distribution, particularly of tobacco products and alcoholic beverages, has historically been reserved by law to government. From a purely tax point of view that abstracts from regulatory functions and ownership issues, differences between fiscal monopolies and private-licensing-cum-excise systems appear to be small. There is a presumption that countries with an inefficient excise department would probably not collect more revenue from a fiscal monopoly, while a country with a well-administered excise service is not likely to need a monopoly for revenue purposes. An advantage of fiscal monopolies is that their pricing mechanism can reflect government income distribution policies more accurately than would be possible through separate excise taxation. But it may be more efficient to have the greater institutional competition inherent in the separation of a government's taxing function and the production of excisable goods in the private sector.

In developing countries excise systems may contribute substantially to certainty in taxation. By focusing on single commodities and prescribing in detail control and collection procedures that are attuned to the peculiarities of each production process or the way in which a service is rendered, the policymaker leaves no doubt who should be taxed and to what extent. No room is left for an arbitrary determination of the tax liability, a factor of which the

APPENDIX A

EXCISE SYSTEMS

Table A:1 lists the goods and services that are subject to excises for 126 countries. Excisable items are grouped under five headings: "Foods, Nonalcoholic Beverages," "Textiles, Miscellaneous Nonfood Items," "Luxury Goods," "Producer Goods," and "Services." These correspond to the classification in Chapter 2. Producer goods are defined to include raw materials and intermediate goods that are inputs for other goods, as well as capital goods such as plant, machinery, and equipment. Services include the provision or sale of water, gas, and electricity that are provided by public utilities in most countries, but by private enterprise in some, and that may be legally defined as the delivery of a good.

Because they are taxed in virtually all countries, traditional excise goods (tobacco products, alcoholic beverages, petroleum products), entertainment services, and motor vehicles are not identified separately in the table. These items are included, however, for the purpose of determining the "Nature of Excise System" in each country. As shown in Chapter 2, excise systems may be of the limited, intermediate, or extended type, depending upon the number of goods and services included in the base. In the case of extended excise systems, a representative sample has been drawn of the goods subject to excise.

Table A:1 also gives each country's denotement of its excise system, such as *taxe unique* (francophone Africa), consumption tax (Afghanistan, Caribbean, Central America, Egypt, Somalia, Sudan), additional tax (Jordan), commodity tax (Far East), purchase tax (Israel), or luxury tax (Spain, Uruguay), and the products for which it operates a fiscal monopoly. All information is the latest available—the beginning of 1977 has been used as cut-off point—but some source material was older and sometimes incomplete.

Table A:1. Excise Systems, 1977

Country	Nature of Excise System	Foods, Nonalcoholic Beverages	Textiles, Miscellaneous Nonfood Items	Luxury Goods	Producer Goods	Services
Afghanistan	Intermediate; includes consumption tax; monopoly of tobacco, sugar, petroleum	Sugar, soft drinks, vegetable oil, honey, macaroni	Textiles, shoes, soap	--	Cement, batteries, plastics, steel products	--
Algeria	Limited; monopoly of tobacco, matches	Bread, flour, meat, soft drinks	Matches	--	--	Transportation of passengers, freight
Argentina	Intermediate	Sugar, meat, cereals, cider, soft drinks	Matches, lighters, playing cards	Cosmetics, perfumery, other luxury goods	Tires, hides	Insurance, transportation, travel, news agencies
Australia	Limited	Butter, fat, meat, wheat, canned fruit	Matches, wool	--	Coal	Fire insurance
Austria	Intermediate; monopoly of tobacco, spirits, salt	Salt, milk, meat, grain, starch products, soft drinks	--	--	--	Insurance, fire protection, transportation, advertisement, tourism
Bahamas	Limited	--	--	--	--	Travel, hotel rooms
Bahrain	No excises	--	--	--	--	--
Bangladesh	Extended	Tea, sugar, biscuits, edible oil, soft drinks	Matches, textiles, soap	Cosmetics, perfumery, appliances	Cement, paints, paper, batteries, steel	Hotel receipts
Barbados	Extended; includes consumption tax	Salt, mineral water, fruit and vegetable juices	Stationery, washing agents, stoves	Jewelry, radios, TV sets washing machines, water heaters, AC units, phonograph records, cars	Cement, varnish, lacquers, paints, enamels, natural gas	Hotel, restaurant receipts
Belgium	Limited	Sugar, confectionery, soft drinks	--	--	--	Insurance, advertisement
Bolivia	Limited; monopoly of tobacco, alcohol, matches	Sugar, rice, soft drinks	--	--	Minerals, gold, silver	Insurance, banking
Botswana[1]	Limited	--	Matches	--	--	--
Brazil	Limited; petroleum monopoly	--	--	--	Minerals	Insurance, banking, electricity, travel
Burma	Limited	Sugar, salt, soft drinks	Matches	Silver	--	Hotels, restaurants
Burundi	Limited	Soft drinks	--	--	--	--
Cameroon[2]	Intermediate; includes taxe unique	--	Textiles, shoes	--	Paints	Insurance, credit balances

Table A:1 (continued). Excise Systems, 1977

Country	Nature of Excise System	Foods, Nonalcoholic Beverages	Textiles, Miscellaneous Nonfood Items	Luxury Goods	Producer Goods	Services
Canada[3]	Limited; spirits monopoly	--	Matches, lighters, playing cards, smokers' accessories	Jewelry, precious and semi-precious stones, clocks, watches, cars, boats	--	Insurance
Central African Republic[2]	Intermediate; includes taxe unique and domestic consumption tax	--	Shoes, textiles	--	Paints	Insurance, credit balances
Chad	Intermediate; includes taxe unique	Sugar, livestock	--	--	--	--
Chile	Limited	Coffee, icecream, soft drinks	Matches, playing cards	--	Minerals, coal, tires	Electricity, restaurants, hotels, travel
China	Extended; includes commodity tax; monopoly of tobacco, alcoholic beverages	Sugar, salt, meat, soft drinks, flavoring essence	Matches, textiles, leather	Cosmetics, jewelry, appliances, radios, TV sets	Cement, steel, plastics, sheet glass, timber, paper	Electricity
Colombia	Limited; monopoly of alcohol, salt, emery	--	--	--	--	Hotels, international travel
Congo, People's Republic of[2]	Intermediate; includes taxe unique	Soft drinks	Textiles, shoes	--	Paints	Insurance, railroad fares
Costa Rica	Extended; includes consumption tax; alcoholic beverages monopoly	Coffee, sugar, flour, soft drinks	Matches	Cosmetics, appliances, TV sets, cameras, sound equipment	Cement, building materials, tires	Air, railway transportation
Cyprus	Limited; monopoly of alcohol, salt	Salt, soft drinks	Matches	--	--	Air travel
Dahomey	Limited	Wheat flour, soft drinks	--	--	Cement	Insurance
Denmark	Intermediate	Coffee, tea, chocolate, sugar, confectionery, icecream, soft drinks	Matches, lighters, playing cards, pharmaceuticals	Cosmetics, perfumery, radios, TV sets, phonograph records, cars	Paper board, lamps, fuses	Insurance, restaurants
Dominican Republic	Intermediate	Soft drinks, fruits	Matches, textiles, shoes, leather, china, glass	Jewelry, AC units, automobiles	Wire, fuel, paper	International travel, insurance, telephone, hotel accommodation
Ecuador	Limited	Sugar, soft drinks	--	--	--	Banking, maritime transport of passengers and freight

Table A:1 (continued). Excise Systems, 1977

Country	Nature of Excise System	Foods, Nonalcoholic Beverages	Textiles, Miscellaneous Nonfood Items	Luxury Goods	Producer Goods	Services
Egypt	Extended; includes consumption tax, tax on consumer durables	Sugar, coffee	Cotton, wool	--	Cement	--
El Salvador	Intermediate; includes consumption tax	Sugar, wheat flour, soft drinks, vegetables	Matches, textiles	Cosmetics, appliances, AC units, phonographs	--	Insurance, international travel
Equatorial Guinea	No excises	--	--	--	--	--
Ethiopia	Intermediate; monopoly of tobacco, matches, cigarette paper	Sugar, salt, soft drinks	Textiles, footwear	Perfumery	Iron, steel, plastic, rubber products	Construction
Fiji	Limited	--	--	--	--	Hotel receipts
Finland	Intermediate; includes consumer durables; alcoholic beverages monopoly	Confectionary, margarine, butter, milk, soft drinks	Matches, pharmaceuticals	Ornaments, furs, carpets, clocks, watches, appliances, TV sets, radios, cameras, musical instruments, cars, motorcycles, boats, airplanes	--	Insurance, travel
France	Intermediate; monopoly of tobacco, alcohol, matches, gunpowder	Coffee, tea, sugar, vegetable oil, meat, cereals, tropical products, soft drinks	Matches	Cosmetics, perfumery, jewelry	Powders, explosives	Insurance, transportation, heating, electricity
Gabon 2/	Intermediate; includes taxe unique	--	--	--	Paints, plywood	Shipping construction
Gambia, The	Limited	--	--	--	--	Airports, hotel beds
Germany, Federal Republic of	Intermediate; monopoly of spirits, matches	Coffee, tea, sugar, saccharin, salt, icecream, soft drinks, acetic acid	Matches, playing cards	--	Light bulbs, tubes	Insurance, transportation, fire protection
Ghana	Extended	Cocoa, sugar, salt, edible oil, mineral water	Matches, textiles, soap, glassware, furniture, footwear	Cosmetics, radios, TV sets, appliances, automobiles	Paper, chemicals, paints, metal products	Airports, foreign travel, hotels, and restaurants
Greece	Extended; monopoly of matches, cigarette paper, salt, kerosene, saccharine, playing cards, emery	Coffee, sugar, cheese, oil, fats	Detergents, brushes, matches, playing cards	Jewelry, furs, washing machines, AC units, cameras, toys	Skins, metals, wood, kaolin, dynamite, soda	Insurance, banking, passenger transport, restaurants

Table A:1 (continued). Excise Systems, 1977

Country	Nature of Excise System	Foods, Nonalcoholic Beverages	Textiles, Miscellaneous Nonfood Items	Luxury Goods	Producer Goods	Services
Grenada	Extended; includes consumption tax	Confectionary, icecream	Matches, soap	Cosmetics, perfumery, jewelry, carpets, watches, appliances, radios, sound equipment	Cement	Hotel receipts, travel, telecommunications
Guatemala	Limited	Salt, soft drinks	--	Radios	--	Railroad and airline passages, foreign travel, hotels, boarding houses
Guinea	Limited	Soft drinks	Textiles, footwear	--	Sheet metal, plastics	--
Guyana	Limited	--	Matches	--	--	Insurance, airline tickets, travel
Haiti	Extended; monopoly of tobacco, alcohol, matches, sugar, petroleum products	Sugar, edible oil, butter, cheese, flour, lard	Textiles	Cosmetics	Cement	--
Honduras	Limited	Sugar, soft drinks, forestry products	Matches	--		Insurance, radio cables, airplane fares
Iceland	Intermediate; monopoly of tobacco, spirits, matches	Chocolate, sugar confectionery, fruit juices, soft drinks, chicory	Matches	--	--	Insurance, airplane fares
India	Extended	Coffee, tea, sugar, salt, edible oil, soft drinks	Matches, textiles, soap, medicines, glass, footwear	Cosmetics, perfumery, appliances, AC units, radios, TV sets, films, cameras, sound equipment	Cement, metals, plastics, coal, wood, paper, rubber, batteries, cables, motors	Transportation, travel, electricity
Indonesia	Limited	Sugar, saccharine	--	--	--	--
Iran	Intermediate; monopoly of tobacco, tea, sugar, caviar, petroleum	Tea, sugar, fish, soft drinks	--	Telephones, musical instruments	--	Insurance, railway fares, foreign travel
Iraq	Intermediate	Coffee, tea, sugar, salt	Textiles, detergents	Radios, record players	Cement	Advertisement, brokerage
Ireland	Limited	Mineral water	Matches	--	Tires	Insurance, checks
Israel	Extended; includes purchase tax	Sugar	Playing cards	--	Cement	Foreign travel
Italy	Intermediate; monopoly of tobacco, matches	Coffee, cocoa, sugar, confectionery, margarine, bananas	Matches, lighters	--	--	Insurance, electricity, <u>taxe de séjour</u>
Ivory Coast	Limited	--	--	--	--	Insurance

Table A:1 (continued). Excise Systems, 1977

Country	Nature of Excise System	Foods, Nonalcoholic Beverages	Textiles, Miscellaneous Nonfood Items	Luxury Goods	Producer Goods	Services
Jamaica	Extended; includes consumption tax	Sugar, edible oil, flour, soft drinks	Matches, textiles, soap, footwear	Jewelry, appliances, radios, TV sets, records	Cement, building materials	Travel, taxe de séjour
Japan	Extended; includes commodity tax; monopoly of tobacco, salt, camphor	Coffee, tea, cocoa, sugar, salt, soft drinks	Matches, furniture, carpets, playing cards	Cosmetics, perfumery, jewelry, furs, appliances, clocks, AC units, radios, TV sets, sound equipment, records, sporting goods, books, automobiles	Timber	Travel, meals, lodging, bathing, electricity, gas
Jordan	Extended; includes additional tax	Salt	Matches, textiles	Perfumes, refrigerators, radios, TV sets	Cement, paints	Oil transit dues, airports, hotel rooms, electricity
Kenya	Intermediate	Sugar, biscuits, mineral water	Matches, textiles, soap	--	Paints, distempers	Air travel, hotel accommodation
Korea	Extended; includes commodity tax; monopoly of tobacco, ginseng	Coffee, sugar, meat, soft drinks	Textiles, sewing machines, playing cards	Cosmetics, furs, perfumery, jewelry, appliances, AC units, radios, TV sets, watches, clocks, sound and photographic equipment, cars, motor boats	Cement, metals, chemicals, plastics, wood, paper, rubber, glass, leather, building materials	Travel, electricity, gas, telephone
Kuwait	No excises	--	--	--	--	--
Laos	Limited	--	--	--	--	--
Lebanon	Limited; tobacco monopoly	Salt	--	--	Cement	Oil transit dues, hotel accommodation
Lesotho[1/]	Limited	--	Matches	--	--	Hotel accommodation
Liberia	Limited; includes stumpage tax	Soft drinks	Furniture	Jewelry	Cement, paints, lumber products	Air travel
Libyan Arab Republic	Limited; monopoly of tobacco, sugar, salt	Sugar, salt, fruits, cereals	--	--	--	--
Luxembourg	Limited	Sugar, mineral water	--	--	--	--
Malagasy Republic	Limited; monopoly of tobacco, alcohol	Sugar, candy, edible oil, biscuits	Matches	--	--	Insurance, transportation, airports, taxe de séjour
Malawi	Limited	Sugar, soft drinks	Soap, cotton fabrics	--	--	--

Table A:1 (continued). Excise Systems, 1977

Country	Nature of Excise System	Foods, Nonalcoholic Beverages	Textiles, Miscellaneous Nonfood Items	Luxury Goods	Producer Goods	Services
Malaysia	Intermediate	Sugar, seasonings	Soap, mattresses, matches, playing cards	Household appliances, TV sets	Cement, paints, foam rubber, tires, batteries, lamps	Hotels, restaurants
Mali	Limited	Foodstuffs, peanut oil, soft drinks	Matches, soap, ceramics, chalk	--	--	--
Malta	Limited	Soft drinks	--	--	--	--
Mauritania	Limited	--	--	--	--	--
Mauritius	Limited	Sugar, vinegar, crown corks	Matches	--	--	--
Mexico	Intermediate; petroleum monopoly	Sugar, salt, fish, soft drinks	Matches, textiles, glass	Jewelry, radios, TV sets	Cement, rubber, forestry products	Insurance, transportation, telephone, water, electricity
Morocco	Limited; tobacco monopoly	Sugar, mineral water	Matches	--	Tires	Insurance
Nepal	Extended	Sugar, edible oil, rice, soft drinks, flour	Matches, textiles, utensils, soap, furniture	--	Building materials, jute	Air travel, water, hotels
Netherlands	Limited	Sugar, soft drinks	--	Passenger cars	--	Fire insurance
New Zealand	Limited	Sugar	--	--	--	--
Nicaragua	Extended; includes consumption taxes; monopoly of spirits, matches	Sugar, soft drinks, wheat flour, cork bottle caps	Matches, detergents	Cosmetics, electrical appliances, TV sets, photographic equipment	Cement	Insurance, savings, air travel
Niger	Limited	--	--	--	--	Insurance
Nigeria	Extended	Confectionery, butter, meat, soft drinks, biscuits, flour	Matches, textiles, soap, utensils, furniture, medicines	Cosmetics, jewelry, radios, TV sets, phonographs, records, leather	Cement, paints, steel, aluminum products, construction materials, lamps, batteries	--
Norway	Intermediate; monopoly of spirits, wine	Chocolate, sugar confectionery, soft drinks	Pharmaceuticals, playing cards	Cosmetics, perfumery, jewelry, automobiles	Investment goods	Electricity
Oman	No excises	--	--	--	--	--
Pakistan	Extended	Tea, sugar, salt, edible oil, soft drinks	Matches, textiles, soap, shoe polishes, glass products	Cosmetics, perfumery, household appliances, leather	Cement, steel, plastics, paints, paper, jute, gas, soda ash, batteries, bulbs	Hotels, restaurants, bank checks

Table A:1 (continued). Excise Systems, 1977

Country	Nature of Excise System	Foods, Nonalcoholic Beverages	Textiles, Miscellaneous Nonfood Items	Luxury Goods	Producer Goods	Services
Panama	Limited	Sugar, meat, soft drinks	--	--	--	Insurance, banks, hotels, air travel
Papua New Guinea	Limited	Soft drinks	--	--	--	Airport departures
Paraguay	Limited; alcohol monopoly	Livestock operations, soft drinks	Matches, playing cards	--	--	--
Peru	Limited	Soft drinks	--	--	--	Foreign travel
Philippines	Limited	Saccharine	Matches, playing cards	Film, fireworks	Coal, coke	Insurance, banks, passenger fares
Portugal	Intermediate; monopoly of tobacco, matches	Sugar, salt, fish, bread, soft drinks	Matches, textiles, pharmaceuticals, playing cards	Cosmetics, perfumery	Turpentine	Insurance, transportation, hotels, restaurants
Qatar	No excises	--	--	--	--	--
Rwanda	Limited	--	--	--	--	--
Saudi Arabia	No excises	--	--	--	--	--
Senegal	Limited	Coffee, tea, edible fats, kola nuts, soft drinks	--	--	--	Insurance, electricity
Sierra Leone	Intermediate	Confectionery, salt, soft drinks	Matches, footwear, umbrellas, suitcases	--	Paint, nails, putty, glue, oxygen	Gas, air travel
Singapore	Limited	Sugar	--	Radios, TV sets	--	Electricity, gas, water, telephone, hotel bills, food and drink charges
Somalia	Intermediate; includes consumption tax; monopoly of tobacco, matches	Coffee, sugar, meat	Matches	Cosmetics, perfumery, jewelry, appliances, sound and photographic equipment	--	Insurance
South Africa[1]	Limited	--	Matches, playing cards	--	--	--
Spain	Intermediate; includes luxury tax; monopoly of tobacco, matches, petroleum	Sugar, soft drinks	Matches	Cosmetics, perfumery, jewelry, appliances, TV sets, pleasure boats	--	Telephone, travel
Sri Lanka	Limited; monopoly of spirits, salt	Tea, salt	Matches	--	--	--

Table A:1 (continued). Excise Systems, 1977

Country	Nature of Excise System	Foods, Nonalcoholic Beverages	Textiles, Miscellaneous Nonfood Items	Luxury Goods	Producer Goods	Services
Sudan	Extended; includes consumption tax; sugar monopoly	Sugar, edible oil, wheat flour, macaroni, mineral water	Matches, soap, footwear, utensils	--	Cement, paints	--
Surinam	Limited	--	Matches	--	--	--
Swaziland[1]	Limited	Soft drinks	Matches	--	--	Hotels, restaurants
Sweden	Intermediate; monopoly of tobacco, spirits, wine	Chocolate, confectionery, butter, fats, soft drinks	--	Cosmetics, perfumery, toilet water, jewelry, motor vehicles	Coal, coke	Electricity, fuel, advertisements
Switzerland	Limited; alcohol monopoly	Salt, soft drinks	--	--	--	Insurance, tourism
Syrian Arab Republic	Intermediate; monopoly of tobacco, sugar, salt, cement	Sugar, salt, edible oil, rice	Cotton	Radios, TV sets	Cement	Oil transit dues, electricity
Tanzania	Intermediate	Sugar, salt, dairy products, biscuits, soft drinks	Matches, textiles, soap	Diamonds	Paints, distempers, pyrethrum	--
Thailand	Limited; tobacco monopoly	Soft drinks	Matches, lighters, playing cards	--	Cement	--
Togo	Limited	Sugar	--	--	--	--
Trinidad and Tobago	Extended; includes consumption tax	Coffee, tea, cocoa, edible oil, lard substitutes	Matches, textiles, furniture, cutlery	Appliances, radios, TV sets, watches, phonographs	--	--
Tunisia	Limited; monopoly of tobacco, matches, playing cards, gunpowder	Coffee, tea, salt, spices	Matches, playing cards	Perfumery	--	Railway transportation, fuel
Turkey	Intermediate; monopoly of tobacco, alcoholic beverages, salt, tea, coffee	Sugar, salt	Matches	--	--	Insurance, banking, transportation, communications, construction
Uganda	Intermediate	Sugar, biscuits, mineral water	Matches, textiles, soap	--	Paints, distempers	Hotel accommodation, professional activities
United Arab Emirates	No excises	--	--	--	--	--

Table A:1 (concluded). Excise Systems, 1977

Country	Nature of Excise System	Foods, Nonalcoholic Beverages	Textiles, Miscellaneous Nonfood Items	Luxury Goods	Producer Goods	Services
United Kingdom	Limited	--	--	Passenger cars	--	--
United States 4/	Limited; spirits monopoly	Sugar, fats	Matches	--	--	Air transport, highway tolls, public utilities, telephone
Upper Volta	Limited; tobacco monopoly	Kola nuts, soft drinks				Insurance
Uruguay	Intermediate; includes luxury tax; monopoly of alcohol, petroleum	Soft drinks	Matches	Toilet articles, jewelry, furs, TV tubes, cars	--	Banking, electricity, insurance
Venezuela	Limited; monopoly of matches, cigarette paper	Salt	Matches	--	--	Telecommunications
Western Samoa	No excises	--	--	--	--	--
Yemen Arab Republic	Limited	Salt, soft drinks	--	--	--	Foreign travel
Yemen, People's Democratic Republic of	Limited	Soft drinks, fish, cereals, dates, fruits	Textiles, utensils	Perfumery, rubber foam	Paints	--
Zaïre	Limited	Sugar, mineral waters	Matches	Perfumery	Cement	--
Zambia	Intermediate	Sugar, confectionary, soft drinks, dairy products, maize, biscuits	Textiles, footwear, soap, detergents, cutlery, furniture	Cosmetics, perfumery, radios, TV sets, records	Paints, varnishes, tires, tubes, packing containers, wire, batteries	Hotels, air travel

Sources: Budget documents, reports, laws, etc. Among the major sources used for more than one country in this table are: International Bureau of Fiscal Documentation, African Tax Systems (Amsterdam: 1975), Corporate Taxation in Latin America (1975), and Value Added Taxation in Europe (Guides to European Taxation, Vol. IV, 1975); Fiscalité Africaine (Paris: 1975); Diamond, Foreign Tax and Trade Briefs; Arthur Anderson & Co., Tax and Trade Guides; Ernst & Ernst, International Business Series; Price Waterhouse & Co., Information Guides; Japan Tax Association, Asian Taxation 1973; Angel Q. Yoingco and Ruben F. Trinidad, Fiscal Systems and Practices in Asian Countries (New York: Frederick A. Praeger, 1968); Organisation for Economic Co-operation and Development, Border Tax Adjustments and Tax Structures in OECD Member Countries (Paris: 1968).

1/ In the case of Botswana, Lesotho and Swaziland, South Africa collects the excise duties payable at the import stage together with import taxes and sales taxes, and pays these into a customs union pool, after which they are distributed to the three smaller partners according to agreed formulas.

2/ The excise systems of Cameroon, Central African Republic, Congo, and Gabon include the taxe unique, an excise on goods produced in one member country of the Central African Customs and Economic Union, but marketed also in other member countries. Chad left the Union, but maintained the tax.

3/ The Federal Government in Canada levies excises on tobacco and alcoholic beverages and other products listed in the table. Provincial Governments impose duties on petroleum products and liquor sales; they also operate liquor monopolies at the retail level.

4/ In the United States, the Federal Government collects excises on sugar, telephone services, and air transport. Many states tax public utilities, although mostly under their sales taxes rather than as separate excises. Some states operate liquor monopolies at the retail level.

SALES TAX SYSTEMS

Table B:1 shows the nature and scope of sales taxes in 126 countries. The "Nature of Sales Tax" indicates the trade level at which the tax is imposed as defined in Chapter 2, or that no sales tax is levied. The standard rate denotes the only or the most common sales tax rate in a particular country. All tax rates are expressed as a percentage of the tax-exclusive value of taxable sales which is the practice in most countries; this is also called the effective rate. An asterisk (*) denotes countries that have tax-inclusive or nominal rates. The relationship between the two rates is expressed by the formula:

$$t_e = t_i \frac{1}{1 - t_i}$$ where t_e is the tax-exclusive rate and t_i the tax-inclusive rate.

The treatment of individual commodities or groups of commodities is given under four headings: "Basic Necessities," "Luxury Goods," "Producer Goods," and "Services." These headings correspond to those for excise systems, except that "Basic Necessities" under sales taxes combines the two excise headings "Foods, Nonalcoholic Beverages," and "Textiles, Miscellaneous Nonfood Items." As under excise systems, producer goods include inputs (raw materials and intermediate goods) and capital goods (plant, machinery, and equipment), and services the provision of water, gas, and electricity. Often a representative sample has been drawn in case categories of goods and services included a large number of individual items. The information relates to the beginning of 1977 but sometimes older source material had to be used.

Table B:2 provides a distribution of the various sales tax systems by region and the number of countries that do not have sales taxes.

Table B:1. Sales Tax Systems, 1977

Country	Nature of Sales Tax	Standard Rate as Percentage of Tax-Exclusive Value	Treatment of Basic necessities	Luxury goods	Producer goods	Services
Afghanistan	Sales tax not levied	--	--	--	--	--
Algeria[1]	Manufacturers	25*	Exemption for agricultural products, bread, newspapers, school books, medicines; 7.5 per cent on butter, cereals; 11.1 per cent on sugar, cheese, soap, certain textiles	42.8 per cent on appliances, porcelain, sporting goods; 66.7 per cent on fancy foods, perfumes, small cars; 150 per cent on large cars, caviar, precious objects	Credit for tax paid on inputs and specified capital goods	Not taxed
Argentina[2]	Value-added	16	Exemption for foodstuffs, books, newspapers, medicines	Standard rate	Credit for tax paid on producer goods; credit for capital goods in three annual installments	Taxed at lower rate
Australia	Wholesale	15	Exemption for foods, clothing, footwear, books, medicines; 2.5 per cent on household furnishings, appliances	40 per cent on toilet preparations, perfumery, jewelry, watches, clocks, cars, motorcycles; 50 per cent on phonographic and photographic equipment	Exemption for inputs under suspension rule; direct exemption for capital goods, building materials	Not taxed
Austria	Value-added	18	8 per cent on most foods, books, newspapers, fuel	Standard rate	Credit for tax paid on producer goods; exemption for certain raw materials	Taxed; 8 per cent on passenger transport, professions
Bahamas	Sales tax not levied	--	--	--	--	--
Bahrain	Sales tax not levied	--	--	--	--	--
Bangladesh	Manufacturers	20	Exemption for foodstuffs; 7.5 per cent on malted milk	30 per cent on jewelry, silks, furs, porcelain ware, liquor; 25 per cent on A.C. units, appliances, refrigerators	Exemption for inputs under suspension rule; 7.5 per cent on asbestos, iron, and steel; direct exemption for industrial and agricultural machinery	Not taxed
Barbados	Retail	5	Exemption for foods, newsprint, stationary, kerosine	Standard rate	Exemption for capital goods, building materials, agricultural inputs, transport equipment	Not taxed
Belgium	Value-added	18	6 per cent on foods, soap, medicines, books; 14 per cent on clothing, shoes, fuel, soft drinks	25 per cent on jewelry, perfumery, furs, radios, TV sets, automobiles, weapons, cameras, spirits, cars	Credit for tax paid on producer goods	Taxed; 6 per cent on transportation, cleaning, repairs, hotels; 14 per cent on electricity, construction, engineering

Table B:1 (continued). Sales Tax Systems, 1977

Country	Nature of Sales Tax	Standard Rate as Percentage of Tax-Exclusive Value	Treatment of			
			Basic necessities	Luxury goods	Producer goods	Services
Bolivia	Value-added	5	Exemption for foodstuffs, medicines, fuel, books, newspapers	10 per cent to 20 per cent on luxury goods, appliances	Credit for tax paid on producer goods	Not taxed [3/]
Botswana [4/]	Manufacturers	10	Exemption for food, medicines, clothing; 5 per cent or 7.5 per cent on certain other products	15 per cent on appliances, A.C. units, office machines; 20 per cent on certain other products	Credit for tax paid on certain inputs; exemption for most producer goods	Not taxed
Brazil [5/]	Manufacturers (Federal)	8	Exemption for certain foodstuffs; 4, 5, or 8 per cent on most agricultural products; exemption for medicines, newsprint, handicrafts	Higher rates of 10, 15, or 30 per cent	Credit for tax paid on producer goods	Not taxed
	Value-added (States)	12.3*-17.6*	Exemption for certain foodstuffs	Standard rates	Credit for tax paid on inputs; exemption for industrial capital goods and agricultural producer goods	Not taxed, but covered under separate municipal tax
Burma	Production	10	Exemption for foodstuffs; 5 per cent on other essential goods	Higher rate of 15 per cent	Exemption or lower rate on producer goods	Not taxed
Burundi	Multistage turnover	2	Standard rate; exemption for tea, coffee, cotton	Standard rate	Taxed; exemption for hides	Taxed; 5 per cent on real property
Cameroon	Production [6/]	9.6* [7/]	Exemption for unprocessed foodstuffs, newspapers; 4.6 per cent on handicrafts	Standard rate	Taxed	Taxed; 4.6 per cent on transportation; 12.4 per cent on movie theatres
Canada	Manufacturers (Federal)	12	Exemption for foodstuffs, farm products, children's clothing, medicines, fuel, electricity	Standard rate	Exemption for inputs under suspension rule; capital goods exempted outright; 5 per cent on building materials	Not taxed
	Retail (Provinces)	5-8	Exemption for foodstuffs, medicines, books, newspapers	Standard rate	Exemption for agricultural capital goods	Most services not taxed, but fairly broad coverage in Manitoba
Central African Republic	Production [8/]	11.7* [7/]	Exemption for unprocessed foodstuffs.	Standard rate	Taxed	Taxed at 16.2 per cent; 6.2 per cent on banking; 2.4 per cent on cotton transport; insurance exempt

Table B:1 (continued). Sales Tax Systems, 1977

Country	Nature of Sales Tax	Standard Rate as Percentage of Tax-Exclusive Value	Treatment of			
			Basic necessities	Luxury Goods	Producer goods	Services
Chad	Production	15.6*[7]/	Exemption for certain agricultural products; 12.4 per cent on milk products; 6.4 per cent on edible oil; 4.7 per cent on rice	Standard rate	Taxed	Taxed at 15.6 per cent; 11.7 per cent on construction and rentals; 5.7 per cent on transportation
Chile	Value-added	20	Exemption for basic foodstuffs, newspapers	20 per cent additional tax on luxury goods	Credit for tax paid on producer goods	Taxed; 8 per cent additional tax on transportation
China	Multistage turnover	2	0.6 per cent on foodstuffs	Various rates up to 4 per cent	0.6 per cent on producer goods	Taxed at various rates
Colombia	Manufacturers	15	Exemption for food, medicines, drugs, textbooks, stationary	35 per cent on jewelry, radios, cameras, certain household appliances, automobiles, imported tobacco	Credit for tax paid on inputs; capital goods taxed at 6 per cent (few at 15 per cent); exemption for agricultural inputs and machinery	Taxed
Congo, People's Republic of	Production[9]/	15.2*	Exemption for unprocessed foodstuffs; 7.5 per cent on clothing, beverages	Standard rate	Taxed	Taxed; 4.7 per cent on river transportation; 7.5 per cent for restaurants, movies, highway transportation; exemption for insurance
Costa Rica	Value-added	8	Exemption for foodstuffs, kerosene, medicines, textbooks	Standard rate	Credit for tax paid on producer goods; direct exemption for agricultural inputs and machinery	Not taxed, except restaurants, night clubs, repair of motor vehicles
Cyprus	Sales tax not levied	--	--	--	--	--
Dahomey	Manufacturers	15.6*[7]/	Exemption for unprocessed agricultural and forestry products	Standard rate	Taxed, but subsequent deduction for physically incorporated inputs; exemption for unprocessed raw materials.	Taxed; exemption for insurance
Denmark	Value-added	15	Exemption for private use of gas, water, electricity, newspapers	Standard rate	Credit for tax paid on producer goods	Taxed; exemption for banking, insurance, education, health
Dominican Republic	Sales tax not levied	--	--	--	--	--

Table B:1 (continued). Sales Tax Systems, 1977

Country	Nature of Sales Tax	Standard Rate as Percentage of Tax-Exclusive Value	Treatment of			
			Basic necessities	Luxury Goods	Producer goods	Services
Ecuador	Value-added	4	Exemption for foods, medicines, newspapers, books	Standard rate	Credit for tax paid on producer goods, except new buildings	Taxed; 10 per cent on some luxury services
Egypt	Sales tax not levied	--	--	--	--	--
El Salvador	Sales tax not levied	--	--	--	--	--
Equatorial Guinea	Multistage turnover	3	Exemption for foods, textbooks, newspapers	10 per cent on cosmetics, jewelry, appliances, musical instruments, liquor, automobiles	Taxed	Taxed
Ethiopia	Production[10]	5	Exemption for basic foodstuffs, coffee, tailor-made suits, ice	Standard rate	Exemption of inputs for incorporation in other manufactures	Not taxed
Fiji	Sales tax not levied	--	--	--	--	--
Finland	Wholesale	12.4*	Exemption for essential goods, fuel, newspapers	Standard rate	Exemption for inputs under suspension rule	Not taxed, except insurance, repair and service shops
France	Value-added[11]	17.6	7 per cent on certain foods	33.3 per cent on jewelry, furs, phonographic and photographic equipment, motor vehicles, radios	Credit for tax paid on producer goods	Taxed; 7 per cent on hotel accommodation, cultural activities
Gabon	Production[12]	7.5*	Exemption for unprocessed agricultural products, fish	Standard rate	Taxed; exemption for timber	Taxed at 16.3 per cent; 3.6 per cent on construction; exemption for insurance
Gambia, The	Sales tax not levied	--	--	--	--	--
Germany, Federal Republic of	Value-added	11	5.5 per cent on foodstuffs, books, newspapers	Standard rate	Credit for tax paid on producer goods	Taxed; 5.5 per cent on public transport, professions, cultural activities
Ghana	Manufacturers	11.5	Exemption for foodstuffs, educational materials; 5 per cent on textiles	Standard rate	Exemption for inputs under suspension rule; direct exemption for capital goods	Not taxed; 5 per cent on building materials
Greece	Manufacturers	8	Exemption or lower rates on foodstuffs, agricultural products	Standard rate	Taxed, but subsequent deduction for inputs, but not capital goods	Not taxed

Table B:1 (continued). Sales Tax Systems, 1977

Country	Nature of Sales Tax	Standard Rate as Percentage of Tax-Exclusive Value	Treatment of			
			Basic necessities	Luxury goods	Producer goods	Services
Grenada	Sales tax not levied	--	--	--	--	--
Guatemala	Sales tax not levied	--	--	--	--	--
Guinea	Manufacturers	7.5*	Exemption for unprocessed agricultural products	Standard rate	Taxed, but subsequent deduction for physically incorporated inputs	Taxed at 5.3 per cent, but 7.5 per cent on construction
Guyana	Manufacturers	10-20	Exemption for unprocessed foods; lower rates on several products	25 per cent on jewelry, refrigerators, cars; 30 per cent on records, photographic equipment; 45 per cent on phonographs	Exemption for inputs under suspension rule; 3 per cent on capital goods	Not taxed
Haiti	Sales tax not levied	--	--	--	--	--
Honduras	Value-added	3	Exemption for basic foodstuffs, medicines, livestock, forestry products	Standard rate	Credit for tax paid on producer goods; exemption for industrial and agricultural machinery	Not taxed, except entertainment, hotels, restaurants
Iceland	Retail	20	Exemption for milk, salt, newspapers	Standard rate	Not taxed, except lubricating oil, chemicals for printing, cleaning	Exempt, except hotels, restaurants, laundries, hairdressing, entertainment, electricity, passenger transport, insurance, advertisement
India 13/	Manufacturers	5-7	Exemption for fresh milk, vegetables, eggs, poultry, books, newspapers	Higher rates of 10 per cent to 15 per cent	Exemption for raw materials or excluded under suspension rule; some taxed at 1 per cent to 2 per cent	Not taxed
Indonesia	Production	10	Generally taxed, except fresh milk, vegetables, eggs, poultry, books, newspapers	Special higher rates	Taxed at lower rates	Generally not taxed
Iran	Sales tax not levied	--	--	--	--	--
Iraq	Sales tax not levied	--	--	--	--	--

Table B:1 (continued). Sales Tax Systems, 1977

Country	Nature of Sales Tax	Standard Rate as Percentage of Tax-Exclusive Value	Treatment of			
			Basic necessities	Luxury goods	Producer goods	Services
Ireland	Value-added	20	Exemption for foods, medicines, clothing, footwear, fuel, electricity; 10 per cent on books, newspapers	35 per cent on motor vehicles; 40 per cent on radios, TV sets, phonographs, records	Credit for tax paid on producer goods; 10 per cent on building materials, office machines, capital goods	Taxed; exemption for insurance, banking, education, health, public transportation
Israel	Value-added	8	Exemption for unprocessed fruits and vegetables, books, newspapers; lower rates for essentials	Standard rate	Credit for tax paid on producer goods	Taxed; except entertainment, hotels, vehicle hire; 6 per cent on banking and insurance
Italy	Value-added	12	6 per cent on basic foodstuffs, wine, pharmaceuticals, soft drinks, fuel	18 per cent on luxury fabrics; 30 to 35 per cent on jewelry, perfumes, furs, motor vehicles	Credit for tax paid on producer goods	Taxed; 6 per cent on gas, electricity
Ivory Coast	Manufacturers	20.5*	Exemption for unprocessed agricultural products, foodstuffs, newspapers, books; 9.3 per cent on fabrics	33.3 per cent on cosmetics, jewelry, alcoholic beverages	Credit for tax paid on producer goods, except new industrial buildings, transport equipment, furniture; 9.3 per cent on ships	Taxed at 3.1 per cent; 6.4 per cent on some services; exemption for insurance, transportation
Jamaica	Sales tax not levied	--	--	--	--	--
Japan	Sales tax not levied	--	--	--	--	--
Jordan	Sales tax not levied	--	--	--	--	--
Kenya	Manufacturers	15	Exemption for animal and vegetable products, pharmaceuticals	20 per cent on appliances, cameras, sound equipment, cars	Exemption for inputs under suspension rule; direct exemption for capital goods, fertilisers	Not taxed
Korea	Multistage turnover	1-2	Exemption for agricultural products, salt, newspapers, books 0.5 per cent on certain other products	Higher rates up to 3.5 per cent	Taxed	Taxed; 1 per cent on banking, 3.5 per cent on restaurants, recreation
Kuwait	Sales tax not levied	--	--	--	--	--

Table B:1 (continued). Sales Tax Systems, 1977

Country	Nature of Sales Tax	Standard Rate as Percentage of Tax-Exclusive Value	Treatment of			
			Basic necessities	Luxury goods	Producer goods	Services
Laos	Production	7.2*	Exemption for agricultural products	17.6 per cent on perfumery, jewelry, luxury textiles	Taxed	Taxed; exemption for banking, insurance
Lebanon	Sales tax not levied	--	--	--	--	--
Lesotho 4/	Manufacturers	10	Exemption for food, medicines, clothing; 5 per cent or 7.5 per cent on certain other products	15 per cent on appliances, A.C. units, office machines; 20 per cent on certain other products	Credit for tax paid on certain inputs; exemption for most producer goods	Not taxed
Liberia	Sales tax not levied	--	--	--	--	--
Libyan Arab Republic	Sales tax not levied	--	--	--	--	--
Luxembourg	Value-added	10	2 per cent on cereals, bread, milk, pharmaceutical products; 5 per cent on other foods, medicines, fuels, books, newspapers	Standard rate	Credit for tax paid on producer goods	Taxed; 5 per cent on transportation, liberal professions, cultural activities, advertising
Malagasy Republic	Manufacturers	13.6*	Exemption for basic foodstuffs, liquid fuel, school supplies, newspapers; 6.4 per cent on certain other products	Standard rate	Credit for tax paid on producer goods, except transport equipment, furniture, housing; exemption for many inputs	Taxed; 6.4 per cent on insurance, banking, transportation, electricity, construction
Malawi	Production	15	Exemption for basic foodstuffs	Standard rate	Exemption for capital goods	Not taxed
Malaysia	Manufacturers	5	Exemption for foodstuffs and other basic necessities	10 per cent on perfumery, jewelry, tobacco products, alcoholic beverages	Exemption for inputs under suspension rule; direct exemption for many capital goods	Not taxed
Mali	Manufacturers	25*14/	Exemption for foodstuffs, printed matter; 10 per cent on imported foodstuffs	40 per cent on imported luxury goods	Taxed, but subsequent deduction for physically incorporated inputs; 40 per cent deduction for buildings and public work projects	Taxed at 17.6 per cent; 14.9 per cent on construction; 6.4 per cent on transportation; exemption for insurance, banking
Malta	Sales tax not levied	--	--	--	--	--

Table B:1 (continued). Sales Tax Systems, 1977

Country	Nature of Sales Tax	Standard Rate as Percentage of Tax-Exclusive Value	Treatment of			
			Basic necessities	Luxury goods	Producer goods	Services
Mauritania	Manufacturers	9.9*	Exemption for basic consumer goods; 4.2 per cent on certain other products	Standard rate, but 33.3 per cent on luxury imports	Taxed, but subsequent deduction for physically incorporated inputs	Taxed at 13.6 per cent
Mauritius	Sales tax not levied	--	--	--	--	--
Mexico	Multistage turnover	4	Exemption for basic foodstuffs, fuel, books, newspapers	10 per cent on cosmetics, jewelry, furs, watches, sporting goods, photographic equipment, cars; 5 to 30 per cent on cars, yachts, aircraft	Taxed	Taxed, except banking, insurance, transportation, 15 per cent night clubs, restaurants
Morocco	Manufacturers	17.6*	Exemption for basic foodstuffs, newspapers, books; various reduced rates	25 per cent on jewelry, alcoholic beverages	Credit for tax paid on producer goods, except transport equipment, furniture, nonindustrial buildings	Taxed at 4.2 per cent to 9.9 per cent; 6.8 per cent on utilities; exemption for banking, insurance
Nepal	Retail/wholesale	8	Lower rate on clothing, soap, glass products	12 per cent on cosmetics, jewelry, appliances, radios, phonographs, films, watches	7 per cent on cement and paints	Not taxed
Netherlands	Value-added	18	4 per cent on foodstuffs, medicines, newspapers, books, soap, fuel	Standard rate	Credit for tax paid on producer goods	Taxed; 4 per cent on public transportation, lawyers, advertisements, hotels, restaurants
New Zealand	Wholesale	20	Exemption for agricultural products, wide range of consumer goods	40 per cent on perfumery, toilet preparations, jewelry, motor vehicles; 50 per cent on photographic and phonographic equipment	Exemption for inputs under suspension rule; direct exemption for capital goods	Not taxed
Nicaragua 15/	Retail/wholesale	6	Exemption for foodstuffs, medicines, certain clothing, printed matter	Standard rate	Exemption for agricultural inputs, machinery, cement	Taxed
Niger	Manufacturers	22*	Exemption for unprocessed goods; 2.6 per cent on products of local origin	Higher rate of 42.9 per cent	Taxed but subsequent deduction for physically incorporated inputs	Taxed at 15.6 per cent; 6.4 per cent on tourist activities; exemption for insurance
Nigeria	Sales tax not levied	--	--	--	--	--

Table B:1 (continued). Sales Tax Systems, 1977

Country	Nature of Sales Tax	Standard Rate as Percentage of Tax-Exclusive Value	Treatment of			
			Basic necessities	Luxury goods	Producer goods	Services
Norway	Value-added	20	Exemption for books, newspapers; 11.1 per cent on fish	Standard rate	Credit for tax paid on producer goods	Taxed; exemption for insurance, banking, health, education
Oman	Sales tax not levied	--	--	--	--	
Pakistan	Manufacturers	20	Exemption for foodstuffs, utensils, kerosene, books, newspapers; also reduced rates varying from 7.5 per cent to 10 per cent	25 per cent to 30 per cent on luxury goods	Exemption for most producer goods under suspension rule; also credit for tax paid on inputs and exemption for many capital goods	Not taxed
Panama	Value-added	5	Exemption for agricultural products, pharmaceuticals	Standard rate	Credit for tax paid on producer goods	Not taxed
Papua New Guinea	Sales tax not levied	--	--	--	--	--
Paraguay	Retail/wholesale	3	Exemption for basic foodstuffs, medicines, certain clothing	10 per cent on jewelry, furniture, electric appliances, automobiles	Exemption for inputs under suspension rule; direct exemption for capital goods	Not taxed
Peru	Manufacturers	20	Exemption for foodstuffs; lower rates of 1, 2, and 3 per cent	40 per cent on cosmetics, perfumery, jewelry, furs, beverages, luxury textiles	Conditional credit of 20-50 per cent of the tax paid on inputs	Taxed at 2 per cent to 11 per cent; 3 per cent on construction
Philippines	Production	7	Exemption for unprocessed agricultural products; 2 per cent on sugar, coconut oil; 5 per cent on processed foodstuffs	70 per cent to 200 per cent on luxury goods; 40 per cent on semi-luxuries	Taxed, but deduction for imports taxed at same rate as final product; exemption for mineral products	Taxed
Portugal	Wholesale	10	Exemption for basic foodstuffs, medicines, books, newspapers	Higher rates of 20, 30, and 40 per cent on cosmetics, jewelry, furs, alcoholic beverages, pleasure boats	Exemption for producer goods under suspension rule; direct exemption for most capital goods	Not taxed
Qatar	Sales tax not levied	--	--	--	--	--
Rwanda	Sales tax not levied	--	--	--	--	--
Saudi Arabia	Sales tax not levied	--	--	--	--	--
Senegal	Manufacturers	12.4*	Exemption for unprocessed agricultural products, foodstuffs, newspapers, books; 4.2 per cent on certain other goods	Standard rate, but 33.3 per cent on luxury imports	Credit for tax paid on producer goods, except buildings, transport equipment, furniture	Taxed at 9.3 per cent, exemption for insurance, banking, transportation

Table B:1 (continued). Sales Tax Systems, 1977

Country	Nature of Sales Tax	Standard Rate as Percentage of Tax-Exclusive Value	Treatment of			
			Basic necessities	Luxury goods	Producer goods	Services
Sierra Leone	Sales tax not levied	--	--	--	--	--
Singapore	Sales tax not levied	--	--	--	--	--
Somalia	Sales tax not levied	--	--	--	--	--
South Africa 4/	Manufacturers	10	Exemption for food, medicines, clothing; 5 per cent or 7.5 per cent on certain other products	15 per cent on appliances, A.C. units, office machines; 20 per cent on certain other products	Credit for tax paid on certain inputs; exemption for most producer goods	Not taxed
Spain	Multistage turnover	2	Exemption for bread, meat, farm products, books, newspapers	Standard rate	Taxed; exemption for fishing vessels	Taxed at 2.7 per cent; exemption for education
Sri Lanka	Production	5	Exemption for basic foodstuffs, books; 1 per cent on certain other products	15 per cent to 35 per cent on cosmetics, jewelry, radios, appliances, utensils, and other luxury goods	Taxed at lower rates; exemption for capital goods	Taxed, except insurance, banking, education
Sudan	Sales tax not levied	--	--	--	--	--
Surinam	Sales tax not levied	--	--	--	--	--
Swaziland 4/	Manufacturers	10	Exemption for food, medicines, clothing; 5 per cent or 7.5 per cent on certain other products	15 per cent on appliances, A.C. units, office machines; 20 per cent on certain other products	Credit for tax paid on certain inputs; exemption for most producer goods	Not taxed
Sweden	Value-added	17.6*	Exemption for newspapers, fuel medicines	Standard rate	Credit for tax paid on producer goods	Taxed; 9.9 per cent on immovable property; 3.1 per cent on hotels and restaurants; exemption for banking, professional services, electricity
Switzerland	Retail/wholesale	5.6/8.4	Exemption for food products, water, fuel, medicines, newspapers	Standard rate	Exemption for inputs under suspension rule; 4.4 per cent on capital goods	Not taxed; 3.3 per cent on building materials

Table B:1 (continued). Sales Tax Systems, 1977

Country	Nature of Sales Tax	Standard Rate as Percentage of Tax-Exclusive Value	Treatment of			
			Basic necessities	Luxury goods	Producer goods	Services
Syrian Arab Republic	Sales tax not levied	--	--	--	--	--
Tanzania	Manufacturers	12	Exemption for foodstuffs, books; 10 per cent on some items	Higher rates of 15, 18, 24, 40 and 50 per cent	Exemption for inputs under suspension rule	Not taxed
Thailand	Production	7	Exemption for poultry, livestock, garden products, tapioca, manioc	Higher rates of up to 40 per cent on refrigerators, TV sets, cameras, watches, automobiles	Inputs taxed at 1.5 per cent; exemption for capital goods	Taxed at various rates
Togo	Manufacturers	11.1*	Exemption for foodstuffs	Standard rate	Taxed, but subsequent deduction for physically incorporated inputs	Taxed at 8.7 per cent
Trinidad and Tobago	Sales tax not levied	--	--	--	--	--
Tunisia	Manufacturers 16/	16.8*	Exemption for basic foodstuffs	Higher rates of 28.9, 43.7, 59.7 per cent	Taxed, but subsequent deduction for inputs; exemption for capital goods	Taxed at 6.2 per cent; 2.4 per on construction; 6.4 per cent on gas, electricity
Turkey	Manufacturers 17/	Various	Not taxed	Higher rates	Taxed, but subsequent deduction for inputs on percentage basis; capital goods not taxed	Not taxed
Uganda	Manufacturers	10	Exemption for basic foodstuffs, footwear; 5 per cent on bicycles, sewing machines, hurricane lamps	Higher rates of 15, 20 per cent	Exemption for inputs under suspension rule; also direct exemption for many inputs, agricultural machinery, fertilizers, building materials	Not taxed 18/
United Arab Emirates	Sales taxes not levied	--	--	--	--	--
United Kingdom	Value-added	8	Exemption for food, fuel, books, newspapers, medicines, children's clothing	12.5 per cent on jewelry, furs, appliances, radios, TV sets, photographic equipment, caravans, boats, aircraft, gasoline	Credit for tax paid on producer goods	Taxed; exemption for insurance, banking, education, health
United States	Retail (45 States and the District of Columbia)	2.5-7	Generally taxed	Standard rate	Generally exemption for raw materials; some capital goods are taxed	Treatment varies; some States tax public utility services and virtually all States hotel and motel services

Table B:1 (continued). Sales Tax Systems, 1977

Country	Nature of Sales Tax	Standard Rate as Percentage of Tax-Exclusive Value	Treatment of			
			Basic necessities	Luxury goods	Producer goods	Services
Upper Volta	Manufacturers	21.9*	Exemption for agricultural products	Standard rate	Taxed, but subsequent deduction for physically incorporated inputs	Taxed; exemption for insurance
Uruguay	Value-added	20	Exemption for unprocessed agricultural products; 7 per cent on processed foodstuffs, fruit juices, medicines, newspapers books	Standard rate	Credit for tax paid on producer goods; 7 per cent on fertilisers, lubricants	Taxed; 7 per cent on construction, insurance, hotels, restaurants
Venezuela 19/	Sales tax not levied	--	--	--	--	--
Western Samoa	Sales tax not levied	--	--	--	--	--
Yemen Arab Republic	Sales tax not levied	--	--	--	--	--
Yemen, People's Democratic Republic of	Sales tax not levied	--	--	--	--	--
Zaïre	Production	10	Exemption for agricultural products	Standard rate	Taxed, but exemption for capital goods; 50 per cent deduction for construction	Taxed; 4 per cent on transportation; exemption for rentals, medical services
Zambia	Sales tax not levied	--	--	--	--	--

Sources: See Table A:1. An asterisk (*) after the standard rate means that it is legally defined as a tax-inclusive or nominal rate.

1/ In addition, local governments in Algeria levy (i) a turnover tax on industrial and commercial activities at 2.5 per cent; (ii) a tax on professional activities at 6 per cent; and (iii) a turnover tax on services at 6 per cent, but with higher rates on restaurants and rentals (7.5 per cent), hairdressers (15 per cent), and beauty salons (27 per cent).
2/ Each of the 24 departments in Argentina also imposes a 1.1 per cent gross receipts tax with surcharges ranging from 20 per cent to 600 per cent.
3/ Bolivia has a separate sales tax on services rendered at rates of 2 per cent to 10 per cent.
4/ The manufacturers sales taxes of Botswana, Lesotho, and Swaziland are identical to the South African sales tax. At the import stage South Africa collects the sales tax together with import taxes and excises in a customs union pool and distributes these to the three smaller partners according to agreed formulas.
5/ Brazil also imposes a gross receipts tax at 0.75 per cent.
6/ In addition, a manufacturers sales tax is levied in East Cameroon at a rate of 6.4 per cent; services are not taxed, except construction.

Table B:1 (concluded). Sales Tax Systems, 1977

Footnotes continued:

7/ Includes additional taxes or surcharges imposed on the same base and earmarked for local governments or special agencies or funds.

8/ The Central African Republic also levies a transaction tax at 1.01 per cent* on goods and services not subject to the production tax or excises.

9/ The Congo also levies an additional sales tax applied at 5.3 per cent* to the first sale of a good and at 3.1 per cent* to the first rendering of a service; the bases of the two taxes are somewhat different.

10/ Ethiopia also levies a 2 per cent turnover tax.

11/ France also levies a tax on services (TPS) at a rate of 9.2 per cent, but a taxpayer may elect to pay the value-added tax instead. Moreover, a retail sales tax is imposed at the local level at 2.8 per cent on goods and certain services exempted from TPS; the rate on entertainment and hotel accommodation is 9.3 per cent.* The custom of imposing a separate tax on services instead of integrating the levy with the main variant of the sales tax is also followed in a number of French-speaking West African countries; however, in this table these taxes are listed under the heading "Services."

12/ In addition, Gabon administers a 1 per cent turnover tax on commercial and industrial activities not covered by the production tax.

13/ The sales tax picture in India is extremely complicated. There are not only single-point and multipoint taxes, but two states also operate mixed single-point and double-point systems. In addition, states with multipoint systems impose various special single-point taxes particularly on luxuries and semiluxuries. Finally, a central sales tax is levied on the interstate sale of goods which are chargeable at 3 per cent in the state of origin.

14/ The tax-inclusive rate applies to imports only.

15/ Nicaragua also imposes a gross receipts tax at 0.2 per cent.

16/ Includes consumption tax levied at varying rates.

17/ Also known as production and expenditure tax. In addition, Turkey imposes a retail sales tax on certain goods and services, called "operation tax."

18/ The Ugandan Sales Tax Act provides for the taxation of services by statutory order, but so far this provision has not been applied.

19/ Local governments impose a gross receipts tax, generally at a rate of 0.5 per cent.

Table B:2. Distribution of Sales Tax Systems

Nature of Sales Tax	North and West Africa	Central Africa	East and South Africa	Middle East	Asia and Far East	Caribbean and Central America	South America	Europe, North America and Australasia	Total Number of Countries [1]	Percentage Distribution [2] All	Percentage Distribution [2] Users
Countries with sales tax systems	13	8	9	1	14	5	11	26	87	67	100
Turnover tax	--	2	--	--	3	--	--	2	7	5	8
Production tax	--	6	2	--	6	--	--	--	14	11	16
French-type	(--)	(5)	(--)	(--)	(1)	(--)	(--)	(--)	(6)	(5)	(7)
Other	(--)	(1)	(2)	(--)	(5)	(--)	(--)	(--)	(8)	(6)	(9)
Manufacturers tax	13	--	7	--	4	--	4	4	32	25	37
Suspension system	(1)	(--)	(3)	(--)	(4)	(--)	(1)	(1)	(10)	(8)	(11)
Subtraction technique											
Physical deduction	(7)	(--)	(--)	(--)	(--)	(--)	(--)	(--)	(7)	(5)	(8)
Other	(1)	(--)	(--)	(--)	(--)	(--)	(--)	(2)	(3)	(2)	(3)
Tax credit principle	(4)	(--)	(4)	(--)	(--)	(--)	(3)	(1)	(12)	(9)	(14)
Wholesale tax	--	--	--	--	--	--	--	4	4	3	5
Retail/wholesale tax	--	--	--	--	1	1	1	1	4	3	5
Retail tax	--	--	--	--	--	1	--	3	4	3	5
Value-added tax	--	--	--	1	--	3	6	12	22	17	25
EEC model	(--)	(--)	(--)	(--)	(--)	(--)	(--)	(12)	(12)	(9)	(14)
Other	(--)	(--)	(--)	(1)	(--)	(3)	(6)	(--)	(10)	(8)	(11)
Countries without sales tax systems	5	1	4	15	3	8	2	4	42	33	--
Total	18	9	13	16	17	13	13	30	129	100	100

1/ Three countries--Canada, Brazil, and India--are represented twice in this column as each operates two different forms of sales taxation.
2/ Figures may not add because of rounding.

APPENDIX C

TAX REVENUE STATISTICS

Tables C:1 and C:2 show the structure of indirect tax revenues and the relative importance of excises on goods, services, and motor vehicles in 82 countries; figures are based on three-year averages. Table C:3 indicates the years and levels of government covered.

The coverage and computation of the excise data are discussed in Chapter 3. Receipts from sales taxes include those from sales taxes levied on imports. Export duties include revenues from oil and mining operations collected in the form of income taxes or royalties. Stamp and registration duties are taxes on capital and financial transactions, except succession and gift duties (considered to be direct taxes); in European and francophone countries these taxes may include a large property tax element; in Central and South American countries stamp duties often resemble sales taxes and excise duties. Finally, "indirect taxes" is the sum of excises, sales taxes, import duties, export taxes, stamp and registration duties, and other indirect taxes (for instance, business license taxes); no other definition is implied.

Excise and other tax data are mainly taken from budget documents, statistical abstracts, or other official government sources. For industrial countries the main reference has been Organisation for Economic Co-operation and Development, *Revenue Statistics of OECD Member Countries 1965–71* (Paris, 1973); for francophone African countries mention should be made of John R. Hill, "Sales Taxes in Francophone Africa," Ph.D. dissertation (Urbana: University of Illinois, 1974). In a few cases use has been made of unpublished (nonconfidential) data supplied to the International Monetary Fund by member governments.

Gross national product (GNP) and per capita income data are computed from International Monetary Fund, *International Financial Statistics*, vol. 27 (February 1974). In the absence of data on GNP, GDP, which includes income produced domestically that accrues to nonresidents but excludes income received from abroad by residents, is used for Chad, Dahomey, Iran, Liberia, Mali, Nepal, Nigeria, Senegal, Singapore, Syria, Uganda, and Upper Volta.

	Per Capita GNP (U.S. dollars)	Total Tax to GNP Ratio	Total indirect taxes	Selective taxes on goods, services, and motor vehicles			Total selective taxes and sales taxes	Import duties	Export duties	Stamp and registration duties	Other indirect taxes
				Total	Traditional excise goods	Sales taxes					
Argentina	1,036	10.5	69.4	32.0	(25.1)	17.2	49.2	10.5	5.1	4.2	0.4
Australia	2,709	27.0	35.7	19.1	(13.5)	7.3	26.4	4.4	--	3.1	1.8
Austria	1,969	26.9	52.4	19.0	(12.6)	25.3	44.3	6.0	--	1.1	1.0
Barbados	531	26.4	50.2	18.6	(14.1)	--	18.6	30.2	--	0.8	0.6
Belgium	2,698	24.4	53.3	15.1	(11.9)	31.1	46.2	3.9	--	3.2	--
Bolivia	176	8.2	80.9	13.5	(11.0)*	6.3	19.7	44.8	10.8	4.2	1.3
Brazil	411	22.9	84.9	16.7	(14.6)1/	50.3	66.9	3.4	4.0	1.8	8.7
Canada	3,879	29.0	38.8	12.3	(6.9)	16.1	28.4	3.2	--	--	7.2
Chad	79	13.6	70.5	17.7	(9.4)*	14.2	31.9	25.0	10.6	2.5	0.5
Chile	801	20.0	74.5	9.4	(8.0)1/*	32.3	41.6	11.4	15.8	5.4	0.2
China	370	17.8	78.1	41.6	(20.9)	5.9	47.5	26.2	--	4.5	--
Colombia	326	11.5	52.1	15.5	(14.3)	7.7	23.2	16.9	5.6	4.6	1.7
Costa Rica	537	13.5	74.1	23.5	(16.7)	15.3	38.8	27.2	6.0	1.3	0.9
Cyprus	890	13.3	70.4	37.0	(24.2)	--	37.0	29.8	0.3	1.4	1.8
Dahomey	83	14.3	77.1	9.8	(8.7)2/*	3.8	13.6	56.3	5.3	1.1	0.8
Denmark	3,013	36.4	45.1	24.6	(16.3)	17.9	42.5	1.5	--	1.0	--
Dominican Rep.	356	15.9	80.0	28.7	(20.3)*	9.7	28.7	42.4	4.5	2.0	2.3
Ecuador	312	12.7	84.4	15.6	(11.3)	--	25.3	31.5	20.5	5.0	2.0
El Salvador	295	10.4	73.9	28.0	(21.3)	--	28.0	24.1	14.4	5.6	1.8
Ethiopia	70	9.0	73.0	26.2	(17.3)	15.8	42.0	20.2	8.9	1.5	0.4
Finland	2,220	29.7	50.3	25.2	(18.0)	19.6	44.9	3.2	0.6	1.6	--
France	2,946	21.5	67.3	21.0	(16.1)	38.0	59.0	1.5	--	2.4	4.3
Germany	3,072	23.1	47.2	20.6	(16.0)	22.0	42.7	2.2	--	1.1	1.2
Ghana	237	16.7	82.4	21.3	(13.4)	7.9	29.2	16.6	36.3	0.1	0.2
Greece	1,118	17.4	78.7	31.2	(22.7)	12.2	43.4	10.7	--	21.4	3.3
Guatemala	359	8.0	83.4	28.1	(23.3)	--	28.1	25.2	5.2	23.9	1.0
Honduras	270	11.0	77.3	28.1	(22.7)	7.4	35.5	29.0	10.0	--	2.8
India	89	12.3	78.7	50.8	(24.3)	15.0	65.8	8.3	1.9	2.7	--
Indonesia	97	10.3	82.0	19.1	(17.5)	12.1	31.2	19.8	29.5	1.3	0.1
Iran	387	17.2	85.1	10.0	(7.7)	--	10.0	20.5	53.5	1.0	0.1
Ireland	1,377	27.9	57.6	40.8	(36.3)	11.3	52.1	4.4	--	1.1	0.1
Israel	1,656	29.0	55.1	11.8	(8.4)*	12.5	24.2	16.3	--	4.3	10.3
Italy	1,729	19.1	69.7	35.7	(24.8)	21.8	57.5	3.9	--	7.6	0.7
Ivory Coast	323	19.1	82.6	9.9	(9.2)*	26.5	36.5	23.4	20.1	1.5	1.1
Jamaica	675	20.2	68.2	28.4	(19.0)	--	28.4	21.5	15.4	2.8	--

Table C:1 (continued). Selected Countries: Structure of Indirect Tax Revenue, 1969-71

	Per Capita GNP (U.S. dollars)	Total Tax to GNP Ratio	Total indirect taxes	Selective taxes on goods, services, and motor vehicles: Total	Traditional excise goods	Sales taxes	Total selective taxes and sales taxes	Import duties	Export duties	Stamp and registration duties	Other indirect taxes
							In Per Cent of Total Tax Revenue				
Japan	1,644	18.4	40.1	25.8	(16.7)	--	25.8	3.1	--	3.0	8.2
Kenya	133	15.1	58.0	33.7	(26.1)	--	33.7	20.2	0.9	1.4	1.8
Korea	253	15.3	72.9	37.5	(18.2)	7.5	45.0	13.2	--	5.4	9.3
Lebanon	566	9.8	74.9	23.5	(18.7)	--	23.5	41.9	9.2	--	0.4
Liberia	274	--	74.6	7.1	(4.9)2/*	--	7.1	32.2	30.5	0.4	4.4
Malagasy Rep.	134	15.0	79.4	18.3	(18.2)*	19.6	37.9	33.9	5.6	--	2.0
Malaysia	363	16.7	66.5	34.7	(21.6)	--	34.7	14.8	13.2	--	3.7
Mali	55	12.2	85.9	11.4	(6.7)*	24.0	35.3	21.7	7.6	2.3	19.0
Mauritania	80	13.5	78.2	9.9	(9.1)3/*	25.2	35.2	14.0	25.1	2.1	1.7
Mauritius	236	18.0	74.9	37.0	(31.1)	--	37.0	22.1	8.8	4.6	2.4
Mexico	637	9.5	59.8	16.8	(7.1)*	10.6	27.4	9.9	1.5	1.5	19.6
Morocco	232	16.7	77.8	23.1	(17.2)	26.5	49.6	17.2	2.0	6.4	2.6
Nepal	88	4.4	77.1	15.6	(11.1)2/*	14.7	30.3	36.6	5.8	3.8	0.6
Netherlands	2,482	26.1	43.2	14.7	(10.8)	22.0	36.8	4.5	--	1.4	0.5
New Zealand	2,200	26.3	34.4	14.4	(13.3)4/	8.3	22.7	9.5	--	0.9	1.2
Nicaragua	445	8.9	79.8	41.2	(26.6)	8.3	49.4	25.5	2.4	2.1	0.3
Niger	100	8.8	62.4	9.0	(7.6)*	28.3	37.3	16.1	5.7	2.4	0.8
Nigeria	124	22.7	93.0	13.6	(5.7)	--	13.6	20.8	58.4	0.1	--
Norway	2,858	30.5	55.4	21.1	(12.5)	30.9	52.1	2.2	--	0.2	0.9
Pakistan	103	11.9	83.9	38.3	(23.9)	6.3	44.5	17.5	16.4	2.0	3.4
Panama	713	14.3	58.9	27.8	(16.0)5/	--	27.8	22.4	2.7	3.9	2.0
Paraguay	248	10.5	78.3	19.6	(17.5)5/	5.0	24.5	36.1	2.8	14.3	0.7
Peru	435	14.9	63.0	15.0	(9.7)*	--	15.0	24.3	--	23.7	--
Philippines	207	10.0	68.6	15.7	(14.2)6/	21.4	37.0	17.8	6.2	1.6	6.0
Portugal	685	17.0	64.5	29.3	(12.7)6/	11.9	41.2	12.0	0.1	11.1	--
Senegal	198	18.3	74.2	18.5	(16.4)*	34.4	52.9	11.5	5.5	2.6	1.7
Sierra Leone	150	12.7	73.9	26.3	(24.2)	--	26.3	34.6	12.9	0.1	--
Singapore	945	13.6	50.1	40.3	(24.0)	--	40.3	5.6	--	3.0	1.2
Somalia	--	--	88.6	31.3	(13.1)2/*	--	31.3	47.8	4.4	4.9	0.2
South Africa	774	15.7	47.1	18.6	(16.5)	7.2	25.7	10.2	7.7	3.5	

Table C:1 (concluded). Selected Countries: Structure of Indirect Tax Revenue, 1969-71

	Per Capita GNP (U.S. dollars)	Total Tax to GNP Ration	Total indirect taxes	In Per Cent of Total Tax Revenue							
				Selective taxes on goods, services, and motor vehicles			Total selective taxes and sales taxes	Import duties	Export duties	Stamp and registration duties	Other indirect taxes
				Total	Traditional excise goods	Sales taxes					
Sri Lanka	168	17.4	81.1	27.4	(24.0)	10.7	38.0	10.1	30.8	1.0	1.2
Sweden	4,063	33.5	37.4	21.5	(13.6)	12.8	34.3	2.6	--	0.5	--
Switzerland	3,405	18.3	38.5	19.7	(13.4)	9.4	29.1	6.9	--	2.5	--
Syrian Arab Rep.	279	14.7	76.3	18.0	(9.6)	--	18.0	17.3	32.0	5.0	4.0
Tanzania	87	15.1	65.3	31.4	(21.8)	11.3	42.7	17.6	4.2	0.5	0.3
Thailand	191	12.4	86.1	28.1	(22.3)	21.3	49.4	27.1	8.2	0.7	0.6
Trinidad & Tobago	787	17.5	52.1	21.9	(9.3)2/*	--	21.9	19.9	9.4	0.9	0.1
Tunisia	270	21.8	86.5	17.4	(15.3)7/	24.6	42.0	6.1	15.8	3.6	19.1
Turkey	388	19.5	67.8	30.3	(19.2)	20.3	50.6	10.4	1.1	5.7	--
Uganda	116	13.3	80.5	28.6	(18.0)	16.3	44.9	15.7	19.3	0.6	--
United Kingdom	2,234	31.4	35.0	24.9	(21.2)	7.7	32.5	1.5	--	0.8	0.1
United States	4,698	23.8	24.3	15.3	(8.2)	6.5	21.9	1.0	--	0.2	1.2
Upper Volta	60	10.4	74.5	11.8	(11.2)*	21.4	33.3	35.2	3.8	2.2	--
Uruguay	852	12.4	85.5	26.7	(17.2)	19.4	46.1	14.4	6.1	18.1	0.7
Venezuela	962	22.0	92.2	7.8	(7.3)	--	7.8	6.1	69.9	0.9	7.5
Zaire	103	25.3	73.9	6.1	(5.4)*	7.7	13.8	18.6	41.3	--	0.3
Zambia	378	31.4	79.0	10.4	(9.6)2/*	--	10.4	9.5	56.7	0.1	2.5

*Not including revenues collected on traditional excise goods in the form of import duties, and in addition in francophone African countries revenues collected on such goods in the form of sales taxes.

1/ Part of the sales tax attributable to traditional excise goods.
2/ Not including receipts from the following traditional excise goods: tobacco products: Dahomey, Liberia, Trinidad and Tobago; hydrocarbon oils: Nepal, Somalia, Zambia.
3/ Including excises on sugar and tea.
4/ Including motor vehicle taxes.
5/ Including excises on soft drinks.
6/ Including excises on sugar and essences.
7/ Including minor excises on gunpowder and playing cards.

Table C:2. Selected Countries: Relative Importance of Selective Taxes on Goods, Services, and Motor Vehicles, 1969-71

In percent of total receipts

	Tobacco products	Alcoholic beverages	Hydrocarbon oils	Total traditional excise goods	Sugar	Soft drinks	Other foods and non-alcoholic beverages	Total foods and non-alcoholic beverages	Textiles and miscellaneous non-food items	Luxury goods	Producer goods	Total selective taxes on goods
Argentina	27.1	6.5	44.9	78.5	0.1	2.2	--	2.3	--	1.5	--	82.2
Australia	19.4	29.5	21.8	70.6	--	--	1.3	1.3	--	--	--	72.0
Austria	20.7*	12.7*	33.0	66.4	--	4.8	5.2	10.0	--	--	--	76.4
Barbados	4.6	30.5	40.3	75.5	--	6.0	--	6.0	--	0.3	0.6	82.3
Belgium	19.7	12.1	47.3	79.0	0.4	1.7	--	2.1	--	--	--	81.2
Bolivia 1/	32.8	46.0	2.8	81.6≈	--	2.1	--	2.1	--	--	--	83.7
Brazil 1/	35.8	8.7	43.0	87.5	--	--	--	--	--	--	--	87.5
Canada	5.8	17.0*	33.6	56.4	--	--	--	--	--	--	--	56.4
Chad	14.4	18.5	20.2	53.2≈	--	--	--	--	--	--	--	56.4
Chile 1/	40.3	7.3	37.6	85.1≈	--	--	--	--	--	--	--	53.2
China	23.6* 2/	15.6* 2/	11.1	50.3	4.3	1.3	9.6	15.3	4.5↑	7.8	9.4^	85.1
Colombia	26.1	29.2*	36.7	92.0	--	--	1.5	1.5	--	--	--	87.3
Costa Rica	14.5	31.6*	25.0	71.1	0.8	3.9	1.2	5.9	--	--	3.4^	93.5
Cyprus	30.5	8.0*	26.7	65.2	--	--	0.6	0.6	--	--	--	80.4
Dahomey	...	35.9	53.3	89.3	--	--	--	--	--	--	--	65.9
Denmark	25.4	23.3	17.6	66.3	2.6	1.3	0.5	4.5	0.7	2.0	--	89.3
Dominican Republic	27.8	37.4	5.6	70.7≈	--	1.0	--	1.0	--	--	--	73.4
Ecuador	17.5	17.1	38.0	72.5	2.5	7.0	--	9.5	--	--	--	71.7
El Salvador	16.2	36.0	23.9	76.1	6.8	--	--	6.8	--	--	--	82.0
Ethiopia	5.0*	21.4	39.5	65.9	12.0	--	7.7	19.7	10.4↑	--	--	82.9
Finland	17.1	32.5*	21.6	71.1	1.3	1.1	2.6	5.1	6.1	--	--	96.0
France	13.3*	14.0*	49.2	76.5	0.8	0.3	1.5	2.6	--	0.2	--	82.3
Germany	23.9	18.5*	35.3	77.8	0.4	0.3	3.6	4.3	--	--	--	79.3
Ghana	17.8	12.3	33.1	63.1	--	--	16.8	16.8	--	--	--	82.1
Greece	27.8	10.6	34.3	72.7	7.0*	--	--	7.0	--	--	--	80.0
Guatemala	16.2	38.9	27.7	82.8	--	4.3	--	4.3	--	--	--	79.7
Honduras	11.6	51.2	17.8	80.6	3.1	3.1	--	6.2	--	--	--	87.1
India	10.7	8.4	28.8	47.9	5.5	0.2	2.5	8.2	11.6↑	1.3	13.4	86.8
Indonesia 3/	50.6	0.6	40.5	91.7	8.3	--	--	8.3	--	--	--	82.4
Iran	16.6*	9.3	50.7	76.5								100.0

In per cent of total receipts

	Tobacco products	Alcoholic beverages	Hydro-carbon oils	Total tradi-tional excise goods	Sugar	Soft drinks	Other foods and non-alcoholic beverages	Total foods and non-alcoholic beverages	Textiles and miscellaneous non-food items	Luxury goods	Producer goods	Total selective taxes on goods
Ireland	29.4	35.2	24.4	89.1	--	0.6	--	0.6	--	--	--	89.7
Israel	21.5	8.3_9/	41.5	71.2≈	--	--	--	--	--	--	9.1^	80.4
Italy	19.9*	3.5	46.0	69.4	1.2	--	5.6	6.9	--	--	2.4^	78.7
Ivory Coast	31.5	26.0	35.4	93.0≈	--	--	--	--	--	--	--	93.0
Jamaica	22.6	27.4	16.6	66.7	0.9	1.5	1.6	4.0	3.6†	0.9	0.8^	75.9
Japan	17.8*	20.4	26.2	64.5	1.4	0.3	--	1.7	--	4.5	--	70.8
Kenya	16.3	23.9	37.2	77.4	10.9	1.7	0.1	12.7	3.5	--	0.5	94.2
Korea	20.2*	14.8	13.5	48.5	5.4	0.6	0.2	6.2	7.6†	4.4	6.2	72.9
Lebanon	20.3*	1.7	57.6	79.7	--	--	--	--	--	--	4.2^	83.9
Liberia	...	34.3	34.7	69.0≈	--	--	--	--	--	--	--	69.0
Malagasy Republic	19.9	79.6		99.5≈	--	--	--	--	--	--	--	99.5
Malaysia	21.8	10.5	30.0	62.3	7.7	--	--	7.7	--	--	--	70.0
Mali	16.2_5/	2.5	39.7	58.5≈	--	--	--	--	--	--	--	58.5
Mauritania	67.5/	--	24.0	91.5≈	...	--	6.0	6.0	--	--	--	97.5
Mauritius	24.3	33.9	25.9	84.1	--	--	--	--	--	--	--	84.1
Mexico	16.4	9.2	16.9	42.6≈	0.6	2.4	0.4	3.4	1.9†	--	0.9^	48.7
Morocco	27.5*_6/	--	47.1	74.6	13.2	--	--	13.2	--	--	--	87.7
Nepal	45.9	25.8	...	71.7≈	6.4	--	4.8	11.1	2.1	--	0.4^	85.4
Netherlands	19.7	14.8	38.7_7/	73.1	0.9	--	--	0.9	--	--	--	74.0
New Zealand	28.4	22.5	41.4_7/	92.3	1.1	--	--	1.1	--	--	--	93.4
Nicaragua	20.1	23.7*	20.8	64.6	3.4	5.0	3.6	12.1	--	--	2.8^	79.5
Niger	25.7	23.2	36.0	84.8≈	--	--	--	--	--	--	--	84.8
Nigeria	7.8	12.2	22.2	42.2	--	0.3	--	--	--	--	--	42.5
Norway 8/	14.3	24.8*	20.1	59.2	--	1.3	3.0	4.4	0.2	--	--	63.8
Pakistan 8/	18.1	2.2	42.2	62.5	3.4	0.7	6.9	11.0	12.4†	1.0	7.9	94.9
Panama	8.2	28.7	20.5	57.4	--	--	--	--	--	--	--	57.4
Paraguay	20.3	25.9*_9/	43.0	89.2	--	--	--	--	--	--	--	89.2
Peru	20.2	20.9	23.1	64.3	--	--	--	--	--	--	--	64.3
Philippines	38.2	20.3	32.5_10/	90.9	--	--	--	--	--	--	--	90.9
Portugal	17.7*	3.8	22.1	43.5	--	1.3	0.5	1.8	0.5†	--	--	45.9

Table C:2 (continued). Selected Countries: Relative Importance of Selective Taxes on Goods, Services, and Motor Vehicles, 1969-71

In per cent of total receipts

	Tobacco products	Alco-holic bever-ages	Hydro-carbon oils	Total tradi-tional excise goods	Sugar	Soft drinks	Other foods and non-alcoholic beverages	Total foods and non-alcoholic beverages	Textiles and mis-cellaneous non-food items	Luxury goods	Producer goods	Total selective taxes on goods
Senegal	12.5	8.9	66.9	88.3≃	--	--	--	--	--	--	--	88.3
Sierra Leone	31.8	14.4	46.1	92.3	0.3	--	0.1	0.4	0.5↑	--	0.5	93.7
Singapore	20.0	17.5	22.0	59.5	4.3	--	--	4.3	--	--	--	63.8
Somalia	41.4*	0.4	...	41.8≃	54.0	--	0.4	54.4	--	--	--	96.2
South Africa	30.0	41.6	17.1	88.7	--	--	--	--	--	--	--	88.7
Sri Lanka	40.7	29.7*	17.4	87.9	--	--	6.7	6.7	--	--	--	94.6
Sweden	16.2*	27.9*	19.2	63.3	--	1.7	--	1.7	--	--	--	65.0
Switzerland	19.5	9.3*	39.2	68.0	0.7	1.3	--	2.0	--	--	--	70.0
Syrian Arab Republic	28.4*	3.4	21.2	53.0	15.2*	--	3.4	18.6	--	--	10.0^	81.6
Tanzania	20.9	16.3	32.3	69.5	10.6	1.4	0.3	12.2	5.6↑	--	0.4	87.8
Thailand	30.5*	14.7	34.1	79.4	--	3.2	--	3.2	--	--	1.0^	83.6
Trinidad and Tobago	...	23.2	19.1	42.3≃	--	--	0.1	0.1	--	--	--	42.4
Tunisia	60.2* 11/	--	27.7	87.9	--	--	12.0 12/	12.0	--	--	--	100.0
Turkey	——31.4*——		31.9	63.3	8.2	--	--	8.2	--	--	--	71.5
Uganda	17.3	14.1	31.7	63.1	20.3	1.5	0.1	22.0	6.2↑	--	0.4	91.7
United Kingdom	28.4	22.9	33.9	85.2	--	--	--	--	--	--	--	85.2
United States	14.2	21.2*	18.0	53.4	0.3	--	--	0.3	--	--	--	53.7
Upper Volta	50.7*	17.1	26.9	94.8	--	--	--	--	--	--	--	94.8
Uruguay	25.9	15.4*	23.3	64.5	--	5.1	--	5.1	--	3.2	--	72.8
Venezuela	32.4	45.0	15.8	93.2	--	--	0.1	0.1	--	--	--	93.3
Zaire	20.8	40.0	28.2	89.0≃	1.7	--	--	1.7	--	--	--	90.6
Zambia	24.8	67.7	...	92.5≃	--	--	--	--	--	--	--	92.5

Table C:2 (continued). Relative importance of selective taxes on goods, services, and motor vehicles. Selected countries.

In per cent of total receipts

	Transportation, travel	Insurance, banking	Miscellaneous services	Total selective taxes on services	Gambling, sweepstakes, lotteries	Entertainment	Total selective taxes on services, gambling, and entertainment	Motor vehicle taxes	Non-classified selective taxes	Total selective taxes on goods, services, and motor vehicles
Argentina	--	2.8	--	2.8	1.8°	0.5	5.2	12.6+	--	100.0
Australia	--	1.7	0.5	2.2	8.1°	--	10.3	16.9	0.8	100.0
Austria	6.0	3.6	2.4	12.0	0.4	1.0+	13.3	8.4-	1.9	100.0
Barbados	--	--	--	--	5.0	0.7	5.7	12.0	--	100.0
Belgium	--	5.1	--	5.1	1.4	1.8+	8.2	10.6	--	100.0
Bolivia	--	--	--	--	--	5.2	5.2	8.6-	2.4	100.0
Brazil	1.5	--	7.4Δ	8.9	--	--	8.9	2.5	1.1	100.0
Canada	--	2.8	--	2.8	--	2.0	4.7	38.9	--	100.0
Chad	--	--	--	--	--	--	--	2.9	43.9	100.0
Chile	1.2	--	--	1.2	0.6	5.1	7.0	6.8	1.1	100.0
China	--	--	1.3Δ	1.3	--	3.9	5.2	7.5+	--	100.0
Colombia	--	--	1.0<	1.0	0.3⊕	1.3	2.6	2.1	1.8	100.0
Costa Rica	0.2	--	--	0.2	--	--	0.2	--	19.4	100.0
Cyprus	0.6	--	--	0.6	9.1°	0.5+	10.2	22.5	1.4	100.0
Dahomey	--	--	--	--	--	--	--	10.7	--	100.0
Denmark	--	0.1	1.1<	1.2	0.9	0.2+	2.3	23.7	0.5	100.0
Dominican Republic	2.5	1.0	0.5	4.0	13.1°	1.0+	18.2	10.1	--	100.0
Ecuador	9.0	7.4	--	16.4	--	0.5	16.9	--	1.1	100.0
El Salvador	--	--	--	--	5.4°	--	5.4	6.8	4.9	100.0
Ethiopia	--	--	--	--	1.0⊕	0.3+	1.3	2.0	0.7	100.0
Finland	0.1	1.6	--	1.8	2.7	0.8+	5.3	11.4	1.0	100.0
France	0.1	6.6	3.5Δ	10.2	3.3	1.3+	14.7	5.9-	--	100.0
Germany	1.3	2.3	--	3.6	1.7	0.5+	5.9	11.7-	0.3	100.0
Ghana	1.3	--	0.3<	1.7	0.3	1.2+	3.1	6.3	10.6	100.0
Greece	--	--	1.5	1.5	--	--	1.5	15.4	3.4	100.0

Table C:2 (continued). Selected Countries: Relative Importance of Selective Taxes on Goods, Services, and Motor Vehicles, 1969-71

In per cent of total receipts

	Transportation, travel	Insurance, banking	Miscellaneous services	Total selective taxes on services	Gambling, sweepstakes, lotteries	Entertainment	Total selective taxes on services, gambling, and entertainment	Motor vehicle taxes	Non-classified selective taxes	Total selective taxes on goods, services, and motor vehicles
Guatemala	--	--	--	--	--	--	--	7.2	5.8	100.0
Honduras	--	--	--	--	--	--	--	7.0	6.2	100.0
India	2.9	--	2.7Δ	5.6	0.5°	2.4	8.4	7.8±	1.3	100.0
Indonesia	--	--	--	--	--	--	--	--	--	100.0
Iran	5.0	--	--	5.0	--	--	5.0	8.8—	--	100.0
Ireland	--	0.3	--	0.3	1.6	0.1+	2.1	8.2+	--	100.0
Israel	7.7	--	--	7.7	--	0.9	8.6	11.1	--	100.0
Italy	0.4	2.0	2.1Δ	4.5	3.1	1.3+	8.9	5.7	6.7	100.0
Ivory Coast	--	--	--	--	--	0.9	0.9	6.1	--	100.0
Jamaica	1.6	--	0.8<	2.5	5.0°	2.8+	10.3	9.9+	3.9	100.0
Japan	--	--	8.1	8.1	--	1.6+	9.7	17.3—	2.2	100.0
Kenya	--	--	--	--	--	0.3	0.3	5.5	--	100.0
Korea	9.2	--	4.6Δ	13.8	0.2	6.4+	20.4	6.3±	0.4	100.0
Lebanon	--	--	--	--	0.6	--	0.6	15.5	--	100.0
Liberia	0.9	--	--	0.9	--	1.0	1.9	18.9	10.2	100.0
Malagasy Republic	--	--	--	--	--	--	--	--	--	
Malaysia	--	--	--	--	--	--	--	0.5	2.7	100.0
Mali	--	--	--	--	--	--	--	27.3	--	100.0
Mauritania	--	--	--	--	--	--	--	2.5	41.5	100.0
Mauritius	--	--	--	--	4.7	--	4.7	11.0	0.2	100.0
Mexico	5.4	2.3	15.7Δ	23.5	3.8	--	27.3	8.9+	15.1	100.0
Morocco	--	--	--	--	--	--	--	2.7	9.6	100.0
Nepal	0.8	--	2.8Δ	3.6	--	3.7	7.3	1.3	6.0	100.0
Netherlands	--	0.2	--	0.2	0.2	0.9+	1.3	24.6—	--	100.0
New Zealand	--	--	--	--	6.6	--	6.6	--	--	100.0
Nicaragua	0.8	--	--	0.8	--	0.8	1.6	3.8+	15.2	100.0
Niger	--	--	--	--	--	--	--	2.9	12.2	100.0
Nigeria	--	--	--	--	--	--	--	--	57.5	100.0
Norway	--	--	2.9Δ	2.9	0.3	--	3.1	22.0—	11.1	100.0
Pakistan	--	0.2	0.3<	0.5	--	--	0.5	4.5+	--	100.0

Table 6.2 (continued). Selected countries

In per cent of total receipts

	Transportation, travel	Insurance, banking	Miscellaneous services	Total selective taxes on services	Gambling, sweepstakes, lotteries	Entertainment	Total selective taxes on services, gambling, and entertainment	Motor vehicle taxes	Non-classified selective taxes	Total selective taxes on goods, services, and motor vehicles
Panama	--	--	--	--	42.6°	--	42.6	--	--	100.0
Paraguay	--	--	--	--	--	--	--	--	10.7	100.0
Peru	--	4.2	--	4.2	--	--	4.2	--	31.5	100.0
Philippines	--	--	--	--	--	3.7	3.7	5.4	--	100.0
Portugal	1.6	1.1	10.6	13.4	--	2.4†	15.8	1.1	37.2	100.0
Senegal	--	--	--	--	0.9°	--	0.9	3.1	7.7	100.0
Sierra Leone	--	--	--	--	0.3°	0.6†	0.9	5.3	0.1	100.0
Singapore	--	--	5.9Δ	5.9	3.4	3.7	13.0	19.5	3.7	100.0
Somalia	--	0.4	--	0.4	--	1.5	1.9	1.9	--	100.0
South Africa	--	--	--	--	--	--	--	11.3-	--	100.0
Sri Lanka	--	--	--	--	2.4°	--	2.4	2.9	--	100.0
Sweden	--	--	15.5Δ	15.5	3.3	--	18.8	16.2-	--	100.0
Switzerland	--	--	4.3	4.3	0.1	1.6†	6.0	16.0	8.0	100.0
Syrian Arab Republic	--	--	3.4	3.4	--	--	3.4	15.0	--	100.0
Tanzania	--	--	0.9	0.9	0.2	1.2	2.2	10.0	--	100.0
Thailand	--	--	--	--	8.6°	2.0	10.6	5.0	0.8	100.0
Trinidad and Tobago	--	--	--	--	5.6°	1.5†	7.1	23.0	27.5	100.0
Tunisia	5.6	15.5	1.2	22.2	0.1	--	22.4	2.6	--	100.0
Turkey	--	--	--	--	--	--	--	--	3.6	100.0
Uganda	--	--	1.2<	1.2	0.1	0.5†	1.9	6.4	--	100.0
United Kingdom	--	--	--	--	3.2	--	3.2	11.2	0.4	100.0
United States	15.4	3.4	8.6Δ	27.4	1.6	0.6†	29.7	11.0†	5.6	100.0
Upper Volta	--	--	--	--	--	--	--	--	5.2	100.0
Uruguay	--	13.8	1.3	15.0	9.9°	--	24.9	2.2-	--	100.0
Venezuela	2.3	--	--	2.3	--	--	2.3	4.4	--	100.0
Zaire	--	--	--	--	--	--	--	5.4	4.0	100.0
Zambia	--	--	--	--	--	--	--	7.5	--	100.0

Table C:2 (concluded). Selected Countries: Relative Importance of Selective Taxes on Goods, Services, and Motor Vehicles, 1969-71

In per cent of total receipts

Meaning of symbols:

*   Includes revenue (excises and profits) from fiscal monopolies. In addition to fiscal monopolies of tobacco products, alcoholic beverages, and sugar indicated in the table, data include receipts from the following other monopolies:

    - matches (included under "tobacco products"): France, Germany, Italy, Nicaragua, Portugal, Venezuela;

    - salt (included under "other foods and nonalcoholic beverages"): Austria, Cyprus, Italy, Syria.

≈   Not including revenues collected on traditional excise goods in the form of import duties, and in addition in francophone countries revenues collected on such goods in the form of sales taxes.

╆   Exclusively or mainly revenues from excises on textiles.

‹   Exclusively or mainly revenues from excises on cement.

∆   Exclusively or mainly revenues from selective taxes on public utility services of electricity and gas.

∨   Exclusively or mainly revenues from hotel and restaurant duties.

○   Including national lottery profits.

†   Including receipts from hunting, fishing, and dog licenses.

＋   Including revenues from excises on tires.

—   Including revenues from excises on cars.

Notes:

1/ Taxation of traditional excise goods subsumed by sales tax.
2/ Profits of Tobacco and Wine Monopoly allocated as follows: tobacco products: 60 per cent, alcoholic beverages 40 per cent.
3/ Composition of excise revenues estimated on the basis of breakdown available for earlier years.
4/ Estimate of purchase tax on alcoholic beverages.
5/ Including excises on sugar and tea.
6/ Including excises on biri and narcotics.
7/ Including various taxes on motor vehicles.
8/ Based on provisional actuals for fiscal year 1972-73.
9/ Including excises on soft drinks.
10/ Including excises on sugar and essences.
11/ Including minor excises on gunpowder and playing cards.
12/ Including minor excises on alcoholic beverages, perfumery, tires.

Table C:3. Years and Levels of Government Covered

Country	Fiscal Years	Levels Covered	Country	Fiscal Years	Levels Covered
Argentina	1969–70	A	Mexico	1968–70	A
Australia	1969–71	A	Morocco	1969–71	C
Austria	1969–71	A	Nepal	1972	C
Barbados	1970–71	C	Netherlands	1969–71	A
Belgium	1969–71	A	New Zealand	1970–72	C
Bolivia	1967–69	C	Nicaragua	1969–71	C
Brazil	1969–71	A	Niger	1969–71	C
Canada	1970–72	A	Nigeria	1972	C
Chad	1969	C	Norway	1969–71	A
Chile	1968–70	C	Pakistan	1972–73	A
China	1969–71	A	Panama	1969–71	C
Colombia	1969–71	A	Paraguay	1969–71	C
Costa Rica	1969–71	A	Peru	1969–71	C
Cyprus	1969–71	A	Philippines	1970–71	A
Dahomey	1969–71	C	Portugal	1969–71	A
Denmark	1970–71	A	Senegal	1969–71	C
Dominican Rep.	1969–71	C	Sierra Leone	1971–72	C
Ecuador	1972	C	Singapore	1970–72	A
El Salvador	1969–71	C	Somalia	1969–71	C
Ethiopia	1969–71	C	South Africa	1970–72	C
Finland	1969–71	A	Sri Lanka	1969–71	C
France	1969–71	A	Sweden	1969–71	A
Germany	1969–71	A	Switzerland	1969–71	A
Ghana	1969–71	C	Syrian Arab Rep.	1969–71	C
Greece	1969–71	A	Tanzania	1969–71	C
Guatemala	1969–71	C	Thailand	1969–71	C
Honduras	1969–71	C	Trinidad & Tobago	1969–71	C
India	1970–72	A	Tunisia	1969–71	A
Indonesia	1970–72	C	Turkey	1969–71	C
Iran	1970–71	C	Uganda	1969–71	C
Ireland	1970–72	A	United Kingdom	1970–72	A
Israel	1969–71	C	United States	1969–71	A
Italy	1969–71	A	Upper Volta	1968–70	C
Ivory Coast	1967–69	C	Uruguay	1969–71	C
Jamaica	1971–72	C	Venezuela	1969–71	A
Japan	1969–71	A	Zaïre	1969–71	C
Kenya	1969–71	C	Zambia	1969–71	A
Korea	1969–70	A			
Lebanon	1969–71	C			
Liberia	1970–72	C			
Malagasy Rep.	1969–71	C			
Malaysia	1969–71	C			
Mali	1969–71	A			
Mauritania	1969–71	C			
Mauritius	1969–71	C			

A = all levels.
C = central government; includes also, in some cases, collections on behalf of
        local governments.

NOTES

CHAPTER 1

[1]According to *Webster's Third New International Dictionary*, the word "excise" derives from the Middle Dutch *excijs* which is probably a modification of the Old French *assise*: session, settlement, assessment. For an historic account of excise taxation in Europe, see Günter Schmölders, "Das Verbrauch- und Aufwandsteuersystem," vol. 2, pp. 652–59.

[2]From a reference made by J. van der Poel, who surveys the development of excise taxation in the Netherlands in "De Evolutie der Accijnzen"; the quotation is from p. 1012.

[3]As set forth for instance in Fritz Neumark, *Grundsätze gerechter und ökonomisch rationaler Steuerpolitik*, who distinguishes: (a) budgetary principles; (b) ethical-social policy; (c) impact of tax policy on the private sector; and (d) legal and technical principles of taxation. For an overview of tax principles and theories see also H. J. Hofstra, *Inleiding tot het Nederlands belastingrecht*, chap. 2.

[4]Ferdinand Lassalle, *Die indirekte Steuer und die Lage der arbeitenden Klassen*. The account in this paragraph is adapted from Fritz Neumark, "Lasalles Steuer-Streitschrift, 1863–1963."

[5]The salt excise has always been considered a most inequitable form of taxation and viewed as representing a visible sign of oppression by the imperious overlord. In France, the *gabelle* contributed to the passions of the French revolution. The Indian nationalists used the salt duty as a weapon to arouse hostility against British domination, and Gandhi chose its abolition to spearhead the noncooperation movement. In China it became despised at the turn of the century because foreign governments used it to ensure the payment of principal and interest on loans by their nationals to the Chinese Government.

[6]Schmölders, "Das Verbrauch- und Aufwandsteuersystem," p. 655, who cites J. G. L. Leib, *Wie ein Regent Land and Leut verbessern und sich dadurch in Macht und Ansehen setzen könne* (published in 1705).

[7]James M. Buchanan and Francesco Forte, "Fiscal Choice Through Time: A Case for Indirect Taxation"; also James M. Buchanan, *Public Finance in Democratic Process*, chap. 16.

[8]The optional character of excises, their convenience to the taxpayer, and low administrative costs, were often stressed by early proponents of this form of taxation. For an interesting account of some Anglo-Saxon representatives of this point of view, see Harold M. Groves, *Tax Philosophers*, pt. 2.

[9]Adam Smith, *The Wealth of Nations*, vol. 2, p. 351.

[10]The minimization-of-interference criterion is mentioned in Neumark, *Gründsatze gerechter und ökonomisch rationaler Steuerpolitik*, pp. 256–59. Elsewhere in the professional literature it appears habitually neglected, although at one time it was one of the established principles of a good tax; see, for instance, Joseph A. Schumpeter, *History of Economic Analysis*, p. 404.

[11]Recently this point has been emphasized again by Richard M. Bird, "Optimal Tax Policy for a Developing Country: The Case of Colombia," pp. 49–51.

[12]For differences on the role of the public sector under conditions of socialism or capitalism, see Richard A. Musgrave, *Fiscal Systems*, chap. 1.

CHAPTER 2

[1]For a brief overview and evaluation of taxes on goods and services, see John F. Due, "Sales and Excise Taxes."

[2]"The only essential thing about a scheme of revenue classification is that it should be logical, appropriate to the subject matter and reasonably realistic." Harley L. Lutz, "Revenues, Public," p. 362.

[3]See International Monetary Fund (IMF), *A Manual on Government Finance Statistics*, Draft, pp. 166–68; and Organisation for Economic Co-operation and Development (OECD), *Revenue Statistics of OECD Member Countries, 1965–1973*, pp. 34–38; and pp. 46–47 for a comparison of tax classification systems used by other international organizations. Taxes on goods and services are also referred to as production, purchase and transaction taxes or, more broadly, as consumption taxes, on the assumption that they are borne in relation to consumption expenditures. They are also called expenditure or spending taxes in European tax literature, although in Anglo-Saxon works the last two terms are usually reserved for a direct tax on consumption expenditures collected from individuals on the basis of returns, rather than for the indirect type of "consumption" tax surveyed in this study.

[4]For an interesting discussion see Harley L. Lutz, *Public Finance*, pp. 422–23. The United States Supreme Court upheld the corporation tax introduced in 1909, arguing that it was not direct, but was an excise on the privilege of doing business as a corporation (Flint v. Stone Tracy Company; 220 U.S. 107).

[5]James Coffield, *A Popular History of Taxation*, pp. 74–78.

[6]A wide definition is also used by John F. Due, *Indirect Taxation in Developing Economies: The Role and Structure of Customs Duties, Excises, and Sales Taxes*, chap. 3; and A. R. Prest, *Public Finance in Underdeveloped Countries*, p. 73. Attention is also drawn to the definition of excise in *Webster's Third New International Dictionary* which reads: "a obs: DUTY, TOLL, TAX b: an internal tax, duty, or impost levied upon the manufacture, sale, or consumption of a commodity within a country and usu. forming an indirect tax that falls on the ultimate consumer c: any of various duties or fees levied on producers of excisable commodities d: any of various taxes upon privileges (as of engaging in a particular trade or sport, transferring property, or engaging in business in a corporate capacity) that are often assessed in the form of a license or other fee."

[7]The OECD includes customs and import duties, and export and exchange taxes (these are generally minor levies in its member countries), under selective taxes on goods and services. The IMF, on the other hand, maintains a separate category—taxes on international trade—for these taxes.

[8]This should be distinguished from the practice in some countries (for example, Tanzania, Uganda, and Guyana) of incorporating the Brussels Tariff Nomenclature (BTN) in the sales tax rate structure. This is a matter of easy product identification (much of the revenue is collected at the import stage) rather than an issue affecting the charge to tax. In Malaysia and Barbados the BTN terminology is used in enumerating the sales tax exemptions.

[9]The coverage of the Australian sales tax is aptly characterized in *Taxation Review Committee, Full Report, 31 January, 1975*, p. 514: "The remaining sales tax is scattered in small packets over other categories of consumption expenditure and constitutes a small but uneven levy upon them, too modest to deserve much consideration. Outside the area of motoring, drink and tobacco, taxes on goods and services at the Federal level can be dismissed as a trivial relic."

[10]For two thorough exercises in taxonomy along these lines, see Günter Schmölders, "Das Verbrauch- und Aufwandsteuersystem," pp. 636–52; and J. van der Poel, *Over Accijnzen*. In Germany, classification issues receive an added impetus because excises are constitutionally assigned to the Federal Government. This is also the case in India where it may have contributed to the expansion of the excise system.

[11]See John F. Due, "The Evolution of Sales Taxation, 1915–1972."

[12]For a vigorous defense compare Knut Wicksell, "A New Principle of Just Taxation," p. 89: "It would seem to be a blatant injustice if someone should be forced to contribute toward the cost of some activity which does not further his interests or may even be diametrically opposed to them."

[13]For the German example see Karl Bräuer, "Aufwandsteuern," pp. 13–14. The Pakistan experience is dealt with in chap. 6.

[14]See Roy Blough, *The Federal Taxing Process*, p. 341. Blough adds nonessentiality as another criterion, but this is not entirely consistent with the other characteristics. For a similar listing of requirements see Gerald Heidinger, *Gedanken zur Steuerreform in Österreich*, pp. 62–63.

[15]Examples are Brazil (petroleum products), Ireland (tobacco), Portugal (liquor), Singapore, Switzerland, and Turkey (petroleum products), and the United Kingdom (petroleum products).

[16]Some French-speaking African countries have so-called export sales tax rates, but it would be more appropriate to consider these as export duties. Zaïre collects sales taxes on exports in addition to regular export duties.

[17]Excises collected through affixing stamps on specified products are not considered stamp duties in this study; this is merely a collection technique not affecting the nature of the excise.

[18]For a clear distinction between taxes on the one hand, and fees and charges on the other, see Edwin R. A. Seligman, *Essays in Taxation*, pp. 406–13.

[19]For instance, arack licenses in Sri Lanka. For an opinion that license taxes can be called excises, see Karl Bräuer, "Excise," p. 669.

[20]See OECD, *Border Tax Adjustments and Tax Structures in OECD Member Countries*, p. 18. The classification issue is briefly mentioned by Due, *Indirect Taxation in Developing Economies*, p. 60; for a particular country, Germany, see Günter Schmölders, "Das Verbrauch- und Aufwandsteuersystem," p. 664.

[21]A. C. Pigou, *A Study in Public Finance*, p. 46, as quoted in N. Shilling, *Excise Taxation of Monopoly*, p. 9; see also Shilling, pp. 13–15, for an illuminating graphical exposition of possible excise rate schedules.

[22]Katrine W. Saito, "Petroleum Taxes: How High and Why?" p. 20.

[23]The production tax is not identified as a separate form of sales taxation in other studies. Production taxes can also be described as turnover taxes with anticascading features that, however, are not as systematic and comprehensive in design as those of manufacturers taxes. Elsewhere, this group may be referred to as manufacturers taxes, but it seems better to reserve that designation for the pure single-stage variant.

[24]The French production tax also served as the model for those manufacturers taxes in francophone Africa that use the subtraction technique to eliminate cascade effects, but in this book the connotation "production tax" is reserved for multistage taxes with anticascading features. For a treatment of the sales taxes that replicate the French production tax, see John R. Hill, "Sales Taxation in Francophone Africa."

[25]This question relates to the distinction between exemptions by use and exemptions by type of good. Exemptions by type of good (capital goods) are much easier to administer than exemptions by use (production or consumption), although invariably less closely related to the objective of freeing producer goods from taxation.

[26]This is the consumption type of value-added tax. Under the income type, a deduction for tax on capital goods is allowed on a depreciation basis, and under the product form no deduction at all is given. Furthermore, in giving credit, all value-added taxes use the invoice method of computation, but the same effect may be achieved if value added is ascertained by subtracting from sales the amounts paid for producer goods (subtraction form), or by adding

the components of value added: wages, profits, interest (addition form). For an exposition, see Alan A. Tait, *Value-added Tax*, pp. 2–5.

[27]Value-added taxes should be distinguished from manufacturers taxes operating under the tax credit principle. Manufacturers taxes are not levied on trading activities *per se* and the tax credit variant, like the suspension or subtraction techniques, is an attempt to eliminate cumulative effects. Under value-added taxes, on the other hand, the tax credit principle, or any other method to reach the same effect, is a *conditio sine qua non* in design. Logically, a value-added tax is not concerned with defining manufacturing; in practice this form of sales taxation also extends through the last wholesale stage if not the retail stage. See Due, *Indirect Taxation in Developing Economies*, p. 126, fn. 16. For these reasons the *taxes sur la valeur ajoutée* in Algeria, Ivory Coast, Malagasy Republic, Morocco, Senegal, and Tunisia that are primarily limited to the manufacturing sector, are designated manufacturers taxes using the tax credit principle. A somewhat different approach is followed by George E. Lent, Milka Casanegra, and Michèle Guérard, "The Value-Added Tax in Developing Countries."

[28]All tax rates are expressed as a percentage of the tax-exclusive value of taxable sales, which is the practice in sixty out of eighty-three countries with sales taxes; this is also called the effective rate. Tax-inclusive rates may also be referred to as nominal rates.

[29]Generally these comprise foods, medicines, fuel, books, newspapers, footwear, soap, and certain clothing items.

[30]For a more detailed treatment see Sijbren Cnossen, "Sales Tax and Excise Systems of the World," in particular pp. 193–207.

[31]The Central African Customs and Economic Union (UDEAC) was established in 1964 by Cameroon, Central African Republic, the Congo, and Gabon. (Chad was also a signatory to the agreement, but subsequently left the union.) Under the agreement, the proceeds of the *taxe unique* are allocated among member countries according to their respective share in the consumption of taxable products. See IMF, *Surveys of African Economies*, vol. 1: Cameroon, Central African Republic, Chad, Congo (Brazzaville), and Gabon, chap. 2.

[32]For a description and evaluation, see P. D. Ojha and George E. Lent, "Sales Taxes in Countries of the Far East."

[33]This agreement led, among others, to the imposition of an excise type consumption tax in Barbados, and the modification and extension of consumption and purchase taxes in Jamaica, and Trinidad and Tobago.

[34]See also John F. Due, "Alternative Forms of Sales Taxation for a Developing Country," *Journal of Development Studies*, p. 266.

CHAPTER 3

[1]See Table 3 in Appendix C for exceptions. In most cases where data for local government revenue are not available, the contribution to total tax revenue may be safely assumed to amount to less than 10 per cent, so that its exclusion does not affect the results seriously. On the other hand, it should be borne in mind that local government taxes are often selective.

[2]Generally, excisable goods are not included in the sales tax base, except in continental European and francophone African countries. For European countries sales tax elements could usually be disaggregated, but this was not possible for most French-speaking African countries. An added difficulty in the case of the latter, as well as for South American countries, is that many earmark the whole or part of some excises for specified purposes; so often such receipts do not pass through the government's ordinary budget, but are administered separately.

[3]In most cases import duty receipts are not very important on goods subject to traditional excises, but sometimes fairly substantial duties are collected on unmanufactured tobacco and on those alcoholic beverages such as whisky, brandy, cordials, and liqueurs that, unlike beer, are not produced locally. However, a breakdown of import duty collections on traditional excise goods could generally be obtained.

[4]For fifty-three countries, only 13 per cent of intercountry variation in the excise share is explained when the excise share is regressed against per capita income in hundreds of U.S. dollars (Y_p), but $\bar{R}^2$ rises to 22 per cent when a dummy variable (D) is added that takes a value of one for countries with a religious taboo on alcohol consumption and zero otherwise. The best fit is obtained when the traditional excise share ($T_{tr.ex}/T$) is taken as the dependent variable and regressed on Y_p and D. The equation is (figures in brackets are t-ratios):

$$T_{tr.ex}/T = \underset{(20.04)}{22.55} - \underset{(4.75)}{0.002821\,Y_p} - \underset{(2.87)}{0.05594D};\ \bar{R}^2 = 0.300$$

[5]The shares of total excises and traditional excises, taken separately, are indeed negatively related to the mining share (N_y) and Y_p. For the excise share the level of the explained variance is 21 per cent. For the share of traditional excises the equation is:

$$T_{tr.ex}/T = \underset{(20.13)}{22.27} - \underset{(4.35)}{0.00249\,Y_p} - \underset{(2.64)}{0.4528\,N_y};\ \bar{R}^{-2} = 0.285$$

[6]See Appendix C, Table 1. As expected, the total share of indirect taxes shows less variation between countries than the share of each indirect tax taken separately. However, of all indirect taxes, excises show the most stable

contribution. On the other hand, the shares of export taxes, sales taxes, and import duties—in that order—vary widely from country to country.

[7]The low-income countries are Brazil and the Philippines. In the former, the contribution of the sales tax is exceptionally high and in the latter that of excises exceptionally low. The sales tax share is also higher in the Malagasy Republic, Morocco, Senegal, and Tunisia, but in these countries, which all belong to the low-income category, part of the sales tax is collected on traditional excise goods.

[8]Author's calculations for francophone countries, Burma, Pakistan, and Indonesia; for other countries, see Due, "Alternative Forms of Sales Taxation," p. 266; and Ohja and Lent, "Sales Taxes in Countries of the Far East," p. 558. Obviously, not the full amount of sales tax collections on imports in these countries is in the nature of a supplementary import duty.

[9]For an analysis of Indonesia's sales tax collections, see Sijbren Cnossen, *The Indonesian Sales Tax*, pp. 11–17.

[10]Perhaps the clearest example of this "demonstration effect" of sales taxes is in francophone Africa, where the evolution of the French sales tax in the post-war period can be readily traced. See Hill, "Sales Taxation in Francophone Africa."

[11]The buoyancy coefficient and the various built-in elasticities are usually measured from a simple double logarithmic function: $\log T = \log a + b \log Y$, in which T stands for actual (un)adjusted tax collections and Y for gross national product, the legal base of a tax or some proxy thereof; (b) is then the buoyancy or elasticity coefficient. An important assumption in using this function is that the coefficient is constant with respect to the range of income or the base that are considered.

Separating automatic and discretionary revenue changes is often difficult. Usually a method developed by A. R. Prest is employed, which first adjusts tax receipts by subtracting from (or adding to) the actual yield for each year the estimated amount attributable to the discretionary change in that year, and then excludes the continuing impact of each discretionary change on future years, assuming that this change does not affect the elasticity of the tax. See A. R. Prest, "The Sensitivity of the Yield of Personal Income Tax in the United Kingdom"; also R. J. Chelliah and S. K. Chand, "A Note on Techniques of Adjusting Tax Revenue Series for Discretionary Changes," unpublished.

$$[12]\frac{dT'}{dY} \cdot \frac{Y}{T'} = \frac{dT'}{dB} \cdot \frac{B}{T'} \times \frac{dB'}{dY} \cdot \frac{Y}{B}$$

in which T' is tax collections adjusted for discretionary changes and B the tax base or its proxy.

[13]Raja J. Chelliah, "Trends in Taxation in Developing Countries," pp. 265 and 273; as well as the updating in Raja J. Chelliah, Hessel J. Baas, and Margaret J. Kelly, "Tax Ratios and Tax Effort in Developing Countries, 1969–71." The latter article notes a marginal decline in the share of indirect taxes since 1966–68.

[14]See *Revenue Statistics of OECD Member Countries 1965–73*, Tables 20 and 21, pp. 82–83.

[15]Sales and income tax liabilities could of course be indexed, but there is a presumption that physical controls as exercised under excises would still be more effective in ensuring tax payment. For experience on the use of a combination of interest charges and penalties to adjust for depreciated tax liabilities, see T. Hirao and C. A. Aguirre, "Maintaining the Level of Income Tax Collections under Inflationary Conditions."

[16]For arguments along these lines, see Prest, *Public Finance in Underdeveloped Countries*, pp. 181–201.

[17]The remaining 11 per cent derives from: fuel oil, 5 per cent; lubricating oils, 2 per cent; asphalt and others, 4 per cent.

[18]Data limitations did not permit the inclusion in excise receipts of import duties on motor vehicles, spare parts, and tires for these and other countries.

[19]When wine production per capita (W_p) was added as an independent variable to Y_p and D in an attempt to explain the size of the alcohol excise share (T_{alc}/T), 39 per cent of intercountry variation in revenue was explained:

$$T_{alc}/T = \underset{(11.25)}{7.012} - \underset{(2.38)}{0.0007864Y_p} - \underset{(2.55)}{0.003561W_p} - \underset{(5.53)}{6.253D}; \bar{R}^2 = 0.390$$

When instead of wine, beer production was added, the level of the explained variance was also relatively high (34 per cent); however, the factor was statistically insignificant, although the coefficient had the expected sign. Similar exercises for tobacco and hydrocarbon oils were less successful. Production data were computed from United Nations, *Statistical Yearbook 1972*.

[20]There are sharp differences in consumption patterns of alcoholic beverages in Europe: while Germany consumed 145 liters of beer per head in 1972 and only 22 liters of wine, Italy drank 111 liters of wine per head in the same year and only 13 liters of beer. See "Europe is the World's Bar," Drink Survey, *The Economist*, December 29, 1973. Beer is easier to tax than wine as it is produced in large manufacturing units, while grapes are grown by many small, and usually well-organized, farmers; this may partly explain the difference in excise patterns.

CHAPTER 4

[1]It is difficult to justify progressivity in taxation on ability-to-pay grounds, but James M. Buchanan and Marilyn R. Flowers, in *The Public Finances*, p. 99, point out that it can possibly also be defended or explained on grounds of efficiency or of political coalition formation. Furthermore, it has been stated that greater income equality as an end in

itself is a sufficient justification for progressive taxation. See Harold M. Groves, "Toward a Social Theory of Progressive Taxation"; and Richard M. Bird, "Equity and Taxes in the Carter Report," who emphasizes that the redistributive role of tax systems is inherently small: "If the principal aim in redistributive policy is to 'level up,' to make the poor better off, the main role the tax system has to play is the limited and essentially negative one of not making them poorer."

[2]The classic reference is to Henry C. Simons, *Personal Income Taxation*, but for an up-to-date discussion see Richard Goode, *The Individual Income Tax*, chap. 2.

[3]Nicholas Kaldor, *An Expenditure Tax*, p. 53. More recently, a well known American teacher of tax law has supported this view in a carefully reasoned analysis. See William D. Andrews, "A Consumption-Type or Cash Flow Personal Income Tax," as well as the comment by Alvin C. Warren, Jr., "Fairness and a Consumption-Type or Cash Flow Personal Income Tax," and the reply by Andrews, "Fairness and the Personal Income Tax: A Reply to Professor Warren."

[4]Sometimes the principle appears to be more narrowly interpreted. For instance, at least until 1969, the Central Office of Information, in *The British System of Taxation* (London: Her Majesty's Stationery Office, 1969), p. 4, held that "taxes should be equitable as between one individual and another. That is, taxes should be universal, imposed without distinction of person between citizens similarly placed. This does not mean, for example, that a tax on whiskey is inequitable because nondrinkers do not pay it. But it does mean that all drinkers—the citizens "similarly placed"—should pay it." For an earlier reference to this quotation and a discussion, see Carl S. Shoup, "Tax Tension and the British Fiscal System," p. 22.

[5]Conceptually and terminologically incidence analysis has been greatly influenced by Richard A. Musgrave, *The Theory of Public Finance*, chaps. 10, 15, and 16; see also his: "On Incidence." In addition, see Horst Claus Recktenwald, *Tax Incidence and Income Redistribution*; and Charles E. McLure, Jr., "General Equilibrium Incidence Analysis: The Harberger model after ten years."

[6]The treatment is found in almost every textbook on public finance, but the most detailed is in John F. Due, *The Theory of Incidence of Sales Taxation*; a lucid description is given in Harold M. Groves and Robert L. Bish, *Financing Government*, pp. 37–77.

[7]More precisely the excise will be divided between the consumer and the producer (if the demand and supply slopes are taken with respect to the price axis) in the ratio of the elasticity of supply (E_s) to the elasticity of demand (E_d), or, if "t" is the excise and "dp" the rise in price, then $dp (t - dp) = E_s/E_d$, which transforms into $dp/t = E_s (E_s + E_d)$. This is known as the Dalton formula; see Hugh Dalton, *Principles of Public Finance*, pp. 48–58.

[8]For cases in which full forward shifting is not likely, see Due, *Indirect Taxation in Developing Economies*, pp. 2–3. Also Richard M. Bird, *Taxation and Development*, p. 110; and chap. 6 for a possible exception under monopoly conditions. For a careful statement of the conditions under which partial equilibrium analysis may be employed to ascertain the incidence of an excise, see Carl S. Shoup, *Public Finance*, pp. 9–10.

[9]Oswald Brownlee and George L. Perry, "The Effects of the 1965 Federal Excise Tax Reductions on Prices." See also P. O. Woodward and Harvey Siegelman, "Effects of the 1965 Federal Excise Tax Reduction Upon the Price of Automotive Replacement Parts."

[10]This was also the finding of an earlier study that analyzed the response of prices of electrical appliances to 1954 legislation that reduced the excise from 10 per cent to 5 per cent. See John F. Due, "The Effect of the 1954 Reduction in Federal Excise Taxes Upon the List Prices of Electrical Appliances—A Case Study." Due's conclusions were confirmed, although somewhat less emphatically, in a later study by Harry L. Johnson, "Tax Pyramiding and the Manufacturer's Excise Tax Reduction of 1954."

[11]Musgrave is the originator of the term "differential incidence" and the assumptions under which it is widely used, but he points out that the concept was first used by Knut Wicksell; see *The Theory of Public Finance*, p. 213, fn. 1. Ann F. Friedlaender and John F. Due hold that instead of "equal-yield," the assumption should be that the same aggregate real factor demand is maintained; see their "Tax Burden, Excess Burden, and Differential Incidence Revisited," pp. 320–22. Also Melvyn B. Kraus, "Tax Burden, Excess Burden, and Differential Incidence Revisited: Comment and Extensions;" and the further thoughts of Friedlaender and Due, "Tax Burden, Excess Burden, and Differential Incidence Revisited: Comment and Extensions—A Reply."

[12]For a brief and lucid summation of the hypothesis see Richard A. Musgrave, "Estimating the Distribution of the Tax Burden," pp. 43–46. For the general equilibrium presentation of excise incidence see Charles E. McLure, Jr. and Wayne R. Thirsk, "A Simplified Exposition of the Harberger Model–I: Tax Incidence," as well as "The Harberger Model: Reply," in response to the critique by Benjamin Bridges, Jr., "The Harberger Incidence Model: A Comment." For an account of the present state of the art on tax incidence, see George F. Break, "The Incidence and Economic Effects of Taxation," pp. 122–79.

[13]It will be noted that this use of the concept "effective rate" differs from that employed in chap. 2, where it refers to the excise to (retail) price ratio. Since the terminology in both cases is widely accepted and the meaning clear in the context, no alternative formulation is suggested.

[14]But see Richard M. Bird and Luc Henry De Wulf, "Taxation and Income Distribution in Latin America: A Critical Review of Empirical Studies"; and Luc De Wulf, "Fiscal Incidence Studies in Developing Countries: Survey and Critique."

[15]These and other problems of household budget surveys are dealt with in greater detail in S. J. Prais and H. S. Houthakker, *The Analysis of Family Budgets*.

[16]Not shown in Table 4:1 because the relevant study did not lend itself to tabular summary. See Marian Krzyzaniak and Süleyman Özmucur, "The Distribution of Income and the Short-Run Burden of Taxes in Turkey, 1968," pp. 83, 89. Turkish banking and insurance taxes are also progressive.

[17]Richard C. Webb, *Income Distribution and Government Policy in Peru.*

[18]See Charles E. McLure, Jr., "Taxation and the Urban Poor in Developing Countries."

[19]For a compact review of incidence studies in industrial countries (and the economic effects of various taxes), see Carl S. Shoup, "Quantitative Research in Taxation and Government Expenditures."

[20]Lotteries may be an exception, however. For instance, Michael H. Spiro, "On the Tax Incidence of the Pennsylvania Lottery," p. 57, found that "the lottery tax is regressive for most of the income range except for persons in the income category below \$4,000 per year."

[21]Eric Biørn, "The Distributive Effects of Indirect Taxation: An Econometric Model and Empirical Results Based on Norwegian Data," p. 7.

[22]Thomas W. Calmus, "The Burden of Federal Excise Taxes by Income Classes."

[23]They may become more relevant if, as has been suggested, the dispersion around the average increases as the average income of the income classes rises; see Vito Tanzi, "Redistributing Income through the Budget in Latin America," p. 13.

[24]John F. Due, *Government Finance*, pp. 312-13.

[25]For an explicit treatment of the role of "in-kind consumption" in analyzing the distribution of tax burdens and a view on the changing role of tax policy, see Yukon Huang, "Distribution of the Tax Burden in Tanzania."

[26]For a careful statement on this see Fuat M. Andic and Suphan Andic, *Government Finance and Planned Development: Fiscal Surveys of Surinam and the Netherlands Antilles*, p. 137.

[27]For an appraisal of expenditure incidence studies, see Luc De Wulf, "Do Public Expenditures Reduce Inequality?" For industrial countries it has long been accepted that the expenditure side of the budget is probably the supreme equalizer of the fiscal system. For a recent study see Thomas Franzén, Kerstin Lövgren and Irma Rosenberg. "Redistributional Effects of Taxes and Public Expenditures in Sweden."

[28]It might be pointed out that this is obviously also true when the comparison is between countries at different stages of economic development. For instance, while 20 per cent of total consumption expenditure is spent on food in the United States, the corresponding percentage in Togo is 66 per cent. See Food and Agriculture Organization of the United Nations (FAO), *Income Elasticities of Demand for Agricultural Products*, p. 94.

[29]For a subjective treatment of luxury goods and related excises see Fritz Marbach, *Luxus und Luxussteuer.*

[30]Although the criterion can be formulated more objectively, as in the Philippines where "commodities found in the possession of at least one half of the total number of families can be considered truly essential." See Republic of the Philippines, Joint Legislative-Executive Tax Commission, *12th Annual Report 1970*, p. 43.

[31]L. M. Goreux, *Income Elasticity of the Demand for Food*, p. 3.

[32]For a formulation along these lines, see Malcolm Gillis, "Objectives and Means of Indirect Tax Reform," pp. 569-70, fn. 5.

[33]In addition to a high income elasticity to serve equity purposes and a low price elasticity of demand to safeguard revenue, a low elasticity of supply would be desirable so as to interfere least with resource allocation. The number of goods that would simultaneously satisfy all these requirements is extremely small. Paintings by Dutch masters—Rembrandt, Vermeer, Van Gogh, to name a few—would be examples. The idea is from Alek A. Rozental, "Selective Excises and the Federal Tax Structure," pp. 431-32.

[34]For a rigorous analysis of the possible regressive impact of excises on tobacco products and alcoholic beverages based on data on income or expenditure elasticities and price elasticities, see Charles E. McLure, Jr. and Wayne R. Thirsk, "The Inequity of Taxing Iniquity: A Plea for Reduced Sumptuary Taxes in Developing Countries."

[35]For four countries in Table 4:2 the price elasticities of demand for tobacco products (based on the period 1950-59) are: Italy (-0.82), United Kingdom (-0.04), France (-0.54), and Sweden (-0.41). See Anna P. Koutsoyannis, "Demand Functions for Tobacco," p. 20.

[36]Of course, the tobacco excise itself may also be an important determinant of the expenditure elasticity. Thus, in two countries in Table 4:2—Sri Lanka and Sweden—the excise is so high that tobacco products have become absolute luxuries with expenditure elasticities exceeding unity.

[37]For an interesting, if somewhat outdated, account of tobacco taxation in India, see Government of India, *Report of the Taxation Enquiry Commission 1953-54*, vol. 2, pp. 290-302.

[38]On this see Government of India, *Report of the Central Excise Reorganisation Committee*, p. 142.

[39]The literature on price elasticities is extremely scarce, but see George F. Break, "The Allocation and Excess Burden Effects of Excise and Sales Taxation," pp. 65-68.

[40]M. M. Metwally, "Household Expenditure Patterns: Hamilton, New Zealand," p. 81.

[41]FAO, *Income Elasticities of Demand for Agricultural Products*, pp. 165, 167.

[42]For a proposal along these lines see Arnold C. Harberger, "Issues of Tax Reform for Latin America," pp. 112-13.

[43]This seems to be the case in the small island communities of the East Caribbean, as noted in H.W.T. Pepper, "Transportation Taxes," pt. 1, p. 278. But a recent study of the United States concluded that an increase in the gasoline excise would probably not be regressive; see *A Study of the Quarterly Demand for Gasoline and Impacts of Alternative Gasoline Taxes*, prepared for the Environmental Protection Agency and the Council on Environmental Quality, p. IV. 34.

[44]For two studies that favor such excise systems see Milton Taylor, et. al., *Fiscal Survey of Colombia*, p. 220; and Bird, *Taxation and Development*, p. 111. For an earlier reference, also Hashemite Kingdom of Jordan, *Report of the Royal Fiscal Commission*, unpublished, p. 52.

⁴⁵For a summary see Fuat M. Andic and Arthur J. Mann, "Redesigning Puerto Rico's Tax System: An Overview," p. 188.

⁴⁶Puerto Rico has an intermediate excise system covering traditional excise goods, chewing gum, candies, matches, luxury goods, slot machines, cement, hotel rooms, entertainment and gambling levies, and various motor vehicle taxes, including excises on tires and tubes. See *What You Should Know About Taxes in Puerto Rico 1973*, pp. 24–39.

⁴⁷It is understandable, therefore, that the advisory council to the West German Minister of Finance came out in favor of retaining the excises on traditional excise goods, but of reducing or eliminating the smaller excises that were costly to administer anyway. See *Der Wissenschaftliche Beirat beim Bundesministerium der Finanzen: Entschlieszungen, Stellungnahmen und Gutachten von 1949 bis 1973*, p. 74; and for specific proposals to abolish the excises on sugar, lighting equipment, salt, matches, playing cards, and acetic acid, *Gutachten der Steuerreformkommission 1971*, chap. 10.

CHAPTER 5

¹For a summary of the present status of the welfare debate in the field of public finance with many references to excise taxation, see J. G. Head, "The Welfare Foundations of Public Finance Theory." The analyses of various authors discussed below can all be viewed as applications of the theory of optimal commodity taxation. For a recent survey of the literature, see David F. Bradford and Harvey S. Rosen, "The Optimal Taxation of Commodities and Income."

²The theorem is sometimes referred to as the Joseph-Hicks demonstration following the publication by M. F. W. Joseph, "The Excess Burden of Indirect Taxation;" and the treatment in J. R. Hicks, *Value and Capital*, pp. 330–33. But Buchanan and Forte in "Fiscal Choice Through Time," p. 144, fn. 1, ascribe the theorem to E. Barone, "Studi di economia finanziaria," *Giornale degli economisti* (1912), II, pp. 329–30 in notes. For a summing up of the discussions prior to 1954 see David Walker, "The Direct-Indirect Tax Problem: Fifteen Years of Controversy." Useful for its mathematical presentation is also Palle Schelde Andersen, *Direct Versus Indirect Taxes: A Survey*.

³For an excellent nontechnical exposition see Earl R. Rolph and George F. Break, *Public Finance*, pp. 298–300. For a more technical evaluation, see also Musgrave, *The Theory of Public Finance*, pp. 140–159; and the discussions by Robert L. Bishop, "The Effects of Specific and Ad Valorem Taxes," and Jesse S. Hixson and James B. Ramsey, "A Further Comment on the Effects of Excise Taxes."

⁴Of course, it had long been realized that income and sales taxes in practice exhibited important excise effects on account of their partial coverage and graduated rate structures. Furthermore, Rolph and Break pointed out that partial equilibrium analysis could not really be applied since the effect of an excise on the output of nontaxed goods should also be taken into account. See Earl R. Rolph and George F. Break, "The Welfare Aspects of Excise Taxes."

⁵I. M. D. Little, "Direct versus Indirect Taxes."

⁶Arnold C. Harberger, "Taxation, Resource Allocation, and Welfare"; see also his "The Measurement of Waste."

⁷See Richard A. Musgrave and Peggy B. Musgrave, *Public Finance in Theory and Practice*, p. 459, who point out that the figure may be too high, because it does not take into account the offsetting effects of automotive excises to the free provision of road services, nor the "demerit" elements in sumptuary excises.

⁸Milton Friedman, "The 'Welfare' Effects of an Income Tax and an Excise Tax."

⁹This is referred to as the Pigovian tradition in public finance. Although already analyzed by Marshall, in its present form the argument was first presented in A. C. Pigou, *The Economics of Welfare*, chap. 9. The theorem has led to a great deal of controversy, not so much as regards its theoretical merits as its relevance in the real world, because it is believed that the required excise (or subsidy) on a particular activity can rarely, if ever, be equated to the marginal social damage (benefit) that it generates. For a review see E. J. Mishan, "The Postwar Literature on Externalities: An Interpretative Essay." For a vigorous defense of the Pigovian tradition and the exposition of "a modified approach that recommends itself more for its promise of effectiveness, than its theoretical nicety," even in a world where firms "are neither pure competitors nor profit maximizers," see William J. Baumol, "On Taxation and the Control of Externalities"; the quotation is from pp. 307–08.

¹⁰A cogent formulation of the underlying theory is given in R. G. Lipsey and K. Lancaster, "The General Theory of Second Best"; the quotation is from p. 12.

¹¹For an interesting discussion of the relationship between excess burdens and substitutability, see J. G. Head and C. S. Shoup, "Excess Burden: The Corner Case"; and J. Gregory Ballentine and Charles E. McLure, Jr., "Excess Burden: The Corner Case in General Equilibrium."

¹²See A. B. Atkinson and J. E. Stiglitz, "The Structure of Indirect Taxation and Economic Efficiency;" the quotation is from p. 117. The theorem was first formulated by Frank Ramsey, "A Contribution to the Theory of Taxation."

¹³For the original demonstration of this point see W. J. Corlett and D. C. Hague, "Complementarity and the Excess Burden of Taxation."

¹⁴For an overview compare David Morawetz, "Employment Implications of Industrialisation in Developing Countries: A Survey." On p. 491, Morawetz points out that "a manufacturing sector employing 20% of the labour

force would need to increase employment by 15% per year merely to absorb the increment in a total work force growing at an annual rate of 3%." Several examples in this section are drawn from this article. For an excellent review of the literature, also Shankar N. Acharya, "Fiscal/Financial Intervention, Factor Prices and Factor Proportions: A Review of Issues."

[15]Figures are computed from Biro Pusat Statistik, *Statistik Indonesia,* and *Statistik Industri 1971. Kretek* cigarettes are also made on a small-scale industry basis.

[16]This important aspect is stressed, for instance, in United Nations, *Economic Survey of Asia and the Far East 1969,* pp. 7 and 41.

[17]See W. Arthur Lewis, *Development Planning: The Essentials of Economic Policy,* p. 60.

[18]For a recommendation along these lines, see International Labour Office, *Employment, Incomes and Equality: A Strategy for Increasing Productive Employment in Kenya,* pp. 274–75. In cases where skilled labor is in scarce supply, capital-intensive machine-paced or process-oriented operations may be appropriate, as pointed out by Albert O. Hirschman, *The Strategy of Economic Development,* pp. 151–52.

[19]Morawetz, "Employment Implications of Industrialisation in Developing Countries," p. 525.

[20]Other objectives are to promote the economic development of rural areas and to achieve a more equitable distribution of income. For a survey and critique see Walter R. Mahler, Jr., *Sales and Excise Taxation in India,* pp. 76–86; and *Report of the Central Excise Reorganisation Committee,* pp. 10–16.

[21]Mahler, *Sales and Excise Taxation in India,* p. 83. As a result of the much greater fragmentation of production units, the excise became so cumbersome to administer that the sector was completely exempted in 1963.

[22]The data in this list are based on Mahler, *Sales and Excise Taxation in India,* pp. 78–80.

[23]See *Report of the Central Excise Reorganisation Committee,* p. 61.

[24]For a brief summing up of the major policy issues and alternative forms of incentive taxation, see R. A. Musgrave, A. C. Harberger, and A. Kervyn, "Some Practical Suggestions."

[25]Or better, the provision of road services is excludable and permits rivalry in consumption; this is the opposite of what characterizes pure public goods to which the pricing mechanism cannot be applied. For conceptual differences see Richard A. Musgrave, "Provision for Social Goods." It may be noted that road services differ from other goods as regards specificity with respect to spatial and temporal location, the joint product nature of capacity and quality, the significant economies of scale in production, and government sale of services.

[26]But see John F. Due, "The Relevant Marginal Cost for Establishing Highway User Charges in Developing Economies," unpublished: "Since outlay on new highways is primarily determined by usage of existing roads, highway users are responsible for investment in new highways, and therefore long-run marginal cost is the appropriate basis for highway user charges. Use of the short-run marginal cost would result in excessive highway use and investment in highways (if demand is at all elastic and funds are available), and in constant fluctuations in highway charges if applied, as logic dictates, to each highway separately."

[27]For a comprehensive discussion of road user charges see A. A. Walters, *The Economics of Road User Charges;* and Anthony Churchill, *Road User Charges in Central America.*

[28]Churchill, *Road User Charges in Central America,* p. 66, estimates that passenger cars will consume gasoline in the ratio of 1.0:1.2:1.4 over paved-gravel-dirt roads, whereas the estimated variable maintenance cost of using these roads varies in the ratio of 1:11:33. It should be pointed out that these estimates are for "average" vehicles; the effect of differences in weight and fuel consumption of various types of vehicles is not taken into account.

[29]Walters, *The Economics of Road User Charges,* p. 198, gives as a rule of thumb that if traffic on paved roads is over 75 per cent of total traffic, it is wise to base the vehicle mile tax on the paved highway cost, but if paved roads are so scarce that less than 40 per cent of all traffic is found on them, then vehicle mile taxes should be based on the costs of nonpaved highways.

[30]Roger S. Smith, "Highway Pricing and Motor Vehicle Taxation in Developing Countries: Theory and Practice," p. 465.

[31]Based on figures computed by J. De Weille in *Quantification of Road User Savings,* Churchill, in *Road User Charges in Central America,* p. 72, states that the ratio of tire wear between paved, gravel and earth roads amounts to about 1.0:2.0:3.5 for cars and 1.0:2.0:4.5 for trucks, while the corresponding variation of variable road maintenance costs amounts to 1:11:33.

[32]That urban congestion is a worldwide phenomenon is discerned in "You're never too poor to have a traffic problem," in Business Brief, *The Economist,* September 22, 1973, pp. 84–85. The article discusses also some alternatives to the private car for solving congestion problems such as going underground or making wider use of taxis.

[33]The following two paragraphs are based on Peter L. Watson and Edward P. Holland, "Congestion pricing—the example of Singapore." See also Barry Newman, "Singapore is Waging a War Against Cars and it's Winning." Overall, the scheme is still in an experimental phase; it is closely monitored by the Government of Singapore in cooperation with the World Bank and other agencies.

[34]Smith, "Highway Pricing and Motor Vehicle Taxation in Developing Countries," p. 461. A good study for Canada which attempts to do just that is Z. Haritos, *Rational Road Pricing Policies in Canada.*

[35]This section draws on Allen V. Kneese and Charles L. Schultze, *Pollution, Prices, and Public Policy.* For some counter-argument to Kneese and Schultze, see William J. Baumol and Wallace E. Oates, *The Theory of Environmental Policy;* and for a succinct theoretical exposition also Hugh Macaulay, "Environmental quality, the market, and public finance." For an early contribution to the taxation of energy, see Max Cluseau, "Défense de l'impôt sur l'énergie."

[36]In the United States alone it is estimated that there may be as many as 55,000 major industrial sources of water pollution. Generally, *water pollutants* are distinguished by their environmental assimilating capacities into degradable pollutants such as organic wastes, nondegradable inorganic substances (mercury poisoning of fish and cadmium poisoning of rice are often mentioned as examples), and persistent pollutants such as pesticides and other organic chemicals. *Air pollution* may be caused by mobile agents like automobiles that emit monoxides, hydrocarbons, and nitrogen oxides, and stationary agents such as factories that in addition may emit sulfur oxides; all these toxic fumes are health hazards and have strong corrosive properties.

[37]Kneese and Schultze, *Pollution, Prices, and Public Policy*, p. 91.

[38]Biological oxygen demand (BOD) measures the amount of dissolved oxygen that would be depleted by a specified quantity of organic waste in a given time (usually five days) at a standard temperature (usually 20 degrees centigrade).

[39]The reference is to D. M. Fort and others, "Proposal for a Smog Tax."

[40]For the figures in this paragraph see Gerard M. Brannon, *Energy Taxes and Subsidies*, pp. 119–38. Shorter travel distances, the lower quality of roads and the greater availability of inexpensive and dependable forms of public transportation in European countries may also play a role in explaining the difference in per capita gasoline consumption.

[41]For a view that a corrective excise will reduce rather than increase welfare in the Pareto-efficiency sense, see James M. Buchanan, "External Diseconomies, Corrective Taxes, and Market Structure." For a view that corrective excises fail to confront the complexities of the real world, such as "problems raised by costs of information, regulatory lag, capital intensity of pollution investment, collusive behaviour by dischargers, discontinuities in marginal cost and benefit schedules, as well as the difficulty of setting optimal charges when polluters' marginal damage functions differ and when joint treatment among dischargers is an efficient outcome," see Susan Rose-Ackermann, "Effluent Charges: A Critique."

[42]The argument implies the existence of multiple local optima. For a view that this means that a global optimum cannot be achieved, see Marvin Kraus and Herbert Mohring, "The Role of Pollutee Taxes in Externality Problems."

[43]See "Fires and Fire Losses Classified, 1973," *Fire Journal*, vol. 68 (September 1974), p. 33.

[44]"Bitter Harvest," *Newsweek*, December 28, 1970, p. 20.

[45]See Harold M. Schmeck, Jr., "Alcohol Cost to Nation Put at $25-Billion a Year." For Canada see J. A. Johnson, "Canadian Policies in Regard to the Taxation of Alcoholic Beverages." Although Friedrich Engels contended that alcoholism was a disease of capitalism, some people like to point out that the situation in the U.S.S.R. is not much better. In Russia, most crime appears alcohol-related and more than 60 per cent of all serious industrial, traffic and household accidents can be traced to alcohol. For an interesting account see Peter Osnos, "The Soviet Drinking Problem."

[46]See Jane E. Brody, "Sweden Plans a Nation of Nonsmokers." For evidence that heavy excises and restrictive licenses substantially reduced per capita consumption of alcohol in European countries in the twenties, see D. W. McConnell, "Liquor Traffic," pp. 505–7.

[47]Computed from the data in Appendix C. See also Shoup, *Public Finance*, pp. 272–73: "For any excise tax there are two tax rates that give the same yield, one on the low side of that rate that produces the maximum yield, the other on the high side of that rate. Sumptuary considerations, that is, reduction of negative externalities, dictate use of the high rate, but in fact all sumptuary tax rates are on the low side, when indeed they are not aimed at the maximum yield."

[48]See *The Budget: Speech of the Finance Minister 1959/60*, p. 23.

[49]These reasons do not apply to local retail excises, of course, but in many countries these may be more difficult to administer and coordinate with neighboring jurisdictions than the manufacturer's excise.

[50]See Sally Hey, "Departmental and Municipal Revenues in Colombia: Proposals for Reform," p. 763. To remedy the situation, Hey proposes to establish a national liquor agency to streamline production, pricing and taxing policies and administration, or alternatively to sell departmental distilleries to the private sector and to impose a national liquor excise with the proceeds being distributed to the departments.

[51]Any significance state and local taxes might have is further reduced by their deductibility in computing the federal income tax liability. See John F. Due, "Studies of State-Local Tax Influences on Location of Industry," p. 167.

[52]A major study on tax exporting in the United States is Charles E. McLure, Jr., "The Interstate Exporting of State and Local Taxes"; also by the same author, "Taxation, Substitution, and Industrial Location."

[53]It may be pointed out that this is only so in the case of selective taxes. Under a general sales tax, border tax adjustments whether based on the destination principle or the origin principle should make no difference to international trade. For an exposition of the argument see Harry Johnson and Mel Krauss, "Border Taxes, Border Tax Adjustments, Comparative Advantage, and the Balance of Payments."

[54]See Bela Balassa and Associates, *The Structure of Protection in Developing Countries*, pt. 1.

[55]For a set of comprehensive recommendations on coordination of excises and import duties, see Malcolm Gillis and Charles E. McLure, Jr., "Coordination of Tariffs and Internal Indirect Taxes."

[56]Directives are laid down in Commission of the European Communities, *Proposed Council Directives on Excise Duties and Similar Taxes*. For a useful review, see John Dodsworth, "Excise Duties." For a summary of the present stage of the harmonization measures also "Tax Harmonization in the E.E.C.: A Status Report," *European Taxation*, vol. 14 (August 1974), p. 274.

[57]For two accounts of the major provisions, see K. Millenaar, "Fiscale harmonisatie in de Benelux"; and A. L. C. Simons, "De opheffing van grenzen voor accijnzen en omzetbelasting."

[58]See Ronald Soligo, *Factor Intensity of Consumption Patterns, Income Distribution and Employment Growth in Pakistan*, p. 16, who finds that urban and high-income families have the most labor-intensive consumption pattern, primarily on account of increased expenditures on housing and other construction activities which are labor-intensive processes.

[59]See P. T. Bauer and B. S. Yamey, *The Economics of Under-Developed Countries*, p. 86, fn. 1.

[60]For a strong statement compare Charles E. McLure, Jr., "The Proper Use of Indirect Taxation in Latin America: The Practice of Economic Marksmanship," p. 24: "Arduous efforts to increase the overall progressivity of the tax system through luxury taxation might retard work-effort and saving; it might conceivably reduce the rewards to both saving and work effort to such an extent as to encourage emigration of some of the best-trained and potentially most productive members of the labor force." McLure's article provides a convenient and compact review of many of the issues raised in this chapter.

[61]Shoup, *Public Finance*, p. 592; also p. 593, fn. 22: "Many less developed countries would probably attain a higher rate of growth over a span of several decades if they spent more than they do on high-protein foods for their younger children, even at the cost of a lower level of investment in plant, equipment, and public infrastructure." For an in-depth analysis also Carl S. Shoup, "Production from Consumption." The importance of "productive investment" was already recognized by Alfred Marshall, *Principles of Economics*, p. 229: "A great part of the wages of the working class is invested in the physical health and strength of their children. The older economists took too little account of the fact that human faculties are as important a means of production as any other kind of capital."

[62]Shoup, *Public Finance*, p. 472; see also pp. 473–78.

[63]For an excellent discussion of neutrality, harmony, and conflict of goals, see Neumark, *Grundsätze gerechter und ökonomisch rationaler Steuerpolitik*, pp. 382–402.

CHAPTER 6

[1]For examples of this practice, see Government of Pakistan, *Taxation Enquiry Committee Report*, vol. 1, pp. 180–81; and Ministry of Finance, *Budget Speech for 1965–66*, p. 26.

[2]See *Report of the Central Excise Reorganisation Committee*, pp. 19–20 and 58–59.

[3]Gordon C. Winston, "Overinvoicing, Underutilization, and Distorted Industrial Growth," p. 416. This finding has initiated a review of the accepted beliefs concerning economic development policies as noted in Derek T. Healey, "Development Policy: New Thinking About an Interpretation," with a summary of capacity utilization data from thirteen developing countries (p.785). See also Gordon C. Winston, "Capital Utilisation in Economic Development," in which he argues that higher capacity utilization rates should be recognized explicitly as an alternative to saving, and that policies should be designed specifically to increase these rates, as this "holds great promise for increasing the level and rate of growth of income in underdeveloped countries" (p. 58).

[4]The following is adapted from the more detailed treatment in Sijbren Cnossen, "Capacity Taxation: The Pakistan Experiment."

[5]Under income taxes, depreciation allowances can be employed to increase capacity utilization by permitting higher write-offs for multiple shifts. For references to this practice, see Bird, *Taxation and Development*, p. 86; Richard Slitor, "Reform of the Business Tax Structure: Analysis of Problems and Alternative Remedial Proposals," pp. 484–85; and Lauchlin Currie, *Accelerating Development: The Necessity and the Means*, p. 111.

[6]For a description of agricultural income taxes, see George E. Lent, "Taxation of Agricultural Income in Developing Countries"; and Richard M. Bird, *Taxing Agricultural Land in Developing Countries*, pp. 63–66.

[7]Joan Robinson, *The Economics of Imperfect Competition*, p. 163. In an analysis of Mrs. Robinson's scheme, Benjamin Higgins proposed as an alternative "a tax on profits in excess of a fair return on utilized capacity," which in his view would approximately attain the same objective and be easier to administer than the tax-and-bounty scheme. As long as the rate of net (after tax) profits rises with output, it would be advantageous "not only to utilize existing plant and equipment more fully but to operate the part that is utilized as efficiently as possible." See Benjamin Higgins, "Fiscal Control of Monopoly"; the quotations are from p. 319 and p. 321.

[8]See Klaus Knorr and William J. Baumol, eds., *What Price Economic Growth?*; in particular the contributions by William D. Carmichael and Richard E. Quandt in chapters 4 and 5.

[9]See Vito Tanzi, "Theory of Tax Structure Development and the Design of Tax Structure Policy for Industrialization," pp. 66–67.

[10]For a critique see Richard Bird, "A Tax Incentive for Sales: The Canadian Experience."

[11]Official statements on the rationale of the tax may be found in Ministry of Finance, *The Budget Speech for 1961–62*, pp. 23–24; "A Talk by the Secretary, Ministry of Finance, Broadcast from Radio Pakistan, Rawalpindi, on 12th June 1966," *Pakistan Budgets 1966–67*, p. 205; *The Budget 1969–70*, p. 33; and *The Budget in Brief 1972–73*, p. 28.

[12]This form of excise taxation is not entirely new. In the cradle of the modern excise, the Netherlands in the seventeenth century, the excise was often converted to an annual levy on manufacturers and sellers. See P. J. A. Adriani and J. van Hoorn, Jr., *Het Belastingrecht: Zijn Grondslagen en Ontwikkeling*, p. 354.

[13]For a conceptual treatment, see Richard E. Gift, *Estimating Economic Capacity: A Summary of Conceptual Problems*; and Almarin Phillips, "An Appraisal of Measures of Capacity."

[14]See Pakistan Ministry of Industries and Natural Resources, *Report of the Textile Industry Capacity Committee*, unpublished. According to the *Budget Speech for 1967–68*, p. 15, the Committee would be guided by certain broad principles that would take account of "the national average annual production of each statutory category of fabrics or yarn on a per loom or per spindle basis, the average production of the unit itself, the production of a comparable unit, and . . . changes in production because of technological improvements, normal growth or other such factors."

[15]To permit the cotton fabric industry to catch up with the new standards, a country-wide rebate of 20 per cent of capacity was allowed for the first year after the tax came into operation, and 10 per cent for the second year. See S.R.O. No. 61(R)/68, rule 3, *Gazette of Pakistan*, April 22, 1968, p. 198. No rebate was granted to units that had already achieved the prescribed efficiency standard, as indicated by their average annual output for the preceding three years. Moreover, units whose production exceeded the recommended capacity were taxed on the basis of average actual annual output.

[16]S.R.O. No. 61(R)/68, rule 3(9)-(11). Further implementing rules prescribed that each manufacturer had to maintain a daily account of each working shift, showing inter alia their time of commencement and termination, the number of looms worked, and the quantities of each category of cotton fabrics manufactured during the shift.

[17]S.R.O. No. 61(R)/68, rules 4 and 5.

[18]In United Nations, Economic and Social Council, *The Tax System of Pakistan: Studies in Tax Reform Planning*, p. 40, Nurul Islam suggests that capacity tax rates could be adjusted automatically by linking them to price changes. Interestingly, such a system applies to land revenue collections in the Sind Province of Pakistan, permitting adjustments of tax liabilities in step with changes in the average market price of agricultural products over a specified period. See J. Russell Andrus and Azizali F. Mohammed, *The Economy of Pakistan*, p. 342.

[19]For the evidence see *Budget Speech for 1966–1967*, p. 16. The collusion argument was also voiced by the Finance Secretary on June 13, 1964 (*Pakistan Budgets, 1964–65*, p. 211) and is referred to in Winston, "Capital Utilisation in Economic Development," p. 60.

[20]Amotz Morag, "Some Economic Aspects of Two Administrative Methods of Estimating Taxable Income," p. 180.

[21]See *Dawn*, November 22, 1972, and *Gazette of Pakistan*, October 14, 1972. At present, capacity tax is applied to two industries: cotton textiles (147 factories) and sugar (24 mills). See Government of Pakistan, *Taxation Structure of Pakistan*, p. 5. The industry breakdown is from Ministry of Finance, *Monthly Statistical Bulletin*, vol. 23 (January-February 1975).

[22]This would seem an appropriate form of analysis in the Pakistan situation, because the Government did not increase the tax liabilities of the excisable industries through the imposition of the capacity tax (see "Central Finance Minister Defends the Budget in the National Assembly," in *Budget of Pakistan, 1966–67*, p. 71). Therefore, their supply and demand schedules or those of related industries, should not have been appreciably affected. Moreover, factors of production would probably not change if incomes declined, in view of the specialized nature of the taxed industries. Finally, the number of untaxed substitutes to which demand could be diverted was small.

[23]In "Capital Utilisation in Economic Development," p. 57, Winston notes: "In making it more expensive to let plant sit idle, the tax may increase utilisation through an income effect on entrepreneurial utility maximisation such that managerial input may increase as profits are reduced." For supporting arguments he refers to Tibor Scitovsky, *Welfare and Competition: The Economics of a Fully Employed Economy*, pp. 142–47.

[24]For an excellent summary of the conditions under which the taxation of capital goods might be required see Richard M. Bird, "Sales Taxation and Development Planning," pp. 261-63.

[25]For Pakistan, the prevalence of oligopolistic tendencies is argued persuasively by many authors. For example, see Mohammed Yaqub, "The Elasticity of Taxes in a Developing Country—A Case Study of Pakistan," unpublished (Karachi: Pakistan Institute of Development Economics, 1966), as quoted in M. Z. Farrukh, "Tax Concessions to Industries—An Overview of Pakistan's Experience," unpublished, p. 26. Also Stephen R. Lewis and Sarfraz Khan Qureshi, "The Structure of Revenue from Indirect Taxes in Pakistan," p. 498.

[26]See Ghulam Mohammed Radhu, "The Relation of Indirect Tax Changes to Price Changes in Pakistan."

[27]See also *Budget Speech for 1970–71*, p. 13, in which the Government of Pakistan indicated that it expected that the duty on paper and paperboard would be paid out of profits and would not be passed on to the consumer.

[28]See Winston, "Capital Utilisation in Economic Development," p. 55.

[29]Winston, "Capital Utilisation in Economic Development," pp. 43–49. Other studies support the hypothesis regarding the negative correlation between imported raw materials and capacity utilization. See, for instance, Pakistan Central Statistical Office, *Report of Survey on Capacity Utilization by Manufacturing Industries 1965*, Annexure B; and Warren Hogan, "Capacity Creation and Utilisation in Pakistan Manufacturing Industry," pp. 36–38, who also lists the inefficiencies in policies and planning, both of government and private enterprise, as well as some forms of technological or demand determinism often associated with capacity underutilization. For an analysis of Pakistan's import substitution policies, see also Stephen R. Lewis, Jr., *Pakistan: Industrialization and Trade Policies*, in particular chapter 5.

[30]For an analysis of this phenomenon, see Gordon C. Winston, "Overinvoicing, Underutilization, and Distorted Industrial Growth." Earlier, the practice was signaled in *Budget Speech, 1965–66*, p. 24. It was facilitated by an overvalued exchange rate that made imports artificially cheap, import duty exemptions, and a liberal system of depreciation allowances—up to 35 per cent on plant and machinery in the first year of installation, which further reduced the cost of capital goods.

[31]For a review of these measures, see IMF Middle Eastern Department, "Pakistan's Stabilization Program Includes Devaluation of Rupee and Export Duties," *IMF Survey*, November 6, 1972, pp. 103–104.

CHAPTER 7

[1]For an overview of public monopolies, see Herbert Gross, "Monopolies, Public."

[2]State marketing boards, primarily found in developing countries, often transfer substantial revenues to government. Although their main purpose is to facilitate the production and export of agricultural products, they are frequently used as a convenient vehicle for the imposition of export duties. Agricultural price support agencies, for instance, are found in the EEC; the levies imposed on agricultural imports, although primarily meant for protective purposes, make a sizable contribution to the Community's budget. On the other hand, price support agencies may also be involved with the payment of heavy subsidies, as is the case with the Pakistan wheat schemes.

[3]The most detailed reviews of fiscal monopolies are probably found in German tax literature. For some useful introductory articles, see Karl Bräuer, "Monopol als Form der Besteuerung"; and Karl-Heinrich Hansmeyer, "Finanzmonopole." Recently, the phenomenon has been exhaustively treated by Otto Gandenberger, in *Das Finanzmonopol.*

[4]Parliamentary feelings were pointedly expressed by Culpepper in the 1640 debates: "These men, like the frogs of Egypt, have gotten possession of our dwelling, and we have scarce a room free from them. They sup in our cup, they dip in our dish, they sit by our fire; we find them in the dye-vat, the wash-bowls, and the powdering tub; they share with the butler in his box; they have marked and sealed us from head to foot. They have a vizard to hide the brand made by that good law in the last parliament of king James; they shelter themselves under the name of a corporation; they make bye-laws which serve their turns to squeeze us and fill their purses." See Stephen Dowell, *History of Taxation and Taxes in England*, vol. 1, pp. 208–209.

[5]See Martin Norr, "Tobacco Taxes at Home and Abroad," p. 842. Napoleon apparently was struck by the revenue potential of tobacco when his eye caught the brilliant jewels and attire of a tobacco manufacturer's wife during a reception at the imperial court.

[6]For a history see M. Marcus, "Taxation of Tobacco and Spirits in Sweden."

[7]See "State Monopolies of Turkey," p. 3.

[8]George F. Break and Ralph Turvey, *Studies in Greek Taxation*, p. 207.

[9]Bräuer, "Monopol als Form der Besteuerung," p. 624. In *Finanzmonopol*, p. 39, Gandenberger finds Bräuer's terminology inadequate, and distinguishes between monopolies with or without enterprise characteristics, calling the first production monopolies (for example, the Austrian tobacco monopoly) and the second "eingeschobene Monopole" (for example, the German alcohol monopoly). Gandenberger does not consider typical wholesale functions such as transportation, sorting and selling, as entrepreneurial in nature.

[10]Exceptions are the Swedish alcohol monopoly and the Spanish petroleum monopoly.

[11]For a description, see Harvard Law School, *Taxation in France*, pp. 257–59; as well as Ministère de l'Economie et des Finances, *Le Système Fiscal Français*, p. 115.

[12]For a brief account, see Gandenberger, *Finanzmonopol*, pp. 18–22.

[13]Shoup Mission, *Report on Japanese Taxation*, vol. 2, p. 156; and FAO, *Ad Hoc Government Consultation on Tobacco*, p. 10.

[14]For an interesting account, see Wilhelm Grotkopp, "Match Industry."

[15]See J. Harvey Perry, *Taxation in Canada*, pp. 211–16.

[16]*Report of the Taxation Inquiry Commission*, pp. 148–53.

[17]See Juanita Amatong, "The Revenue Importance of Government Lotteries," mimeograph.

[18]This point is stressed by Julian L. Simon, "State Liquor Monopolies," pp. 366–67.

[19]For excise data referred to in this paragraph, see Appendix C.

[20]See S. C. Bakkenist as well as M. R. Israel, "Régie or Free Enterprise."

[21]See Sijbren Cnossen, "Tax System and Reform," mimeograph, p. 28.

[22]See *An Outline of Japanese Taxes 1973*, pp. 182–94; and Virginia G. Watkin, *Taxes and Tax Harmonization in Central America*, pp. 453–55.

[23]On this see also Hansmeyer, "Finanzmonopole," p. 581.

[24]Compare Gross, "Monopolies, Public," p. 623.

[25]For a brilliant, not wholly favorable, sociological study on industrial monopolies and clerical agencies, based on the French experience, see Michel Crozier, *The Bureaucratic Phenomenon*.

[26]Break and Turvey, *Studies in Greek Taxation*, p. 209.

[27]Joseph Pincus, *The Economy of Paraguay*, p. 302.

[28]J. J. Hauvonen, "A Note on Oriental Tobacco," mimeograph, pp. 4–5.

[29]United Nations Department of Economic Affairs, *Public Finance Information Papers: Italy*, pp. 26–27.

[30]Recently, the Ceylonese Taxation Commission favored this form of organization; see *Report of the Taxation Inquiry Commission*, p. 151.

[31]See Article 37 of the Rome Treaty; for an account, Gandenberger, *Finanzmonopol*, pp. 117–47.

[32]Simon, "State Liquor Monopolies," pp. 365–77.

[33]Hauvonen, "A Note on Oriental Tobacco," pp. 4–5.

[34]A combination of the first and second options was practised in Japan in the immediate postwar period, when cheap cigarettes were rationed, but more expensive brands sold in the market; see Shoup Mission, *Japanese Taxation*, p. 157.

[35]Such pricing policies are not possible under all fiscal monopolies, of course. Owing to the homogeneity of the product, the tax impact of the Venezuelan cigarette paper monopoly, for instance, is definitely regressive; see Carl S. Shoup, Director, *The Fiscal System of Venezuela: A Report*, p. 259.

[36]This point is strongly advanced by Masao Kambe, "State Monopoly as a Method of Taxing Consumption."

[37]For a discussion of this aspect in the case of the Syrian fiscal monopolies, see D. K. Stout, "Report on Taxation in the Syrian Arab Republic," unpublished, pp. 23–25.

[38]Even when this is not the case as, for instance, in Lebanon where contractual provisions anticipate full monopolization, the government may hesitate to take the last step. Under the original contract, the *Régie Co-Intéressee des Tabacs et Tombacs* was allowed to deduct a fixed amount from its annual profits to amortize part of its shares and pay interest at 5 per cent on outstanding shares. At the expiration of the contract in 1966, the régie's assets would become the property of the Lebanese Government. However, the assets have not yet been transferred, and the concession has been renewed on an annual basis. See Raja S. Himadeh, *The Fiscal System of Lebanon*, pp. 68–70.

[39]Ministry of Finance, *Report of the Board of Inquiry on the Japanese Monopoly System*.

[40]Also Ursula K. Hicks, *Development Finance: Planning and Control*, p. 64.

[41]Prest, *Public Finance in Underdeveloped Countries*, p. 132.

CHAPTER 8

[1]For a succinct statement to this effect, see Carl S. Shoup, "Tax Policy in Developing Economies," unpublished, pp. 15–16: "Policymakers and administrators alike can recognize that the degree of adaptation, the range of successful policy formulation, depends largely on advances in administration. As tax administration becomes more and more efficient, policymakers can consider a wider and wider range of possible tax patterns, or combinations. . . . Tax administration creates the possibility of true tax policy, that is, allows some freedom of choice in policy formulation. . . . In its widest sense, tax administration is the key to tax policy." Reprinted in part in Patrick J. Kelley and Oliver Oldman, *Readings on Income Tax Administration*, p. ix.

[2]See Stanley Surrey, "Tax Administration in Underdeveloped Countries," p. 498.

[3]Two major exceptions should be noted: an excellent analysis of excise operations in the United Kingdom, in James Crombie, *Her Majesty's Customs and Excise*; and a very valuable country study, in Government of India, *Report of the Central Excise Reorganisation Committee*; several examples in this chapter are drawn from the latter.

[4]See Perry, *Taxation in Canada*, p. 331: "The habitat of the excise man is the brewery, the distillery, and the cigar, tobacco, and cigarette factory. Not only are these his native surroundings but in many instances they provide his abode during his working hours, since in some of the larger establishments . . . a staff of half a dozen or more employees of the Department is almost constantly on the premises."

[5]This aspect of excise control is taken very seriously, as is evident for instance, in East African excise legislation that empowers the authorities to revoke or suspend any license, where they are satisfied that "the factory is so designed, equipped, or sited, as to render difficult the supervision thereof for excise purposes." See East African Common Services Organization, *Excise Management Act, 1952*, section 12(1).

[6]An annual license may not be sufficient in the case of manufacturers of spirits and beer, who often require a special permit for each run of production.

[7]*Report of the Central Excise Reorganisation Committee*, pp. 48–49.

[8]John C. Chommie, *The Internal Revenue Service*, p. 155. In Sweden, it is estimated that 25 per cent of all alcohol consumption derives from illicit production; see Colin Narbrough, "Swedes Do Battle Against Illicit Home Brew"; and Richard F. Janssen, "More Europeans Begin making their own booze."

[9]For this reason, each excise levy is usually legislated separately. For an unsuccessful attempt to standardize various forms of excise procedures, see *Report of the Central Excise Reorganisation Committee*, p. 24.

[10]Technical definitions are the rule here. Thus, for the alcohol excise, "proof spirit" is defined as that mixture of alcohol and distilled water which, at the temperature of 51 degrees Fahrenheit, weighs exactly 12/13 of the weight of an equal measure of distilled water at the same temperature. The expression "proof" is said to originate in the days when the "gunpowder test" was applied to alcohol as a rough measurement of the excise liability. For this purpose gunpowder was saturated with alcohol and then ignited: a flash indicated that the mixture was "overproof," the absence of a flash that it was "underproof."

[11]Sometimes all these functions have to be performed with regard to the same product, as in the Canadian case where the excise duty on spirits is computed in five different ways, whichever yields the greatest amount of revenue. The methods involved are based on calculations of the amount of grain in the manufacture of spirits, the alcoholic content during the course of manufacture, the amount of spirits drawn off into the receivers, and the quantity of spirits cleared for consumption after the prescribed period of storage. Moreover, each of these calculations must be made for each run of production. See Perry, *Taxation in Canada*, p. 333.

[12]For an interesting description of this trend in one country, see Harold C. Wilkenfeld, *Taxes and People in Israel*, pp. 68–71.

[13]For a description and critique, see *Report of the Central Reorganisation Committee*, pp. 51–52. Also Pakistan Ministry of Finance, *Central Taxes in Pakistan: A Decade of Development and Self Effort*, p. 16.

[14]Crombie, *Her Majesty's Customs and Excise*, p. 35. He continues: "If it is not possible to define clearly, so isolating what it is desired to charge, it is better not to charge at all." For an interesting discussion of

various definitions used in the United States, see M. Slade Kendrick, *Public Finance, Principles and Problems*, pp. 364–69.

[15]*Report of the Central Excise Reorganisation Committee*, pp. 184–85.

[16]*Report of the Central Excise Reorganisation Committee*, pp. 141–42. Obviously, standard exemptions for waste yarn and samples, or tolerances in measuring the length of yarn are not distinguishable from rate adjustments, but in practice they serve to allay a certain degree of taxpayer dissatisfaction. For this reason, a tax report on Liberia recommends that a small allowance for breakage should be granted to soft drink bottlers. See Carl S. Shoup, Director, *The Tax System of Liberia*, p. 133.

[17]This point is stressed in *Taxation in New Zealand, Report of the Taxation Review Committee*, p. 374.

[18]To some extent, this is also inevitable if the specific rate is graduated according to price and quality: although Arabica coffee is considered superior to Robusta and Liberia coffee, inferior blacks and bits of Arabica may fetch a lower price; similarly, there is little difference between air-cured tobacco (often taxed lower) and low-grade flue-cured tobacco (taxed higher).

[19]Floor-stock taxes are usually despised by the trading community; for a reference on this in connection with the supplementary banderoling of cigarettes in Germany at the time of the galloping inflation of the early twenties, see Karl Bräuer, "Tabaksteuer," p. 1,234.

[20]For instance, the price of cigarettes would be higher in remote areas. Purportedly for this reason, Brazilian retailers have been unwilling to sell cigarettes at the fixed retail price, and the suggestion has been made to base the tax on the manufacturer's price. See Carl S. Shoup, *The Tax System of Brazil*, p. 68. During an unsuccessful experiment in Pakistan, excise rates were reduced for products which carried the retail price printed on them, and confiscatory rates were imposed if the product was subsequently sold for a higher price. See Cnossen, "Capacity Taxation: The Pakistan Experiment," p. 148.

[21]Because of the distorting effects on distribution channels, the Canadian Royal Commission on Taxation concluded that the excise levies should be kept on a specific basis; Due, *Indirect Taxation in Developing Economies*, p. 61, fn. 2.

[22]*Report of the Central Excise Reorganisation Committee*, p. 43. In India, some excisable commodities are taxed on a specific or ad valorem basis, whichever yields the highest amount of revenue; clearly, that approach cannot be recommended from an administrative point of view.

[23]See *Report of the Central Excise Reorganisation Committee*, pp. 10–16 and 65–79; Mahler, *Sales and Excise Taxation in India*, pp. 76–86; and D. T. Lakdawala and K. V. Nambiar, *Commodity Taxation in India*, pp. 64–66.

[24]Crombie, *Her Majesty's Customs and Excise*, p. 37.

[25]A major exception are the wine producers in southern European countries. Because there are all sizes of growers, France does not tax the production stage, but instead imposes the excise on the shipment of wine, and in view of the great variations in quality, price, and alcohol content, the duty is based on volume rather than value; see *Taxation in France*, pp. 242–45.

[26]An interesting suggestion made in India is that products should not be taxed if, for the country as a whole, more than 75 per cent of output is generated in small-scale establishments; see *Report of the Central Excise Reorganisation Committee*, p. 76.

[27]In Nigeria, soap is successfully taxed through an excise on caustic soda. See John F. Due, *Taxation and Economic Development in Tropical Africa*, p. 97. For other interesting examples on how to deal with the small producer problem under excise taxation, see Government of Pakistan, *Taxation Enquiry Committee Report*, vol. 1, pp. 177–88.

[28]For a comprehensive treatment see John F. Due, *State and Local Sales Taxation: Structure and Administration*, pp. 81–100. Recently a list approach to the taxation of services was advocated by the Carter Commission; see "Sales Taxes and General Tax Administration," pp. 56–69. For a summary of administrative issues under the United States retail sales taxes, see Robert N. Schoeplein, "Problems in Administering a Sales Tax on Services."

[29]See Malcolm Gillis, "Reform of Municipal Indirect Taxes, Service Taxation and Stamp Duties," pp. 667–69. The problem of buying airline tickets outside the country (for instance, for an extension of a journey) is a shortcoming of the proposal, for which there is no easy solution.

[30]For an interesting account of betting activities in the United Kingdom stressing evasion by small firms and control problems, see C. Hood, "The Development of Betting Taxes in Britain."

[31]For an interesting account of the Canadian experience, see *Tax Administrators News*, vol. 38, no. 10 (October 1974), pp. 114–15. Also Due, *Indirect Taxation in Developing Economies*, pp. 66–67.

[32]See David M. Winch, *The Economics of Highway Planning*, p. 126.

[33]A detailed examination of the operational requirements of the schemes is found in United Kingdom, Ministry of Transport, *Road Pricing: The Economic and Technical Possibilities*; and in Kiran U. Bhatt, *Road Pricing Technologies: A Survey*.

[34]It is interesting that these, and other problems so prevalent under the excise systems operated on the Indian subcontinent, were also voiced with regard to the old U.S. excises at the time of the *Hearings of the* (Forand) *Subcommittee on Excise Tax Technical and Administrative Changes* (Report of the Subcommittee, 84th Congress, 2nd Session, 1956), as recapitulated in John F. Due, *Sales Taxation*, pp. 246–48.

[35]Government of India, *Report of the Excise Reorganisation Committee*, p. 24. For an authoritative comment on this situation and a proposal to replace the excise system with a manufacturers sales tax, see S. Bhoothalingam, *Final Report on Rationalisation and Simplification of the Tax Structure*, pp. 4–14.

[36]Crombie, *Her Majesty's Customs and Excise*, p. 17.

CHAPTER 9

[1]See Musgrave, *Fiscal Systems*, pp. 125-67; and Harley H. Hinrichs, *A General Theory of Tax Structure Change During Economic Development*, pp. 63-96.

[2]For instance, in a U.S. survey on the fairness of alternative forms of taxation, only 1.1 per cent of the respondents thought that tobacco taxes were "wrong in principle," while 8.4 per cent described income taxes in this way. See H. Cantril, ed., *Public Opinion 1935-1948*, p. 383, quoted in Warren A. Law, "Tobacco Taxation in the Revenue System," p. 373.

[3]See Amilcare Puviani, *Die Illusionen in der öffentlichen Finanzwirtschaft*, which has an introduction by Günter Schmölders. See also, Schmölders, *Finanz- und Steuerpsychologie*; and Buchanan, *Public Finance in Democratic Process*, chap. 10.

[4]Schmölders, *Finanz- und Steuerpsychologie*, pp. 67-71, provides evidence on the *Unmerklichkeit* of several excises in Germany. For instance, only 14 per cent of all respondents in a survey correctly estimated the amount of the excise included in the retail price of cigarettes. Interestingly, underestimation increased in higher-income groups. For evidence that the knowledge of reductions in federal excises effected in the United States in 1954 was neither widespread nor accurate, see Robert Ferber, "How Aware are Consumers of Excise Tax Changes?"

[5]For a vigorous defense of (general) excise taxation on these grounds, see Harley L. Lutz, "The Place and Role of Consumption Taxes in the Federal Tax Structure," pp. 560-74.

[6]For an interesting reference see J. M. Vincent, "Sumptuary Legislation."

[7]Early attitudes toward tobacco consumption are a useful illustration. Before its discovery as a lucrative source of revenue, the use of tobacco in Spanish churches was prohibited by papal encyclical; in Bern the authorities ranked the sin of taking tobacco second only to adultery, in Russia smokers had their noses cut off, in Turkey they were beheaded, and the American puritans considered smoking an ungodly recreation. See Dowell, *History of Taxation and Taxes in England*, vol. 4, pp. 248-50. For a recent reference, see also Edward M. Brecher, et al., *Licit and Illicit Drugs*, chap. 23.

[8]See Richard Goode, "Reconstruction of Foreign Tax Systems," pp. 122-24.

[9]For a good study of the interactional process, see Jonathan Levin, "The Effects of Economic Development on the Base of a Sales Tax: A Case Study of Colombia."

[10]Nicholas Kaldor recommended an expenditure tax for India in *Indian Tax Reform, Report of a Survey*, and for Sri Lanka in *Suggestions for a Comprehensive Reform of Direct Taxation*. India enacted the expenditure tax in 1957, repealed it in 1962, but re-enacted it in 1964, finally repealing it in 1966. Sri Lanka introduced the tax in 1959, but repealed it in 1961. In both countries the revenue yield of the tax was negligible and it was beset by administrative difficulties. Apparently the tax will be given another try in Sri Lanka: see *Budget Speech 1976*, p. 49. Recently, administrative aspects have been re-examined by Patrick L. Kelley, "Is an Expenditure Tax Feasible?" and by Richard E. Slitor, "Administrative Aspects of Expenditures Taxation." Both authors give a qualified endorsement of the feasibility of the tax in the U.S. setting.

[11]For a view that the incidence of a sales tax may be progressive see Malcolm S. Gillis, *Sales Taxation in a Developing Economy: The Chilean Case*. The old Israeli wholesale sales tax is an example of a highly graduated tax with twenty-three different rates varying from 2 per cent to 150 per cent.

[12]For this reason, value-added taxes in Scandinavian countries include most essentials in the tax base and apply the standard (uniform) rate to them. For an example of the argument, see Norwegian Ministry of Finance, *Norwegian Long-Term Programme, 1970-73*, pp. 125-31.

[13]That rate differentiation is possible under a value-added tax is pointed out by Carl S. Shoup, *The Value-Added Tax*, pp. 40-42.

[14]Richard M. Bird, "Public Finance and Inequality," p. 4

[15]Luc De Wulf, "Fiscal Incidence Studies in Developing Countries," p. 237.

[16]Musgrave and Musgrave, in *Public Finance in Theory and Practice*, pp. 450-51, point out that the greater substitutability among particular items within a product group rather than among groups of products is an argument in favor of general product taxes, because the tendency to generate excess burdens may be expected to be smaller.

[17]See José Maria Naharro, "Production and Consumption Taxes and Economic Development," p. 285.

[18]For an excellent treatment of the influence of various taxes on consumption and saving, see Richard Goode, "Taxation of Saving and Consumption in Underdeveloped Countries"; also Douglas Dosser, "Indirect Taxation and Economic Development."

[19]Leading one author to conclude that economic development, particularly in its early stages, is more often hurt by conspicuous saving than by conspicuous consumption. See Dirk J. Wolfson, "The Fiscal Policy Aspect of Development Strategy," p. 9.

[20]Break, *The Incidence and Economic Effects of Taxation*, p. 234.

[21]For an example in the Soviet Union, see Gunnar Myrdal, *Asian Drama: An Inquiry into the Poverty of Nations*, p. 1918.

[22]Shoup points out that "our knowledge of how the economic and social system responds to one or another stimulus or deterrent is as yet so imperfect and the system-wide approach is still so unfamiliar, that there is little even to report on so far." *Public Finance*, p. 466.

[23]McLure, "The Proper Use of Indirect Taxation in Latin America," p. 32.

[24]Richard Goode, "Anti-inflationary Implications of Alternative Forms of Taxation," pp. 157-58.

[25]See, for instance, Alan T. Peacock and John Williamson, "Consumption Taxes and Compensatory Finance."

²⁶For a reference see Otto Eckstein, "Indirect Versus Direct Taxes: Implications for Stability Investment," p. 52, fn. 6.

²⁷See Albert G. Hart, *Defense without Inflation*, pp. 104–109; and John F. Due, "Excise and Sales Taxes as Anti-inflationary Measures." For a not wholly encouraging analysis of the Canadian experience, see Jared Sparks, "Canadian Excise Taxes and Inflation Control."

²⁸See William H. Branson, "The Use of Variable Tax Rates for Stabilization Purposes." For earlier references, see E. Cary Brown, "Analysis of Consumption Taxes in Terms of the Theory of Income Determination," p. 76; and Goode, "Anti-inflationary Implications of Alternative Forms of Taxation." p. 156.

²⁹In France, oil refineries and major storage depots are deemed to be "extraterritorial" by legal fiction, and for purposes of the excise levy the clearance of petroleum products for domestic consumption is equivalent to an act of importation. See *Taxation in France*, p. 239.

³⁰Excises and customs duties share these characteristics with export duties, property taxes, and agricultural land taxes, that are often also assessed on the basis of physical qualities.

³¹Auditors are extremely scarce in developing countries, as pointed out by Due, *Indirect Taxation in Developing Economies*, p. 161.

³²The vital importance of certainty in taxation is still best expressed by Smith, *The Wealth of Nations*, pp. 350–51: "The tax which each individual is bound to pay ought to be certain, and not arbitrary. . . . Where it is otherwise, every person subject to the tax is put more or less in the power of the tax-gatherer, who can either aggravate the tax upon any obnoxious contributor, or extort, by the terror of such aggravation, some present or perquisite to himself."

³³Shoup, *Public Finance*, pp. 217–18.

BIBLIOGRAPHY

BOOKS AND PAMPHLETS

Adler, John H., Eugene R. Schlesinger and Ernest C. Olson. *Public Finance and Economic Development in Guatemala*. Stanford University Press, 1952. Reprinted by Greenwood Press, Westport, Connecticut, 1970.

Adriani, P. J. A. and J. van Hoorn. *Het Belastingrecht: Zijn Grondslagen en Ontwikkeling*. Amsterdam: L. J. Veen's, 2nd ed., 1954.

Andersen, Palle Schelde. *Direct Versus Indirect Taxes: A Survey*. Aarhus: Skrifter fra Aarhus Universitets Økonomiske Institut, no. 25, 1971.

Anderson, Arthur & Co. *Tax and Trade Guides*. Washington, D.C., Pamphlet Series.

Andic, Fuat M. and Suphan Andic. *Government Finance and Planned Development: Fiscal Surveys of Surinam and the Netherlands Antilles*. San Juan: University of Puerto Rico, 1968.

Andrus, Russell J. and Azizali F. Mohammed. *The Economy of Pakistan*. Stanford, California: Stanford University Press, 1958.

Balassa, Bela, and Associates. *The Structure of Protection in Developing Countries*. Baltimore: Johns Hopkins Press, 1971.

Bauer, P. T. and B. S. Yamey. *The Economics of Under-Developed Countries*. London: James Nisbet & Co., 1957.

Baumol, William J. and Wallace E. Oates. *The Theory of Environmental Policy*. Englewood Cliffs, New Jersey: Prentice-Hall, 1975.

Bhatt, Kiran. *Road Pricing Technologies: A Survey*. Washington, D.C.: Urban Institute, 1974.

Bhoothalingam, S. *Final Report on Rationalisation and Simplification of the Tax Structure*. New Delhi: Ministry of Finance, 1968.

Bird, Richard M. *Taxation and Development: Lessons from Colombian Experience*. Cambridge, Massachusetts: Harvard University Press, 1970.

———. *Taxing Agricultural Land in Developing Countries*. Cambridge: Harvard University Press, 1974.

——— and Oliver Oldman, eds. *Readings on Taxation in Developing Countries*. Baltimore: Johns Hopkins Press. First ed., 1964; rev. ed., 1967; 3rd ed., 1975.

——— and John G. Head, eds. *Modern Fiscal Issues: Essays in honor of Carl S. Shoup*. Toronto: University of Toronto Press, 1972.

Blough, Roy. *The Federal Taxing Process*. New York: Prentice-Hall, 1952.

Brannon, Gerard M. *Energy Taxes and Subsidies*. Cambridge, Massachusetts: Ballinger Publishing Company, 1974.

Break, George F. and Ralph Turvey. *Studies in Greek Taxation*. Athens: Contos Press, 1964.

Brecher, Edward M., et al. *Licit and Illicit Drugs*. Mount Vernon, New York: Consumers Union, 1972.

Buchanan, James M. *Public Finance in Democratic Process*. Chapel Hill: University of North Carolina Press, 1967.

——— and Marilyn R. Flowers. *The Public Finances*. Homewood, Illinois: Richard D. Irwin, 4th ed., 1975.

Chommie, John C. *The Internal Revenue Service*. New York: Frederick A. Praeger, 1970.

Churchill, Anthony. *Road User Charges in Central America* (World Bank Occasional Paper Number Fifteen). Baltimore: Johns Hopkins Press, 1972.

Cnossen, Sijbren. *The Indonesian Sales Tax*. Deventer, The Netherlands: Kluwer, 1973.

Coffield, James. *A Popular History of Taxation*. London: Longman, 1970.

Crombie, James. *Her Majesty's Customs and Excise*. London: Allen & Unwin, 1962.

Crozier, Michel. *The Bureaucratic Phenomenon*. Chicago: University of Chicago Press, 1964.

Currie, Lauchlin. *Accelerating Development: The Necessity and the Means*. New York: McGraw-Hill, 1965.

Dalton, Hugh. *Principles of Public Finance*. New York: Augustus M. Kelly, Reprints of Economic Classics, 1967.

De Weille, J. *Quantification of Road User Savings* (World Bank Staff Occasional Paper Number 2). Baltimore: Johns Hopkins Press, 1966.

Diamond, Walter H., ed. *Foreign Tax and Trade Briefs*. New York: Matthew Bender, looseleaf, 1976.

Dowell, Stephen. *History of Taxation and Taxes in England*, 4 vols. London: Longmans, Green and Co., 1888.

Due, John F. *The Theory of Incidence of Sales Taxation*. New York: King's Crown Press, 1942. Reprinted by Russell & Russell, New York, 1971.

Due, John F. *Sales Taxation*. Urbana: University of Illinois Press, 1959.

_____. *Government Finance: An Economic Analysis*. Homewood, Illinois: Richard D. Irwin, 1963.

_____. *Taxation and Economic Development in Tropical Africa*. Cambridge: MIT Press, 1963.

_____. *Indirect Taxation in Developing Economies: The Role and Structure of Customs Duties, Excises, and Sales Taxes*. Baltimore: Johns Hopkins Press, 1970.

_____. *State and Local Sales Taxation; Structure and Administration*. Chicago: Public Administration Service, 1971.

_____ and Ann F. Friedlaender. *Government Finance: Economics of the Public Sector*. Homewood, Illinois: Richard D. Irwin, 5th ed., 1973.

Environmental Protection Agency and the Council on Environmental Quality. *A Study of the Quarterly Demand for Gasoline and Impacts of Alternative Gasoline Taxes*. Lexington, Massachusetts: Data Resources, Inc., December 1973.

Ernst & Ernst. *International Business Series*. United States, Pamphlet Series.

Fiscalité Africaine. Paris, looseleaf.

Gandenberger, Otto. *Das Finanzmonopol*. Heidelberg: Quelle & Meyer, 1968.

Ghai, Dharam P. *Taxation for Development: A Case Study of Uganda*. Nairobi: East African Publishing House, 1966.

Gift, Richard E. *Estimating Economic Capacity: A Summary of Conceptual Problems*. Lexington: University of Kentucky Press, 1968.

Gillis, Stephen Malcolm. *Sales Taxation in a Developing Economy: The Chilean Case*. Ph.D. dissertation (Urbana: University of Illinois, 1968). Ann Arbor, Michigan: University microfilms, 1969.

_____ and Richard A. Musgrave, eds. *Fiscal Reform for Colombia: Final Report and Staff Papers of the Colombian Commission on Tax Reform*. Cambridge: Law School of Harvard Unviersity, 1971.

Gillispie, W. Irwin. *The Incidence of Taxes and Public Expenditures in the Canadian Economy*. Studies of the Royal Commission on Taxation, no. 2. Ottawa: Queen's Printer, 1966.

Goode, Richard. *The Individual Income Tax*. Washington, D.C.: Brookings Institution, rev. ed., 1976.

Groves, Harold M. *Tax Philosophers*. Donald J. Curran, ed. Madison: University of Wisconsin Press, 1974.

Groves, Harold M. and Robert L. Bish. *Financing Government*. New York: Holt, Rinehart & Winston, 7th ed., 1973.

Harberger, Arnold C. *Taxation and Welfare*. Boston: Little, Brown & Company, 1974.

Haritos, Z. *Rational Road Pricing Policies in Canada*. Ottawa: Canadian Transport Commission, 1973.

Hart, Albert G. *Defense Without Inflation*. New York: Twentieth Century Fund, 1951.

Harvard Law School, International Program in Taxation. *Taxation in Australia*. Boston: Little, Brown & Co., 1958.

_____. *Taxation in Brazil*. Boston: Little, Brown & Co., 1959.

_____. *Taxation in Colombia*. Chicago: Commerce Clearing House, 1964.

_____. *Taxation in France*. Chicago: Commerce Clearing House, 1966.

_____. *Taxation in the Federal Republic of Germany*. Chicago: Commerce Clearing House, 2nd ed., 1969.

_____. *Taxation in India*. Boston: Little, Brown & Co., 1960.

_____. *Taxation in Italy*. Chicago: Commerce Clearing House, 1964.

————. *Taxation in Mexico.* Boston: Little, Brown & Co., 1957.

————. *Taxation in Sweden.* Boston: Little, Brown & Co., 1959.

————. *Taxation in the United States.* Chicago: Commerce Clearing House, 1963.

Heidinger, Gerald. *Gedanken zur Steuerreform in Österreich.* Wien: Institut für Finanzwissenschaft und Steuerrecht, 1971.

Hicks, J. R. *Value and Capital.* Oxford: Clarendon Press, 2nd ed., 1946.

Hicks, Ursula K. *Development Finance; Planning and Control.* New York: Oxford University Press, 1965.

Higgins, Benjamin. *Economic Development.* New York: W. W. Norton & Co., rev. ed., 1968.

Himadeh, Raja S. *The Fiscal System of Lebanon.* Beirut: Khayat, 1961.

Hinrichs, Harley H. *A General Theory of Tax Structure Change During Economic Development.* Cambridge: The Law School of Harvard University, 1966.

Hirschman, Albert O. *The Strategy of Economic Development.* New Haven and London: Yale University Press, 12th pr., March 1968.

Hofstra, H. J. *Inleiding tot het Nederlands belastingrecht.* Deventer, Netherlands: Kluwer, 3rd. ed., 1974.

International Bureau for Fiscal Documentation. *Value Added Taxation in Europe.* Amsterdam: Guides to European Taxation, vol. 4, looseleaf, 1976.

————. *African Tax Systems.* Amsterdam, looseleaf, 1974.

Japan Tax Association. *Asian Taxation 1974.* Tokyo, 1975.

Joint Tax Program. *Problems of Tax Administration in Latin America.* Baltimore: Johns Hopkins Press, 1965.

————. *Fiscal Policy for Economic Growth in Latin America.* Baltimore: Johns Hopkins Press, 1965.

Kaldor, Nicholas. *Indian Tax Reform: Report of a Survey.* New Delhi: Government of India Press, 1956.

————. *Suggestions for a Comprehensive Reform of Direct Taxation.* Colombo: Government Press, 1960.

————. *An Expenditure Tax.* London: Unwin University Books, 4th. ed., 1965.

Kelley, Patrick J. and Oliver Oldman, eds. *Readings on Income Tax Administration.* Mineola, New York: Foundation Press, 1973.

Kendrick, M. Slade. *Public Finance, Principles and Problems.* Cambridge: Riverside Press, 1951.

Kneese, Allen V. and Charles L. Schultze. *Pollution, Prices, and Public Policy.* Washington, D.C.: Brookings Institution, 1975.

Knorr, Klaus and William J. Baumol, eds. *What Price Economic Growth?* Englewood Cliffs, N.J.: Prentice Hall, 1961.

Lakdawala, D. T. and K. V. Nambiar. *Comodity Taxation in India.* Bombay: Popular Prakashan, 1972.

Lewis, W. Arthur. *Development Planning: The Essentials of Economic Policy.* New York: Harper & Row, 1966.

Lewis, Stephen R., Jr. *Pakistan: Industrialization and Trade Policies.* Oxford: Oxford University Press, 1970.

Lutz, Harley L. *Public Finance.* New York: D. Appleton-Century Co., 1947.

Magnet, Jacques. *Les Finances Publiques Tunisiennes.* République Tunisienne: Ecole Nationale d'Administration, 1969.

Mahler, Walter R., Jr. *Sales and Excise Taxation in India.* Bombay: Orient Longman, 1970.

Marbach, Fritz. *Luxus and Luxussteuer.* Bern: A. Francke, 1948.

Marshall, Alfred. *Principles of Economics,* 2 vols. London: Macmillan, 9th ed., 1961.

Musgrave, Richard A. *The Theory of Public Finance.* New York: McGraw-Hill, 1959.

———— and Carl S. Shoup, eds. *Readings in the Economics of Taxation.* Homewood, Illinois: Richard D. Irwin, 1959.

————. *Fiscal Systems.* New Haven: Yale University Press, 1969.

————, ed. *Broad-Based Taxes: New Options and Sources.* Baltimore: Johns Hopkins University Press, 1973.

_____ and Peggy B. Musgrave. *Public Finance in Theory and Practice.* New York: McGraw-Hill, 1973.

Myrdal, Gunnar. *Asian Drama: An Inquiry into the Poverty of Nations,* 3 vols. New York: Pantheon House, 3rd pr., 1968.

Neumark, Fritz. *Grundsätze gerechter and ökonomisch rationaler Steuerpolitik.* Tübingen: J. C. B. Mohr (Paul Siebeck), 1970.

Perry, J. Harvey. *Taxation in Canada.* Toronto: University of Toronto Press, 1961.

Pigou, A. C. *The Economics of Welfare.* London: Macmillan, 4th ed., 1946.

_____. *A Study in Public Finance.* London: Macmillan, 3rd ed., 1951.

Pincus, Joseph. *The Economy of Paraguay.* New York: Frederick A. Praeger, 1968.

Prais, S. J. and H. S. Houthakker. *The Analysis of Family Budgets.* Cambridge: Cambridge University Press, 2nd pr., 1971.

Prest, A. R. *Public Finance in Theory and Practice.* London: Weidenfeld and Nicholson, 4th ed., 1970.

_____. *Public Finance in Underdeveloped Countries.* New York: John Wiley, 2nd ed., 1972.

Price Waterhouse & Co. *Information Guides.* United States, Pamphlet Series.

Puviani, Amilcare. *Die Illusionen in der öffentlichen Finanzwirtschaft* (Teoria dell'illusione finanziaria). Berlin: Duncker & Humblot, Finanzwissenschaftliche Forschungsarbeiten, vol. 22, 1960.

Recktenwald, Horst Claus. *Tax Incidence and Income Redistribution.* Detroit: Wayne State University Press, 1971.

Robinson, Joan. *The Economics of Imperfect Competition.* London: Macmillan, 1950.

Rolph, Earl R. and George F. Break. *Public Finance.* New York: Ronald Press, 1961.

Sahota, G. S. *Indian Tax Structure and Economic Development.* London: Asia Publishing House, 1961.

Schmölders, Günter. *Finanz- und Steuerpsychologie.* Reinbek, Germany: Rowohlts Deutsche Enzyklopädie, 1970.

Schumpeter, Joseph A. *History of Economic Analysis.* New York: Oxford University Press, 1954.

Scitovsky, Tibor. *Welfare and Competition: The Economics of a Fully Employed Economy.* Homewood, Illinois: Richard D. Irwin, 1952.

Seligman, Edwin R. A. *Essays in Taxation.* New York: Macmillian, 9th ed., 1921.

Shilling, N. *Excise Taxation of Monopoly.* New York: Columbia University Press, 1969.

Shoup, Carl S., Director. *The Fiscal System of Venezuela: A Report.* Baltimore: Johns Hopkins Press, 1959.

_____. *The Tax System of Brazil.* Rio de Janeiro: Vargas Foundation, 1965.

_____. *Public Finance.* Chicago: Aldine Publishing Company, 1969.

_____, Director, *The Tax System of Liberia.* New York: Columbia University Press, 1970.

_____. *The Value-Added Tax.* Athens: Center of Planning and Economic Research, 1973.

Shoup Mission, *Report on Japanese Taxation.* Tokyo, 1949.

Simons, Henry C. *Personal Income Taxation.* Chicago: University of Chicago Press, 1938.

Smith, Adam. *The Wealth of Nations,* 2 vols. Edwin Cannan, ed. London: Methuen University Paperbacks, 1961.

Soligo, Ronald. *Factor Intensity of Consumption Patterns, Income Distribution and Employment Growth in Pakistan.* Houston: Rice University, Program of Development Studies, Paper No. 44, 1973.

Tait, Alan A. *Value-added Tax.* London: McGraw-Hill, 1972.

Tax Foundation. *Federal Excise Taxes* (Project Note No. 40). New York, 1956.

Taylor, Milton, et al. Joint Tax Program, *Fiscal Survey of Colombia.* Baltimore: Johns Hopkins Press, 1965.

Van der Poel, Jr. *Over Accijnzen.* Haarlem, Netherlands: F. Bohn, 1927.

Wallich, Henry, and John Adler. *Public Finance in a Developing Country: El Salvador—A Case Study.* Cambridge: Harvard University Press, 1951.

Walters, A. A. *The Economics of Road User Charges* (World Bank Occasional Paper Number Five). Baltimore: Johns Hopkins Press, 1968.

Watkin, Virginia G. *Taxes and Tax Harmonization in Central America.* Cambridge: Law School of Harvard University, 1967.

Webb, Richard C. *Income Distribution and Government Policy in Peru.* Cambridge: Harvard University Press, forthcoming.

Wilkenfeld, Harold C. *Taxes and People in Israel.* Cambridge: Harvard University Press, 1973.

Winch, David M. *The Economics of Highway Planning.* Toronto: Toronto University Press, 1963.

Yoingco, Angel Q. and Ruben F. Trinidad. *Fiscal Systems and Practices in Asian Countries.* New York: Frederick A. Praeger, 1968.

ARTICLES AND CONTRIBUTIONS TO BOOKS

Acharya, Shankar N. "Fiscal Financial Intervention, Factor Prices and Factor Proportions: A Review of Issues," *Bangladesh Economic Studies,* vol. 3 (October 1975), pp. 429–64.

Andic, Fuat M. and Arthur J. Mann. "Redesigning Puerto Rico's Tax System: An Overview," *Bulletin for International Fiscal Documentation,* vol. 29 (May 1975), pp. 186–99.

Andrews, William D. "A Consumption-Type or Cash Flow Personal Income Tax," *Harvard Law Review,* vol. 87 (April 1974), pp. 113–88.

———. "Fairness and the Personal Income Tax: A Reply to Professor Warren," *Harvard Law Review,* vol. 88 (March 1975), pp. 931–46.

Atkinson, A. B. and J. E. Stiglitz. "The Structure of Indirect Taxation and Economic Efficiency," *Journal of Public Economics,* vol. 1 (April 1972), pp. 97–119.

Bakkenist, S. C. "Régie or Free Enterprise," in *World Tobacco Congress, Proceedings I.* Amsterdam, 1951, pp. 71–74.

Ballentine, J. Gregory and Charles E. McLure, Jr. "Excess Burden: The Corner Case in General Equilibrium," *American Economic Review,* vol. 66 (December 1976), pp. 944–46.

Baumol, William J. "On Taxation and the Control of Externalities," *American Economic Review,* vol. 62 (June 1972), pp. 307–22.

Biørn, Eric. "The Distributive Effects of Indirect Taxation: An Econometric Model and Empirical Results Based on Norwegian Data," *Swedish Journal of Economics,* vol. 77 (no. 1, 1975), pp. 1–11.

Bird, Richard M. "A Tax Incentive for Sales: The Canadian Experience," *National Tax Journal,* vol. 18 (September 1965), pp. 48–67.

———. "Sales Taxation and Development Planning—Colombia," in Gustav F. Papanek, ed., *Development Policy—Theory and Practice.* Cambridge: Harvard University Press, 1968, pp. 239–66.

———. "Equity and Taxes in the Carter Report," in Canadian Tax Foundation, *Report of the Twentieth Tax Conference,* 1967. Toronto, 1968, pp. 256–64.

———. "Optimal Tax Policy for a Developing Country: The Case of Colombia," *Finanzarchiv,* vol. 29 (no. 1, 1970), pp. 30–53.

——— and Luc Henry De Wulf. "Taxation and Income Distribution in Latin America: A Critical Review of Empirical Studies," *IMF Staff Papers,* vol. 20 (November 1973), pp. 639–82.

———. "Public Finance and Inequality," *Finance and Development,* vol. 11 (March 1974), pp. 2–4, 34.

Bishop, Robert L. "The Effects of Specific and Ad Valorem Taxes," *Quarterly Journal of Economics,* vol. 82 (May 1968), pp. 198–218.

Bobrowski, Luis, and Samuel Goldberg. "Presión Tributaria por Niveles de Ingreso: Un Análisis Comparativo," in *Finanzas Públicas: Segundas Jornadas, 1969* (Córdoba, Argentina, 1970), pp. 391–445.

Bradford, David F. and Harvey S. Rosen. "The Optimal Taxation of Commodities and Income," *American Economic Review,* vol. 66, no. 2 (May 1976), pp. 94–101.

Branson, William H. "The Use of Variable Tax Rates for Stabilization Purposes," in Musgrave, ed., *Broad-Based Taxes,* pp. 267–85.

Bräuer, Karl. "Aufwandsteuern," "Monopol als Form der Besteuerung," and "Tabaksteuer," *Handwörterbuch der Staatswissenschaften.* Jena: Gustav Fisher, 1925, pp. 10–19, 623–27, 1213–38.

Bräuer, Karl. "Excise," in *Encyclopaedia of the Social Sciences.* New York: Macmillan, 1935, pp. 669–71.

Break, George F. "Allocation and Excess Burden Effects of Excise and Sales Taxes," in U.S. Congress (88:2), *Excise Tax Compendium,* pt 1, pp. 65–72.

_____. "The Incidence and Economic Effects of Taxation," in *The Economics of Public Finance* (Essays by Alan S. Blinder and Robert M. Solow, George F. Break, Peter O. Steiner, and Dick Netzer). Washington, D.C.: Brookings Institution, 1974, pp. 119–237.

Bridges, Benjamin, Jr. "The Harberger Incidence Model: A Comment," *National Tax Journal*, vol. 38 (December 1975), pp. 462–66.

Brody, Jane E. "Sweden Plans a Nation of Nonsmokers Starting with Children Born in 1975," *New York Times* (June 3, 1975), p. 16.

Brown, E. Cary, "Analysis of Consumption Taxes in Terms of the Theory of Income Determination," *American Economic Review*, vol. 40 (March 1950), pp. 74–89.

Brownlee, O. H. "User Prices vs. Taxes," in *Public Finances: Needs, Sources, and Utilization* (A Report of the National Bureau of Economic Research). Princeton: Princeton University Press, 1961, pp. 421–37.

Brownlee, Oswald and George L. Perry. "The Effects of the 1965 Federal Excise Tax Reductions on Prices," *National Tax Journal*, vol. 20 (September 1967), pp. 235–49.

Buchanan, James M. "External Diseconomies, Corrective Taxes, and Market Structure," *American Economic Review*, vol. 59 (March 1969), pp. 174–77.

_____ and Francesco Forte. "Fiscal Choice Through Time: A Case for Indirect Taxation, *National Tax Journal*, vol. 17 (September 1964), pp. 144–57.

Calmus, Thomas W. "The Burden of Federal Excise Taxes by Income Classes," *Quarterly Review of Economics and Business*, vol. 10 (Spring 1970), pp. 17–23.

Chelliah, Raja J. "Trends in Taxation in Developing Countries," *IMF Staff Papers*, vol. 18 (July 1971), pp. 224–331.

_____, Hessel J. Baas, and Margaret R. Kelly. "Tax Ratios and Tax Effort in Developing Countries, 1969–71," *IMF Staff Papers*, vol. 22 (March 1975), pp. 187–205.

Cluseau, Max. "Défense de l'impôt sur l'énergie," *Revue de Science et de Législation Financières*, vol. 56 (1954), pp. 261–77.

Cnossen, Sijbren. "Capacity Taxation: The Pakistan Experiment," *IMF Staff Papers*, vol. 21 (March 1974), pp. 127–69.

_____. "The Role and Structure of Sales and Excise Tax Systems," *Finance and Development*, vol. 12 (March 1975), pp. 29–33.

_____. "Sales Tax and Excise Systems of the World," *Finanzarchiv*, vol. 33 (no. 2, 1975), pp. 177–236.

Corlett, W. J. and D. C. Hague. "Complementarity and the Excess Burden of Taxation," *Review of Economic Studies*, vol. 21 (no. 1, 1953–54), pp. 21–30.

De Wulf, Luc. "Taxation and Income Distribution in Lebanon," *Bulletin for International Fiscal Documentation*, vol. 28 (April 1974), pp. 151–59.

_____. "Do Public Expenditures Reduce Inequality?" *Finance and Development*, vol. 11 (September 1974), pp. 20–23.

_____. "Fiscal Incidence Studies in Developing Countries: Survey and Critique," *IMF Staff Papers*, vol. 22 (March 1975), pp. 61–131, 236–37.

Dodsworth, John. "Excise Duties," in Douglas Dosser et. al., *British Taxation and the Common Market*. London: Charles Knight, 1973, pp. 54–88.

Dosser, Douglas. "Indirect Taxation and Economic Development," in Alan T. Peacock and Gerald Hauser, eds., *Government Finance and Economic Development*. Paris: Organisation for Economic Co-operation and Development, 1965, pp. 127–142.

Due, John F. "The Effect of the 1954 Reduction in Federal Excise Taxes upon the List Prices of Electrical Appliances—A Case Study," *National Tax Journal*, vol. 7 (September 1954), pp. 222–26.

_____. "Excise and Sales Taxes as Anti-inflationary Measures," in *Annals of the American Academy of Political and Social Science*, vol. 326 (November 1959), pp. 79–84.

_____. "Studies of State-Local Tax Influences on Location of Industry," *National Tax Journal*, vol. 14 (June 1961), pp. 163–73.

_____. "Administrative Criteria in the Establishment of Sales and Excise Tax Structure," in Joint Tax Program, *Problems of Tax Administration in Latin America*, pp. 413–36.

_____. "Sales and Excise Taxes," in *International Encyclopedia of the Social Sciences*. New York: Macmillan and Free Press, 1968, pp. 550–55.

_____. "Alternative Forms of Sales Taxation for a Developing Country," *Journal of Development Studies*, vol. 8 (January 1972), pp. 263–76.

_____. "The evolution of sales taxation, 1915–1972," in Bird and Head, eds., *Modern Fiscal Issues*, pp. 318–44.

Eckstein, Otto. "Indirect Versus Direct Taxes: Implications for Stability Investment," in U.S. Congress (88:2), *Excise Tax Compendium*, pt 1, pp. 43–55.

Ferber, Robert. "How Aware Are Consumers of Excise Tax Changes?" *National Tax Journal*, vol. 7 (December 1954), pp. 355–58.

Fort D. M., et. al. "Proposal for a Smog Tax," in *Tax Recommendations of the President*, Hearings before the House Committee on Ways and Means, U.S. Congress (91:2), pp. 369–79.

Franzén, Thomas, Kerstin Lövgren and Irma Rosenberg. "Redistributional Effects of Taxes and Public Expenditures in Sweden," *Swedish Journal of Economics*, vol. 77 (no. 1, 1975), pp. 31–55.

Friedlaender, Ann F. and John F. Due. "Tax Burden, Excess Burden, and Differential Incidence Revisited," *Public Finance*, vol. 27 (no. 3, 1972), pp. 312–24.

_____. "Tax Burden, Excess Burden, and Differential Incidence Revisited: Comment and Extentions—A Reply," *Public Finance*, vol. 29 (no. 3–4, 1974), pp. 413–15.

Friedman, Milton. "The 'Welfare' Effects on an Income Tax and an Excise Tax," *Journal of Political Economy*, vol. 60 (February 1952). Reprinted in Milton Friedman, *Essays in Positive Economics*. Chicago: University of Chicago Press, 1953, pp. 100–13.

Gillis, Malcolm. "Reform of Municipal Indirect Taxes, Service Taxation, and Stamp Duties," in Gillis and Musgrave, eds., *Fiscal Reform for Colombia*, pp. 648–91.

_____ and Charles E. McLure, Jr. "Coordination of Tariffs and Internal Indirect Taxes," in Gillis and Musgrave, eds., *Fiscal Reform for Colombia*. Partially reprinted in Bird and Oldman, eds., *Readings on Taxation in Developing Countries*, 3rd ed., 1975, pp. 325–36.

Goode, Richard. "Anti-inflationary Implications of Alternative Forms of Taxation," *American Economic Review*, vol. 42 (May 1952), pp. 147–60.

_____. "Reconstruction of Foreign Tax Systems," in National Tax Association, *Proceedings of the Forty-Fourth Annual Conference on Taxation*. Sacramento, California, 1952. Reprinted in Bird and Oldman, eds., *Readings on Taxation in Developing Countries*, rev. ed., 1967, pp. 121–31.

_____. "Taxation of Saving and Consumption in Underdeveloped Countries," *National Tax Journal*, vol. 14 (December 1961). Reprinted in Bird and Oldman, eds., *Readings on Taxation in Developing Countries*, 3rd. ed., 1975, pp. 273–93.

_____. "Income, Consumption, and Property as Bases of Taxation," *American Economic Review*, vol. 52 (May 1962), pp. 327–34.

Granick, David. "Economic Development and Productivity Analysis: The Case of Soviet Metal-working," *Quarterly Journal of Economics*, vol. 71 (May 1957), pp. 205–33.

Gross, Herbert. "Monopolies, Public," in *Encyclopaedia of the Social Sciences*. New York: Macmillan, 1935, pp. 619–23.

Grotkopp, Wilhelm. "Match Industry," in *Encyclopaedia of the Social Sciences*. New York: Macmillan, 1935, pp. 203–9.

Groves, Harold M. "Toward a Social Theory of Progressive Taxation," *National Tax Journal*, vol. 9 (March 1956), pp. 27–34.

Hansmeyer, Karl-Heinrich. "Finanzmonopole," in *Handwörterbuch der Sozialwissenschaften*. Stuttgart: Gustav Fischer, 1961, pp. 580–85.

Harberger, Arnold C. "Taxation, Resource Allocation, and Welfare," in *The Role of Direct and Indirect Taxes in the Federal Revenue System*. Princeton: Princeton University Press, 1964. Reprinted in Harberger, *Taxation and Welfare*, pp. 25–68.

_____. "The Measurement of Waste," *American Economic Review*, vol. 54 (March 1964). Reprinted in Harberger, *Taxation and Welfare*, pp. 69–85.

_____. "Issues of Tax Reform for Latin America," in Joint Tax Program, *Fiscal Policy for Economic Growth in Latin America*, pp. 110–21.

Head, John G. "The Welfare Foundations of Public Finance Theory," Revista di Diritto Finanziario e Scienza delle Finanze, vol. 24 (September 1965). Reprinted in John G. Head, *Public Goods and Public Welfare*. Durham, North Carolina: Duke University Press, 1974, pp. 3–49.

_____ and C. S. Shoup. "Excess Burden: The Corner Case," *American Economic Review*, vol. 59 (March 1969), pp. 181–83.

Healey, Derek T. "Development Policy: New Thinking About an Interpretation," *Journal of Economic Literature*, vol. 10 (September 1972), pp. 757–97.

Hey, Sally. "Departmental and Municipal Revenues in Colombia: Proposals for Reform," in Gillis and Musgrave, eds., *Fiscal Reform for Colombia*, pp. 736–70.

Higgins, B. "Fiscal Control of Monopoly," in Musgrave and Shoup, eds., *Readings in the Economics of Taxation*, pp. 812–21.

Hill, John R. "Sales Taxation in Francophone Africa," *Journal of Developing Areas*, forthcoming.

Hirao, T. and Aguirre, C. A. "Maintaining the Level of Income Tax Collections under Inflationary Conditions," *IMF Staff Papers*, vol. 17 (July 1970), pp. 277–325.

Hixson, Jesse S. and James B. Ramsey. "A Further Comment on the Effects of Excise Taxes," *Quarterly Journal of Economics*, vol. 86 (November 1972), pp. 684–86.

Hogan, Warren. "Capacity Creation and Utilisation in Pakistan Manufacturing Industry," *Australian Economic Papers*, vol. 7 (June 1968), pp. 28–53.

Hood, C. "The Development of Betting Taxes in Britain," *Public Administration*, vol. 50 (Summer 1972), pp. 183–210.

Huang, Yukon. "Distribution of the Tax Burden in Tanzania," *Economic Journal*, vol. 86 (March 1976), pp. 73–86.

Israel, M. R. "Régie or Free Enterprise," in *World Tobacco Congress, Proceedings I. Amsterdam, 1951, pp. 123–31.*

Janssen, Richard F. "More Europeans begin making their own booze," *Wall Street Journal*, November 25, 1974, p. 6.

Johnson, Harry L. "Tax Pyramiding and the Manufacturer's Excise Tax Reduction of 1954," *National Tax Journal*, vol. 17 (September 1964), pp. 297–302.

_____ and Mel Kraus. "Border Taxes, Border Tax Adjustments, Comparative Advantage and the Balance of Payments," *Canadian Journal of Economics*, vol. 3 (November 1970), pp. 595–602.

Johnson, J. A. "Canadian Policies in Regard to the Taxation of Alcoholic Beverages," *Canadian Tax Journal*, vol. 21 (November-December 1973), pp. 552–64.

Joseph, M. F. W. "The Excess Burden of Indirect Taxation," *Review of Economic Studies*, vol. 6 (June 1939), pp. 226–31.

Kambe, Masao. "State Monopoly as a Method of Taxing Consumption," Kyoto University, *Economic Review*, vol. 7 (July 1932), pp. 1–13.

Karageorgas, D. "The Distribution of Tax Burden by Income Groups in Greece," *Economic Journal*, vol. 73 (June 1973), pp. 436–48.

Kelley, Patrick L. "Is an Expenditure Tax Feasible?" *National Tax Journal*, vol. 23 (September 1970), pp. 237–53.

Koutsoyannis, Anna P. "Demand Functions for Tobacco," *Manchester School of Economic and Social Studies*, vol. 31 (January 1963), pp. 1–20.

Kraus, Marvin and Herbert Mohring. "The Role of Pollutee Taxes in Externality Problems," *Economica*, vol. 42 (May 1975), pp. 171–81.

Kraus, Melvyn B. "Tax Burden, Excess Burden, and Differential Incidence Revisited: Comment and Extensions," *Public Finance*, vol. 29 (no. 3-4, 1974), pp. 404–12.

Krzyzaniak, Marian and Süleyman Özmucur. "The Distribution of Income and the Short-Run Burden of Taxes in Turkey, 1968," *Finanzarchiv*, vol. 32 (no. 1, 1973), pp. 69–97.

Law, Warren A. "Tobacco Taxation in the Revenue System," *National Tax Journal*, vol. 6 (December 1953), pp. 372–85.

Lent, George E., Milka Casanegra and Michèle Guérard. "The Value-Added Tax in Developing Countries," *IMF Staff Papers*, vol. 20 (July 1973), pp. 318–78.

_____. "Taxation of Agricultural Income in Developing Countries," *Bulletin for International Fiscal Documentation*, vol. 27 (August 1973), pp. 324–42.

Levin, Jonathan. "The Effects of Economic Development on the Base of a Sales Tax: A Case Study of Colombia," *IMF Staff Papers*, vol. 15 (March 1968), pp. 30–101.

Lewis, Stephen R., Jr. and Stephen E. Guisinger. "The Structure of Protection in Pakistan," in Bela Balassa and Associates, *The Structure of Protection in Developing Countries.* Baltimore: Johns Hopkins Press, 1971, pp. 223–60.

Lipsey, R. G. and K. Lancaster. "The General Theory of Second Best," *Review of Economic Studies,* vol. 24 (no. 1, 1956–57), pp. 11–32.

Little, I. M. D. "Direct versus Indirect Taxes," *Economic Journal,* vol. 61 (September 1951). Reprinted in Musgrave and Shoup, eds., *Readings in the Economics of Taxation.* Homewood, Illinois: Richard D. Irwin, 1959, pp. 123–31.

Lutz, Harley L. "Revenues, Public," in *Encyclopaedia of the Social Sciences.* New York: Macmillan, 1935, pp. 360–63.

————. "The Place and Role of Consumption Taxes in the Federal Tax Structure," in the U.S. Congress, Joint Committee on the Economic Report (84:1), *Federal Tax Policy for Economic Growth and Stability.* Washington: U.S. Government Printing Office, 1955, pp. 560–74.

Macaulay, Hugh. "Environmental quality, the market, and public finance," in Bird and Head, eds., *Modern Fiscal Issues,* pp. 187–224.

Mansfield, Charles Y. "Elasticity and Buoyancy of a Tax System: A Method Applied to Paraguay," *IMF Staff Papers,* vol. 19 (July 1972), pp. 425–46.

Marcus, M. "Taxation of Tobacco and Spirits in Sweden," Skandinaviska Banken, *Quarterly Review* (July 1940), pp. 73–81.

McConnell, D. W. "Liquor Traffic," in *Encyclopaedia of the Social Sciences.* New York: Macmillan, 1935, pp. 502–9.

McLure, Charles E., Jr. "The Interstate Exporting of State and Local Taxes: Estimates for 1962," *National Tax Journal,* vol. 20 (March 1967), pp. 49–77.

McLure, Charles E., Jr. "Taxation, Substitution, and Industrial Location," *Journal of Political Economy,* vol. 78 (January/February 1970), pp. 112–32.

————. "The Distribution of Income and Tax Incidence in Panama: 1969," *Public Finance Quarterly,* vol. 2 (April 1974), pp. 155–201.

————. "The Incidence of Colombian Taxes: 1970," *Economic Development and Cultural Change,* vol. 24 (October 1975), pp. 155–83.

————. "The Proper Use of Indirect Taxation in Latin America: The Practice of Economic Marksmanship," *Public Finance,* vol. 30 (no. 1, 1975). Partially reprinted in Bird and Oldman, eds., *Readings on Taxation in Developing Countries,* 3rd. ed., pp. 339–49.

————. "General Equilibrium Incidence Analysis: The Harberger model after ten years," *Journal of Public Finance,* vol. 4 (February 1975), pp. 125–61.

————. "Taxation and the Urban Poor in Developing Countries," *World Development,* forthcoming.

———— and Wayne R. Thirsk. "A Simplified Exposition of the Harberger Model—I: Tax Incidence," *National Tax Journal,* vol. 28 (March 1975), pp. 1–27.

————. "The Harberger Model: Reply," *National Tax Journal,* vol. 38 (December 1975), pp. 467–71.

————. "The Inequity of Taxing Iniquity: A Plea for Reduced Sumptuary Taxes in Developing Countries," *Economic Development and Cultural Change,* forthcoming.

Metwally, M. M. "Household Expenditure Patterns: Hamilton, New Zealand," *Economic Record,* vol. 46 (March 1970), pp. 73–85.

Millenaar, K. "Fiscale harmonisatie in de Benelux," *Weekblad voor Fiscaal Recht,* no. 5118 (January 1975), pp. 73–80.

Mishan, E. J. "The Postwar Literature on Externalities: An Interpretative Essay," *Journal of Economic Literature,* vol. 9 (March 1971), pp. 1–28.

Morag, Amotz. "Some Economic Aspects of Two Administrative Methods of Estimating Taxable Income," *National Tax Journal,* vol. 10 (June 1957), pp. 176–85.

Morawetz, David. "Employment Implications of Industrialisation in Developing Countries: A Survey," *Economic Journal,* vol. 84 (September 1974), pp. 491–542.

Musgrave, Richard A. "On Incidence," *Journal of Political Economy,* vol. 61 (August 1953), pp. 306–23.

————. "Estimating the Distribution of the Tax Burden," in Joint Tax Program, *Problems of Tax Administration in Latin America,* pp. 31–102.

_____. "Provision for Social Goods," in J. Margolis and H. Guitton, eds., *Public Economics*. New York: St. Martin's Press, 1969, pp. 124–44.

_____, A. C. Harberger, and A. Kervyn. "Some Practical Suggestions," in International Labour Office, *Fiscal Measures for Employment Promotion in Developing Countries*, Geneva, 1972, pp. 337–42.

_____, Karl E. Case, and Herman Leonard. "The Distribution of Fiscal Burdens and Benefits," *Public Finance Quarterly*, vol. 2 (July 1974), pp. 259–311.

Naharro, José Maria. "Production and Consumption Taxes and Economic Development," in Joint Tax Program, *Fiscal Policy for Economic Growth in Latin America*, pp. 273–320.

Narbrough, Colin. "Swedes Do Battle Against Illicit Home Brew," *Washington Post*, November 17, 1974, H4.

Neumark, Fritz. "Lassalles Steuer-Streitschrift, 1863–1963," *Finanzarchiv*, vol. 23 (no. 1, 1963), pp. 66–81.

Newman, Barry. "Singapore is Waging a War Against Cars and it's Winning," *Wall Street Journal*, November 5, 1976, pp. 1, 20.

Norr, Martin. "Tobacco Taxes at Home and Abroad," *Taxes—The Tax Magazine*, vol. 40 (November 1962), pp. 842–45.

Ojha, P. D. and George E. Lent. "Sales Taxes in Countries of the Far East," *IMF Staff Papers*, vol. 16 (November 1969), pp. 529–79.

Osnos, Peter. "The Soviet Drinking Problem," *Washington Post*, December 29, 1974, B1.

Peacock, Alan T. and John Williamson. "Consumption Taxes and Compensatory Finance," *Economic Journal*, vol. 77 (March 1967), pp. 27–47.

Pepper, H. W. T. "Transportation Taxes," *Bulletin for International Fiscal Documentation*, vol. 29 (July and August 1975), pp. 274–80, 311–16.

Phillips, Almarin. "An Appraisal of Measures of Capacity," *American Economic Review*, vol. 53 (May 1963), pp. 275–92.

Prest, A. R. "The Sensitivity of the Yield of Personal Income Tax in the United Kingdom," *Economic Journal*, vol. 72 (September 1962), pp. 576–96.

Radhu, Ghulam Mohammed. "The Rate Structure of Indirect Taxes in Pakistan," *Pakistan Development Review*, vol. 4 (Autumn 1964), pp. 527–51.

_____. "The Relation of Indirect Tax Changes to Price Changes in Pakistan," *Pakistan Development Review*, vol. 5 (Spring 1965), pp. 54–63.

Ramsey, Frank. "A Contribution to the Theory of Taxation," *Economic Journal*, vol. 37 (March 1927), pp. 46–61.

Rolph, Earl R. and George F. Break. "The Welfare Aspects of Excise Taxes," *Journal of Political Economy*, vol. 57 (February 1949). Reprinted in Musgrave and Shoup, eds., *Readings in the Economics of Taxation*, pp. 110–22.

Rose-Ackermann, Susan. "Effluent Charges: A Critique," *Canadian Journal of Economics*, vol. 6 (November 1973), pp. 512–28.

Roskamp, Karl W. "The Distribution of Tax Burden in a Rapidly Growing Economy: West Germany in 1950," *National Tax Journal*, vol. 16 (March 1963), pp. 20–35.

Rozental, Alek A. "Selective Excises and the Federal Tax Structure," *Southern Economic Journal*, vol. 23 (April 1957), pp. 421–33.

Saito, Katrine W. "Petroleum Taxes: How High and Why?" *Finance and Development*, vol. 12 (December 1975), pp. 17–20, 46.

Schmeck, Harold M., Jr. "Alcohol Cost to Nation Put at $25-Billion a Year," *New York Times*, July 11, 1974, pp. 1, 13.

Schmölders, Günter. "Das Verbrauch- und Aufwandsteuersystem," in *Handbuch der Finanzwissenschaft*, vol. 2. Tübingen: J.C.B. Mohr (Paul Siebeck), 1956, pp. 635–720.

Schnittger, L. "Taxation and Tax Policy in East Africa," in Peter Marlin, ed., *Financial Aspects of Development in East Africa*. New York: Humanities Press, 1970, pp. 27–92.

Schoeplein, Robert N. "Problems in Administering a Sales Tax on Services," in National Tax Association, *Proceedings of the Sixty-Fourth Annual Conference, 1971*. Columbus, Ohio, 1972, pp. 570–82.

Shoup, Carl S. "Production from Consumption," *Public Finance*, vol. 20 (no. 1–2, 1965), pp. 173–202.

———. "Tax Tension and the British Fiscal System," *National Tax Journal*, vol. 14 (March 1961), pp. 1–40.

———. "Quantitative Research in Taxation and Government Expenditures," in National Bureau of Economic Research, *Public Expenditures and Taxation*. New York: Columbia University Press, 1972, pp. 1–60.

Simon, Julian L. "State Liquor Monopolies," in R. Turvey, ed., *Public Enterprise*. Penguin Books, 1968, pp. 365–77.

Simons, A. L. C. "De opheffing van grenzen voor accijnzen en omzetbelasting," *Weekblad voor Fiscaal Recht*, nos. 5121–22 (February 1973), pp. 141–53, 165–72.

Slitor, Richard. "Reform of the Business Tax Structure: Analysis of Problems and Alternative Remedial Proposals," in Gillis and Musgrave, eds., *Fiscal Reform for Colombia*, pp. 463–529.

———. "Administrative Aspects of Expenditures Taxation," in Musgrave, ed., *Broad-Based Taxes*, pp. 227–63.

Smith, Roger S. "Highway Pricing and Motor Vehicle Taxation in Developing Countries: Theory and Practice," *Finanzarchiv*, vol. 33 (no. 3, 1975), pp. 451–74.

Sparks, Jared. "Canadian Excise Taxes and Inflation Control," *Canadian Tax Journal*, vol. 6 (January-February 1958), pp. 71–80.

Spiro, Michael H. "On the Tax Incidence of the Pennsylvania Lottery," *National Tax Journal*, vol. 27 (March 1974), pp. 57–61.

Surrey, Stanley. "Tax Administration in Underdeveloped Countries," in Bird and Oldman, eds., *Readings on Taxation in Developing Countries*, rev. ed., 1967, pp. 497–527.

Tanzi, Vito. "Redistributing Income Through the Budget in Latin America," *Banco Nazionale del Lavoro Quarterly Review*, no. 108 (March 1974), pp. 3–25.

———. "Theory of Tax Structure Development and the Design of Tax Structure Policy for Industrialization," in David T. Geithman, ed., *Fiscal Policy for Industrialization and Development in Latin America*. Gainsville: University of Florida Presses, 1974, pp. 48–67.

Van der Poel, J. "De Evolutie der Accijnzen," *Weekblad voor Fiscaal Recht*, nos. 4682–86; 1963: pp. 1009–14, 1032–40; 1964: pp. 14–18, 37–42, 61.

Vincent, J. M. "Sumptuary Legislation," in *Encyclopaedia of the Social Sciences*. New York: Macmillan, 1935, pp. 464–66.

Walker, David. "The Direct-Indirect Tax Problem: Fifteen Years of Controversy," *Public Finance*, vol. 10 (no. 2, 1955), pp. 153–76.

Warren, Alvin C., Jr. "Fairness and a Consumption-Type or Cash Flow Personal Income Tax," *Harvard Law Review*, vol. 88 (March 1975), pp. 931–46.

Watson, Peter, and Edward P. Holland. "Congestion Pricing—the Example of Singapore," *Finance and Development*, vol. 13 (March 1976), pp. 20–23.

Wicksell, Knut. "A New Principle of Just Taxation," in Richard A. Musgrave and Alan T. Peacock, eds., *Classics in the Theory of Public Finance*. New York: St. Martin's Press, 1967, pp. 72–118.

Winston, Gordon C. "Overinvoicing, Underutilization and Distorted Industrial Growth," *Pakistan Development Review*, vol. 10 (Winter 1970), pp. 405–21.

———. "Capital Utilisation in Economic Development," *Economic Journal*, vol. 81 (March 1971), pp. 36–60.

Wolfson, Dirk J. "The Fiscal Policy Aspect of Development Strategy," *International Development Review*, vol. 15 (no. 3, 1973), pp. 7–12, 34.

Woodward, P. O. and Harvey Siegelman. "Effects of the 1965 Federal Excise Tax Reduction Upon the Price of Automotive Replacement Parts—A Case Study in Tax Shifting and Pyramiding," *National Tax Journal*, vol. 20 (September 1967), pp. 250–57.

PUBLIC DOCUMENTS

Australia. *Taxation Review Committee, Full Report, 31 January 1975*. Canberra: Australian Government Publishing Service, 1975.

Canada. "Sales Taxes and General Tax Administration," *Report of the Royal Commission on Taxation,* vol. 5. Ottawa: Queen's Printer, 1966.

East African Common Services Organization. *Excise Management Act, 1952.* Nairobi: Government Printer, 1963.

European Communities, Commission of the. *Proposed Council Directives on Excise Duties and Similar Taxes.* Brussels: Bulletin of the European Communities, Supplement 3/72, 1972.

France. Ministère de l'Economie et des Finances, *Le Système Fiscal Français.* Paris, 1970.

Germany, Federal Republic of. *Gutachten der Steuerreformkommission 1971* (Schriftenreihe des Bundesministeriums der Finanzen, vol. 17). Bonn: Wilhelm Stollfusz, 1971.

_____. *Der Wissenschaftliche Beirat beim Bundesministerium der Finanzen; Entschliessungen, Stellungnahmen und Gutachten von 1949 bis 1973.* Tübingen: J. C. B. Mohr (Paul Siebeck), 1974.

India, Government of. *Report of the Taxation Enquiry Commission, 1953-54,* 3 vols. New Delhi: Government of India Press, 1955.

_____. *Report of the Central Excise Reorganisation Committee.* Delhi: Government of India Press, 1963.

_____. *Incidence of Indirect Taxation, 1963-64.* New Delhi: Ministry of Finance, 1969.

Indonesia. Biro Pusat Statistik. *Statistik Industri 1971.* (Hasil Pengolahan Data Perusahaan Industri Besar dan Sedang). Jakarta, 1973.

_____. *Statistik Indonesia.* Jakarta, 1974.

International Monetary Fund. *Surveys of African Economies,* 4 vols. Washington, D.C., 1968-71.

_____. *A Manual on Government Finance Statistics (Draft).* Washington, D.C., 1974.

International Labour Office. *Employment, Incomes and Equality: A Strategy for Increasing Productive Employment in Kenya.* Geneva, 1972.

Japan. Ministry of Finance. *Report of the Board of Inquiry on the Japanese Monopoly System.* Tokyo, 1960.

_____. *An Outline of Japanese Taxes 1976.* Tokyo.

New Zealand. *Taxation in New Zealand, Report of the Taxation Review Committee.* Wellington: Government Printer, 1967.

Norway. Ministry of Finance. *Norwegian Long-Term Programme, 1970-73.* Oslo, 1969.

Organisation for Economic Co-operation and Development. *Border Tax Adjustments and Tax Structures in OECD Member Countries.* Paris, 1968.

_____. *Revenue Statistics of OECD Member Countries,* 1968-70, 1965-71, 1965-72, and 1965-73. Paris, 1972, 1973, and 1975.

Pakistan, Government of. Ministry of Finance, Planning and Economic Affairs. *Budget Speech, The Budget in Brief, Explanatory Memorandum on the Budget,* and *Pakistan Budgets.* Karachi and Islamabad, various years.

_____. Central Statistical Office. *Monthly Statistical Bulletin.* Karachi, various issues.

_____. _____. *Report of Survey on Capacity Utilization by Manufacturing Industries 1965,* Annexure B. Karachi: Government of Pakistan Press.

_____. *Taxation Enquiry Committee Report,* 2 vols. Karachi: Government of Pakistan Press, 1961.

_____. Central Board of Revenue. *Tax in Pakistan: A Brief Outline With Particular Reference to Tax Concessions to New Industries and Incentives to Foreign Investment.* Karachi: rev. ed., 1965.

_____. _____. *Central Taxes in Pakistan: A Decade of Development and Self Effort.* Islamabad, 1968.

_____. *Taxation Structure in Pakistan.* Islamabad, 1975.

Philippines, Republic of the. Joint Legislative-Executive Tax Commission. *A Study of Tax Burden by Income Class in the Philippines.* Manila, 1964.

_____. *12th Annual Report 1970.* Manila, 1971.

Puerto Rico, Commonwealth of. Department of the Treasury. *What You Should Know About Taxes in Puerto Rico 1973.* San Juan.

Sri Lanka, Republic of. *Report of the Taxation Inquiry Commission.* Colombo: Government Press, 1968.

_____. *Budget Speech 1976.* Colombo: Department of Government Printing, 1975.

Turkey. "State Monopolies of Turkey," in *Tobacco Affairs.* Istanbul: Monopolies' Press, 1939.

United Kingdom. Ministry of Transport. *Road Pricing: The Economic and Technical Possibilities.* London: Her Majesty's Stationary Office, 1964.

United Nations. Department of Economic Affairs. *Public Finance Information Papers:* Italy. Lake Success, New York, 1950.

―――. *Economic Survey of Asia and the Far East, 1969.*

―――. Economic and Social Council. *The Tax System in Pakistan: Studies in Tax Reform Planning* (July 19, 1971). Revision of a study originally prepared by Nurul Islam, Director, Pakistan Institute of Development Economics, Karachi.

―――. Food and Agriculture Organization of the. *Income Elasticities of Demand for Agricultural Products.* Rome, 1972.

―――. *Ad Hoc Government Consultation on Tobacco.* Izmir, Turkey: November 5–10, 1973; and Rome: June 20–22, 1974.

―――. *Statistical Yearbook 1972.*

United States. U.S. Congress (88:2), House Committee on Ways and Means. *Excise Tax Compendium (Part I) and Federal Excise Tax Structure (Part 2).* Washington, D.C.: U.S. Government Printing Office, 1964.

UNPUBLISHED MATERIAL

Amatong, Juanita. "The Revenue Importance of Government Lotteries." International Monetary Fund, 1968.

Azfar, Jawaid. "The Income Distribution in Pakistan, Before and After Taxes, 1966–67." Ph.D. dissertation. Cambridge: Harvard University, 1972.

Baas, Hessel J. and Daryl A. Dixon. "The Elasticity of the British Tax System, 1950/51–1970/71." International Monetary Fund, 1974.

Chand, Sheetal K. "Tax Revenue Forecasting: An Approach Applied to Malaysia." International Monetary Fund, 1975.

―――― and Bertram A. Wolfe. "The Elasticity and Buoyancy of the Tax System of Peru, 1960–71: An Empirical Analysis." International Monetary Fund, 1973.

Chelliah, R. J. and S. K. Chand. "A Note on Techniques of Adjusting Tax Revenue Series for Discretionary Changes." International Monetary Fund, 1974.

Cnossen, Sijbren. "Tax System and Reform," in *Economic Position and Prospects of the Republic of China,* vol. 2. International Bank for Reconstruction and Development (September 1970).

De Wulf, Luc. Ivory Coast: "Elasticity and Buoyancy of the Ivorian Revenue System." International Bank for Reconstruction and Development, 1975.

Due, John F. "The Relevant Marginal Cost for Establishing Highway User Charges in Developing Economies." Undated.

Farrukh, M. Z. "Tax Concessions to Industries—An Overview of Pakistan's Experience." Cambridge: Harvard University Law School, International Program in Taxation, 1966.

Gandhi, Ved. P. "Indirect Taxes and Personal Income Distribution." Washington, D.C., 1972.

Goreux, L. M. "Income Elasticity of the Demand for Food." Rome: Food and Agricultural Organization of the United Nations, 1959.

Hauvonen, J. J. "A Note on Oriental Tobacco." International Monetary Fund, 1968.

Jordan, Hashemite Kingdom of. *Report of the Royal Fiscal Commission* (August 1960).

Pakistan, Government of. Ministry of Industries and Natural Resources. *Report of the Textile Industry Capacity Committee* (February 1968).

Shoup, Carl S. "Tax Policy in Developing Countries," paper delivered at the Inter-American Center of Tax Administrators, Panama City, May 5, 1967.

Stout, D. K. "Report on Taxation in the Syrian Arab Republic" (November 1965).

INDEX

Ability-to-pay principle, 38. *See also* Progressivity
Adler, John H., 42
Administration of excises: compared to customs administration, 113, 118–19; compared to income tax administration, 4, 112; compared to sales tax administration, 4, 10, 112, 119; conventional method of, 99–110; criteria for, 4, 112–13; presumptive method of, 75–80; and problems with classifications, 103–4; and problems with exemptions, 105–6; and problems with small producers, 107; and problems with specific and ad valorem rates, 104–5; and registration and licensing, 100–101; and supervision and measurement of production, 101–2
Admission charges, 8, 35, 39, 53
Afghanistan, 87, 94
Agriculture, taxes on, 9, 75, 77, 78, 82
Alcoholic beverages, excises on: administration of, 99–102, 163 n. 20, 173 n. 25; coordination of, in Colombia, 70; definitional issues of, 12, 102, 172 n. 10; excess burden of, 57–58; exemptions of, 105; expenditures on, 51; fiscal monopolies of, 87–89, 90–91, 94–95; incidence of, 41–45, 46, 47, 48, 52, 72; psychology of, 40, 111, 112; revenue aspects of, 26, 28, 30–32, 33, 34, 35, 36, 37, 163 n. 19; sumptuary control through, 8, 69–70
Algeria, 85, 87, 94, 162 n. 27
Andic, Fuat M., 166 n. 45
Argentina, 11, 31, 33, 43
Artisan producers. *See* Small businesses
Atkinson, A. B., 57–58
Australia, 8, 32; Taxation Review Committee on, 161 n. 9
Austria, 31, 33, 66, 85, 88, 90, 91, 94
Azfar, Jawaid, 41

Baas, Hessel J., 28
Bahamas, 66
Bangladesh, 26
Banking, 12, 28, 35, 164 n. 16
Barbados, 10, 161 n. 8, 162 n. 33
Baumol, William J., 75, 166 n. 9
Belgium, 31, 71
Benefit principle, 8–9, 62, 70
Benelux, 71
Bénin. *See* Dahomey
Betting and gaming, 8, 12, 28, 30–32, 35, 91, 108, 165 n. 20
Biørn, Eric, 44, 46–47, 165 n. 21
Bird, Richard M., 115, 163 n. 1
Blough, Roy, 161 n. 14
Bobrowski, Luis, 43
Bolivia, 89, 90, 95
Border tax adjustments, 10, 71, 78, 95–96
Brannon, Gerard M., 168 n. 40
Branson, William H., 118
Bräuer, Karl, 85
Brazil, 11, 31, 89, 161 n. 15, 163 n. 7, 173 n. 20
Break, George F., 166 n. 4

Brownlee, Oswald, 164 n. 9
Buchanan, James M., 3, 163 n. 1, 168 n. 41
Burma, 26, 86, 163 n. 8

Calmus, Thomas W., 44, 165 n. 22
Cameroon, 162 n. 31
Canada, 31, 44, 53, 66, 67, 75, 85, 88, 90, 91, 93, 95, 109, 115, 117, 168 n. 45, 172 n. 11; Report of Royal Commission on Taxation and, 173 nn. 21, 28
Capacity taxation. *See* Presumptive excise taxation
Capacity utilization, 74, 81; determinants of, in Pakistan, 82
Capital goods, 59–60, 81, 83
Caribbean Community (Caricom), 17
Case, Karl E., 45
Cement, 13, 27, 33, 34, 37, 42, 76, 87
Central African Republic, 162 n. 31
Certainty in taxation, 4, 119, 121–22
Chad, 162 n. 31
Chand, Sheetal K., 28
Chelliah, Raja J., 27
Chile, 31, 51, 174 n. 11
China, 1, 84, 160 n. 5
China (Taiwan), 17, 29, 30, 33, 34, 51, 52, 88, 90, 92, 94
Churchill, Anthony, 167 nn. 28, 31
Cigarette paper, fiscal monopolies of, 87, 89, 90, 171 n. 35
Classification: of excisable goods and services, 11–12, 102–3; of excise systems, 13; problems with, 103–4; of sales taxes, 15–16
Coffee, 34, 51, 52, 87, 173 n. 18
Colombia, 31, 42, 70, 89, 90, 93, 95, 108
Congestion charges, 62–67; administration of, 109–10; in Singapore, 66–67
Congo, People's Republic of the, 162 n. 31
Cosmetics, perfumery, toilet articles, 1, 8, 13, 39, 53
Costa Rica, 31, 33, 34, 86, 89, 90, 93, 95
Crombie, James, 102, 106, 172 n. 14, 173 n. 36
Cumulative effects: under excise taxation, 22, 61, 105, 106; under sales taxation, 16–17
Cyprus, 29, 31, 33, 34, 35, 87, 90, 94
Czechoslovakia, 68

Dahomey, 91
Dalton, Hugh, 164 n. 7
Denmark, 31, 51
De Wulf, Luc, 28, 42, 115–16
Distribution of excise burdens, 40–48. *See also* Incidence, theory of excise; Progressivity; Regressivity
Dixon, Daryl A., 28
Domestic vs. imported goods, tax treatment of. *See* Border tax adjustments
Dominican Republic, 31, 33, 35
Dowell, Stephen, 171 n. 4, 174 n. 7
Due, John F., 164 nn. 10, 11, 167 n. 26

Library of Congress Cataloging in Publication Data

Cnossen, Sijbren.
   Excise systems.

   Bibliography: p. 176.
   Includes index.
   1. Taxation of articles of consumption.
2. Sales tax. I. Title.
HJ5711.C55   336.2′71   77–1407
ISBN 0–8018–1962–8